Subaltern Sports

Anthem South Asian Studies
Series Editor: Crispin Bates

Subaltern Sports: Politics and Sport in South Asia

Edited by
JAMES H. MILLS

Anthem Press

Anthem Press
An imprint of Wimbledon Publishing Company
75-76 Blackfriars Road, London SE1 8HA

or

PO Box 9779, London SW19 7ZG

www.anthempress.com

This edition published by Anthem Press 2005

British Library Cataloguing in Publication Data
A catalogue record for this book is available from the British Library.

Library of Congress Cataloging in Publication Data
A catalog record for this book has been requested.

1 3 5 7 9 10 8 6 4 2

ISBN 1 84331 167 4 (Hbk)
ISBN 1 84331 168 2 (Pbk)

Typeset by Footprint Labs Ltd, London
www.footprintlabs.com

Printed in India

CONTENTS

ACKNOWLEDGEMENTS

This book has taken a number of years to mature so it feels as if there are more dues to be acknowledged than days since the project was first conceived. The origins of the book lie in the *Football India* conference that Paul Dimeo and I organised at University College Northampton back in 2000. My thanks are extended to all those there who supported our efforts to organize the event and in particular to Professor Peter King and Dr John Hammond who allowed us to see through what, at first sight, must have seemed to be simply a burst of youthful enthusiasm. Then there are those who have encouraged study in the field of sport in South Asia, despite the fact that it seemed to be a marginal, unfashionable or unsuitable project. Apurba Kundu's interest in the topic inspired us to begin collecting contributors and resulted in a special edition of *Contemporary South Asia*, which showed Paul and I the potential of organising publications in the field. Gary Armstrong and Crispin Bates might seem unlikely bed-fellows to those who know them but their different perspectives, from Sports Studies and South Asian history respectively, prompted questions that seemed too interesting not to seek answers for.

The incidental conversations have also egged on this volume. Mario Rodrigues and Novy Kapadia have provided the detail and journalistic energy to discussions and their ability to range across a hundred or more years of India's sporting history is breathtaking. The days that Satadru Sen and I spent watching New Zealand huff-and-puff their way across India in a Test series in 1999 seem not to have been wasted after all. Neither do the afternoons passed in the company of Arunava Chaudhuri and his gang, observing India's national football team similarly toil in England. I am also grateful to Prashant Kidambi for giving me the impression that South Asianists were genuinely interested in sport and to Clare Anderson and Syd Jeffers who organised a stimulating session at Leicester University's Post-Colonialism Research Seminar. I would also like to repeat the thanks expressed many times in the past to the Economic and Social Research Council (ESRC) which has funded so much of my research in recent years.

Finally, I would like to say thanks to Rebecca, Connie and Bea, who are the inspiration behind all my work. I hope that this volume goes some way towards convincing them that my desire to watch sport on the telly, or to sneak off to a football match from time to time, is not simply evidence of slacking.

CONTRIBUTORS TO THIS VOLUME

Joseph Alter is Professor of Anthropology at the University of Pittsburgh. His research is in the field of medical anthropology concentrating on physical fitness, public health, social psychology and the relationship between health, culture and politics broadly defined. Previous publications include *The Wrestler's Body: Identity and Ideology in North India* (University of California Press, 1992) and *Gandhi's Body: Sex, diet and the politics of nationalism* (University of Pennsylvania Press, 2000). In 2004 his most recent research was published as *Yoga in Modern India: The Body between Science and Philosophy* (Princeton University Press).

Paul Dimeo is a Lecturer in Sports Studies at the University of Stirling. He is the co-editor of *Soccer in South Asia: Empire, Nation, Diaspora* (Frank Cass, 2001) and of the special edition of *Contemporary South Asia* (2, 2001) that concentrated on sport in the region and he has published a number of articles and chapters, most recently '"With political Pakistan in the offing": Football and Communal Politics in South Asia, 1887–1947' in the *Journal of Contemporary History* (38, 3, 2003). In 2003 he was awarded a Wellcome Trust for the History of Medicine grant to research the history of doping and anti-doping policy in Britain.

Ramachandra Guha is a historian, biographer and cricket writer. His books include *Savaging the Civilized: Verrier Elwin, His Tribals and India* (University of Chicago Press, 1999) and *Environmentalism: A Global History* (Longman, 2001). His recent work in the history of sport includes editing *The Picador Book of Cricket* (Picador, 2001) and authoring *Corner of a foreign field: the Indian history of a British sport* (Picador, 2003). Now based in Bangalore, he has taught at Yale, Stanford and Berkeley.

James Heitzman is Director, Office of Summer Sessions, University of California, Davis. His publications include *Gifts of Power: Lordship in an Early Indian State* (Oxford University Press, 1997) and his research has been funded by, among others, the Smithsonian Institution Program for International Relations and a Fulbright Senior Research Award. His latest monograph *Network City: Information Systems and Planning in India's Silicon Valley* (Oxford University Press 2003), explores the recent development of Bangalore as a case study of an information society in Asia.

Alex McKay is a Research Fellow at the Wellcome Trust Centre for the History of Medicine at University College London. His research interests focus on Tibet and he is the author of *Tibet and the British Raj: The Frontier Cadre 1904–1947* (Curzon Press, 1997) and editor of the three volume *The History of Tibet* (RoutledgeCurzon, 2003). His work on the history of sport in the region has been published in the *International Journal of the History of Sport* and *Soccer and Society*. He is currently engaged on a study of the encounter between Western and Himalayan medical systems.

James Mills is currently an ESRC Research Fellow and Senior Lecturer in Modern History at the University of Strathclyde. His research interests lie in the history of Britain and its Empire and he has published in the fields of the history of medicine and the history of sport. His work in the former includes the monographs *Cannabis Britannica: Empire, Trade and Prohibition, 1800–1928* (Oxford University Press, 2003) and *Madness, Cannabis and Colonialism* (Palgrave, 2000) and in the latter he was the co-editor of *Soccer in South Asia: Empire, Nation, Diaspora* (Frank Cass, 2001) and of the special edition of *Contemporary South Asia* (2, 2001) that concentrated on sport in the region.

Megan Mills is an independent researcher. She obtained MA degrees in Religious Studies (Toronto) and International Development (Guelph) and her Ph.D. from York University, Toronto. Her research focuses on Anglo-Indians and Anglo-Burmese in Asia and in the diaspora and has been funded by the York University Graduate Development Fund and the Shastri Indo-Canadian Institute. Her publications include 'Some comments on stereotypes of the Anglo-Indians' in the *International Journal of Anglo-Indian Studies* and 'A most remarkable community: Anglo-Indian contribution to sport in India' (1, 1, 1996) in *Contemporary South Asia* (10, 2, 2001).

Peter Parkes is currently Lecturer in Social Anthropology at the University of Kent. His fieldwork has concentrated on the Hindu Kush region of east- ern Afghanistan and northern Pakistan, particularly among the non-Islamic Kalasha (Kalash Kafirs) of Chitral District. Recent publications include 'Kalasha Domestic Society: Practice, Ceremony and Domain' in H. Donnan and F. Selier eds. *Family and Gender in Pakistan* (Hindustan Publishing Corporation, New Delhi, 1997) and the monograph *Kalasha Society: Practice, prestige and enclavement in the Hindu Kush* is forthcoming with Oxford University Press. Peter was the anthropologist involved in making of Granada TV's *Disappearing World* film *The Kalasha: Rites of Spring* (1990).

Satadru Sen is Assistant Professor of History at Washington University in St. Louis. He is the author of *Disciplining Punishment: Colonialism & Convict Society in the Andaman Islands* (Oxford University Press, 2000), co-editor of *Confronting* *the Body: The Politics of Physicality in Colonial and Postcolonial South Asia* (Anthem Press, 2004) and he has published a range of articles about crime, punishment and juveniles in colonial India. His work in the history of sport includes articles on football and cricket in colonial and post-colonial India and in 2004 Manchester University Press published his study of one of India's first great cricketers as the monograph *Migrant Races: Empire, Identity and K.S. Ranjitsinhji.*

Smriti Srinivas is Associate Professor in the Department of Anthropology at the University of California, Davis. Her publications include *The Mouths of People, the Voice of God: Buddhists and Muslims in a Frontier Community of Ladakh* (Oxford University Press, 1998) and *Landscapes of Urban Memory: The Sacred and the Civic in India's High Tech City* (University of Minnesota Press, 2001) which examines the city of Bangalore. Her current work considers the contemporary, transnational religious movement centred on the Indian guru Sathya Sai Baba.

Phillip Zarrilli is Professor of Performance Practice at Exeter University. He began his *kalarippayattu* training with Gurukkal Govindankutty Nayar of the C.V.N. Kalari Thiruvananthapuram in 1977 and has regularly returned to India for additional training ever since. He has published on the physical arts of the country and his books include *Kathakali Dance-Drama: Where Gods and Demons come to Play* (Routledge, 2000) and *When the Body Becomes All Eyes: Paradigms, Discourses and Practices of Power in Kalarippayattu, a South Indian Martial Art* (OUP India, 1998). He has taught abroad, most recently as Professor of Theatre, Folklore and South Asian Studies at the University of Wisconsin-Madison.

INTRODUCTION

James H. Mills

Sports and Subalternity

Subalternity, in this collection, has been interpreted in its widest possible sense. As defined twenty years ago by Ranajit Guha, the concept appears narrow and limited by its origins in Marxist theory (Guha 1982: 1–7). As it has been used over the last two decades it has taken on a broader meaning so that the 'subaltern' is the dominated party in any power relationship and the study of subalternity is of relationships characterised by 'dominance without hegemony'. The importance of the concept of subalternity lies in its recognition of the 'autonomous domain' of the subaltern agent or agents. While dominated, the subaltern is not entirely obliterated and retains values, ideas and modes of action that are not prescribed by the dominant and which can draw upon beliefs and experiences exclusive to the individual or group. In other words the subaltern always has the potential to oppose or resist the dominant as he or she may draw upon alternative values and ideas and can refer back to different experiences and behavioural expectations. As such the position of the dominant group is often a precarious *de facto* arrangement rather than a generally accepted *de jure* agreement (Ludden 2002; Chaturvedi 2000).

Sports invite subalternity. In the first place this is because sports, especially those organized games of the modern period, are all about contest and competition in which victory or defeat are the anticipated outcomes of the exercise. In an ideal world however, it is the competitor with the most suitable combination of skill, prowess, concentration and guile that will triumph. These attributes are not necessarily gifts bestowed by wealth, social status or political manipulation and as such the sporting arena is a world in which societal elites are stripped of their traditional head starts and privileges, and in which they have to face the challenge of others with only the resources of their own bodies to secure ascendancy.[1]

Yet sports invite subalternity in other ways. Preparation for sporting contest often involves a prolonged period of self-absorption in which a focus on training, special diet or even sexual abstinence can demand that an individual or group temporarily withdraws from the usual social obligations and relationships. In other words the 'normal' world can be disrupted and suspended by the status of 'competitor'. The individual may suddenly find that a new body is required as the demands of sporting success fashion the physique in different ways from the demands of labour or reproduction. Indeed, a body unsuited to labour or reproduction, or reluctant to submit to their demands, may suddenly find worth or value, escape even, in sports (see Hong 1997). On the other hand, many sports demand some sort of community activity as this is necessary in order to raise a team or a club. To this end the very process of assembly may present all manner of interesting new possibilities to those gathering ostensibly for the purpose of organizing a game. The experience of unity of purpose and effective communal action can awaken the participants to the potential of coordinated action in other fields.[2]

As a set of activities in which individuals withdraw from their usual social roles, in which they can forge new and unexpected relationships and in which they face challenges where the rules of the society around them do not apply, sports are pregnant with the possibility of contest and resistance. Of course, once the game is over and the contestants and their supporters contemplate a return to the 'real' world, they are forced to consider the prospect of the usual order being reinstated and of the 'normal' rules being reapplied. However, they can retain a vivid impression from the game that those rules do not always apply and that the normal order has been ignored.[3] That these impressions can live long after the game is over is partly down to a particular feature of sports. Participating in or witnessing these contests adds a physical intensity to an experience of reversal or contestation. The exhilarating effect of dopamine and adrenaline in a moment of victory over the team representing a foe or oppressor can add an immediacy and energy to a resentment or rivalry that discussion would struggle to produce.[4]

The spectator adds to the possibilities of sport as subaltern practice as he or she is a witness to – and at times a participant in – the contest, and it is the presence of the spectator that turns an event into a performance; for this reason historians argue that 'the spectacle has always been a potent political weapon' (Harvey 1989: 88). The inspiration drawn by a competitor from a supportive crowd can revitalize his efforts, while intimidation of the opponent can undermine the latter's determination. The relationship between player and spectators can often be based on the identification of the crowd with the competitor, who comes to represent the crowd; his physical trials are seen as manifestations of their daily struggles and difficulties.[5] But there are often instances when a neutral spectator will support one side of the contest because that player or team is considered the underdog and the spectator's support is extended simply because he desires to see the power relations of the moment reversed or undermined. There is a thrill here in such a moment, and a sense that the danger of such a situation is exciting, but safely contained within the parameters of a sporting event.[6]

The spectator's participation converts the game into a spectacle rather than simply a contest between active participants, meaning that the significance of defeat on the field can reverberate far beyond the confines of the pitch or stadium. As witnesses, the spectators carry the story of the setback with them into the community, not simply as a tale to be told but as an experience to be related and relived, animated by traces of the passion and energy that fired them at the spectacle. Today it is not even necessary to be present at the game or in the arena to participate in the experience of the contest, and gathering around the radio set or the television becomes an event in itself. Sporting clashes are now among the most watched and interpreted events in the modern world (Tomlinson 2002: 44) and much of the consumption of these activities through the media is communal. Indeed, the power of the sports event to generate a crowd, whether at the stadium or around the radio or television, can be enough to incite collective agitation. Alternatively those gathered for some other purpose, or in support of a political or social agenda, may find themselves suddenly emboldened or empowered by the passions of sports spectatorship.[7]

If sporting activities invite, even incite, subalternity then they can at the same time act as mechanisms by which subaltern groups are oppressed and through which dominant groups assert their power. The imposition of sporting regimes can be a way of forcing modes of discipline on, and taking control of bodies in, groups reluctant to submit to the rules of work, military discipline or modern educational institutions. Victory at sporting events can be used to carry triumphal messages about the superiority of the group represented by the winning competitors, or more subtle ideas about the benefits of a certain way of life or mode of behaviour. The architecture of a sporting arena (Eichberg 1998: 68–86; Bale 1994; Vertinsky and Bale 2004) or the deliberate management of the experience of the spectacle (Giulianotti 1999: 80–85; Nielsen 1995: 21–44) are often exercises in control or pomp designed to emphasize the competence of the elites. Sporting events have been used to propagate everything: from fascist regimes to multi-national commercial interests; from national identities to racial stereotypes; from colonialism to cultural imperialism (Mangan 2000; Maguire 1999; Sugden and Tomlinson 1998; Armstrong and Giulianotti 2001; Cronin and Mayall 1998; Mills and Dimeo 2003; Klein 1991; Klein 1997). All of this simply enhances the subaltern potential of the player, activity or arena. It is important for historians to examine sport because it is such a volatile and unstable medium, in which all the grand designs of an elite can be publicly mocked or shocked by a moment of individual brilliance or a show of determined teamwork.

Sports in South Asia

It seems particularly appropriate that 'subalternity' should be examined within the sporting practices of South Asia given the significant contributions made to developing the term by academics studying the region. Yet it is only in recent years that serious academic attention has been given to the subject of sport in South Asia. The work carried out in this field was reviewed in detail recently (Mills 2001a) but is briefly worth summarising here. An older gener-ation of historians did display an interest in sports but tended to compile either narrative histories of the formation of clubs and the emergence of star players, or to focus on the role played by British colonizers in introducing and encouraging their games among the locals (Docker 1977; Bose 1990; Cashman 1980; Mangan 1985; Guttman 1994; Mason 1990; Holt 1989). From the late 1980s onwards a greater degree of critical complexity has been brought to the subject. Writers like Nandy, Appadurai and McDonald examined the theme of cricket's indigenization in the postcolonial period and pointed to its central place in a range of emerging positions and identities in the years after Independence in 1947. Nandy (1989) has argued that the underlying rhythms and mythic structures of the game make it profoundly Indian and that it is therefore appropriate that the game should be most enthusiastically appropriated by those from South Asian cultures.

Appadurai and McDonald have instead argued that postcolonial politics and culture explain the rise of cricket in India to the status of the nation's most popular sport. Appadurai points to state support and commercialisation as the driving forces behind the promotion of the game to the masses, who adopted it because 'it became an emblem of Indian nationhood at the same time that it became inscribed, as practice, into the Indian (male) body' (1996: 45). The appropriation of the game has been a self-consciously anti-colonial process argues Appadurai, who concludes that 'cricket gives … the sense of having hijacked the game from its English habitus into the colonies at the level of language, body, and agency as well as competition, finance and spectacle' (46).

McDonald similarly finds that cricket has been a vehicle for the articulation and invention of postcolonial identities insisting that these are less national and more communal in nature. He points to the range of transforming social and economic forces that have swept through India in the 1990s, and argues for the emergence of a 'lumpen middle class' that wishes to express its new wealth and power through extreme Hindu politics. Such politics provide this class with an identity it can assert over minority groups within India, and by which it can challenge others on the international stage. Cricket, as a 'national' sport, is something that the 'lumpen middle class' wish to dominate and control in order to advertize its power: 'due to its place in civil society and as a significant element of popular culture, international one day and test cricket offers fertile terrain for the articulation of Hindu chauvinist and communalist ideologies' (McDonald 1999: 232).

Ramachandra Guha has looked more closely at the history of cricket and the way in which the sport was first used as a vehicle for expressing anti-colonial and nationalist emotions (Guha 1998: 165–9). In 1906, news of the victory of the Hindu team over the European team in Bombay quickly spread beyond the borders of the Bombay Presidency and was celebrated by nationalists across India. Guha quotes an article in the Lahore *Tribune* as an example of how meaning was attached to this victory. The report compared the Indian cricketers with the Japanese soldiers that had made up the first Asian army to defeat a European force in modern times when they had soundly beaten the Russians in 1905. A cricket victory here was represented as more than just a sporting result; it became a symbolic reversal of the discourses of British superiority and it acquired the significance of an important battle in the struggle between Europeans and Asians of the colonial period. Indeed, Guha goes on to develop this theme of how sport articulates – and maybe even exacerbates – political tensions in Indian society by looking at cricket as a site for the development of communal (Muslim and Hindu) identities during the 1930s and 1940s (ibid.: 175–9). Central to this development was the so-called Quadrangular competition. This competition pitted the British against the Muslims, the Hindus and the Others (Parsis, Sikhs and Christians) in Bombay. As the rivalry between Hindu and Muslim political groups intensified in the 1930s, so the games between the teams representing these communities in the Quadrangular took on added significance. Guha notes that 'in towns hundreds of miles from Bombay college students would divide up between classes into Hindu groups and Muslim groups each following the radio commentary from their distinctive point of view'. After a rare Hindu victory in 1939 the celebrations were concluded with a singing of *Bande Maatram*, a hymn with Hindu nationalist overtones. In short, Guha argues that cricket became so important in Indian society in the period before 1947 as this was a time when new identities were emerging and the game was one arena in which they were constructed and articulated (ibid: 189).

While writers like Nandy, Appadurai, Guha and McDonald have looked at the modern sport of cricket, Joseph Alter focused his attention on the indigenous discipline of *Bharatiya kushti* or Indian wrestling in north India. This is an

activity that fuses Hindu sporting traditions dating back to the eleventh century
with Persian martial skills introduced by the Mogul armies after the sixteenth
century. The significance of *Bharatiya kushti* lies in providing an arena for
Indians to challenge, ignore and reinterpret the rules of social and moral
engagement. Alter concludes that 'wrestling only contingently reaffirms per-
vasive cultural themes such as rank and status; more significantly, it opens up
the stage for a protean, maverick revision of these themes' (Alter 1992: 6).

His study of the Indian game *kabaddi* (Alter 2000) offers a contrasting
example to that of wrestling. Both sports have been used as sites for constructions of ideological myths about 'Indian-ness' but the history of each highlights the different versions of 'Indian-ness' that various nationalist groups
were using local games to construct. Wrestling, based on individual efforts and
development, on Indian spiritual exercises and on an Indian diet, was used to
represent 'anti-modern' Indian-ness. This was a version of India manufactured
by reactionary groups that rejected modernity. *Kabaddi* could also be presented as authentically Indian but at the same time it had many of the aspects
of 'modern' sport, especially in its focus on team discipline and coordination.
It therefore appealed to such groups as the RSS[8], the Hindu extremist political organization, that was eager to promote a version of Indian-ness that
emphasized modernity and mobilization. The different histories of the two
games in the twentieth century – wrestling remains obscure while *kabbadi* has
been exhibited at the Olympics – reflects their selection as emblems of two
very different ideological articulations of India's national essence.[9]

A host of recent publications has been concerned to show how sports are
shaped by societies around them in South Asia, while at the same time they
can transform the lives of those in the region. In 1999 James Heitzmann and
Smriti Srinivas published a pair of articles in *The Journal of Sport & Social Issues*
(23,1,1999) that took this theme into the Indian city. Using Bangalore as a
case study they looked at the ways in which sports were used to order and
reorder space in the city, and the competing visions of the Indian metropolis
that each set of sporting activities represented. The city's male population
prepares for its events in traditional Indian gymnasiums and claims the streets,
neighbourhoods and temples of the city during the athletic festivities of the
Karaga celebration. However, the city's elites and planners have been building modern sporting facilities in order to host high-profile tournaments and
have used dubious means to claim the land and resources for these facilities
from local communities in order to expedite their vision of the city's future.
The changing nature of the postcolonial Indian city has impacted upon the
types of sport engaged with in the urban centre while at the same time such
sporting activities have been at the heart of the processes driving conceptual
and environmental changes in the metropolis.

Soccer in South Asia presents a range of stories which suggested that football had been the site of a number of resistance strategies. At the Church Missionary Society School in Srinigar, the game was introduced as a way of disciplining pupils reluctant to develop the ethos – and the bodies – desired by the English schoolmaster. Brutalized into their first game by lathi-wielding masters, the chief concern of the boys was to avoid contact with the ball and its polluting leather surfaces – one boy who failed to evade the offending item was expelled from his home as defiled. Yet the game is still promoted at the school today and the boys annually perform a play that recreates the chaos of that first match, acting out all the roles including the English head and his stick-wielding staff (Mangan 2001: 47–49). Football in Bengal seems just as complex a phenomenon. The ecstatic celebrations of the Calcutta crowd after Mohun Bagan defeated the East Yorkshire Regiment in 1911 presents a troubling paradox: it was at once a moment of resistance, in which the corporal hierarchies constructed by the British were publicly reversed, and at the same time an endorsement of the significance of the foreign sport and its values (Dimeo 2001: 70–72).[10] Such a paradox was prevented in Tibet, despite the fact that British officers and colonial troops took football with them to the kingdom in the 1900s. The game found itself locked in a battle of cultural imperialism with China's *mah-jong* until the Buddhist authorities banned both activities as they sought to resist its creeping influence (McKay 2001: 99). In Goa, football tells another story, flourishing despite, not because of, the European colonizers and securing its place in contemporary Goa as a vehicle for defying the postcolonial Indian state, rather than the colonial Portuguese (Mills 2001b: 87).

Such themes were similarly explored in the collections of essays published as special editions of the journals *Contemporary South Asia* and *Football Studies*. Among the essays in the first collection was one that demonstrated the possibilities and politics of the exceptional sportsman. Kumar Shri Ranjitsinhji was the pre-eminent Indian cricketer of his generation, playing for Cambridge University, Sussex and England. In his article in Contemporary South Asia Satadru Sen shows how the gifts of a player demanded that imperial boundaries be lowered: he was quickly selected to play for Trinity College but at his first game was greeted with icy silence by his team mates. At the same time, however, Sen shows how swift were the attempts made to contain Ranji's position as he was carefully and repeatedly 'Orientalised' in British culture. Ultimately Ranji was able to convert his sporting prowess into political capital, securing the throne of the state of Nawanagar. Here was a man who was allowed to violate the norms of Empire and who successfully used sport as a means of pursuing political ends. Yet Sen wonders just how much satisfaction it brought to a man who he sees as 'like the great American actor Bert

Williams ... a black man performing in a blackface, whose performances were successful, subversive and painful' (Sen 2001: 239; Sen 2004). Recent books return to Ranji, as he is at once a beguiling character and at the heart of fundamental issues about sport and South Asia. Mario Rodrigues addresses the heroic status of Ranji in postcolonial India, where his name adorns the national trophy. Rodrigues sees an irony in the fact that while Ranji 'stands paramount in the pantheon of Indian sporting gods' he did very little for Indian cricket, or indeed for India, as he continued to oppose Indian nationalism and to insist on the rights of South Asia's princes until his death (Rodrigues 2003: 219–248). Ramachandra Guha offers a similar assessment, describing him as 'an arch-loyalist, who cared little for the political aspirations of the ordinary Indian' (2002: 95). While both are right, Sen's account suggests that there are more complex ways of reading this successful Indian sportsman in a period shaped by British colonialism.

The *Football Studies* collection was organized by Paul Dimeo. Much of Dimeo's work has focused on the ways in which it is possible to use the body as an analytical concept in understanding the history of Indian sports. He argues that the body was at the heart of the colonial project to encourage sporting participation among the colonized. This had practical objectives in producing fit and disciplined subject bodies and discursive ends in representing British physical culture as superior to that of local corporal regimes (Dimeo 2002a). However this proved to be a double-edged sword: the body became a site of resistance and sports were identified as spheres of contestation. In victory over British teams the practical and the discursive fused, so much so that one Indian commentator wrote that 'it fills every Indian with joy to know that rice-eating, malaria-ridden Bengalis have got the better of beef-eating, Herculean, booted John Bull' (Dimeo 2004: 43). However, he has also found examples that suggest that the set of discourses identified about South Asian bodies and sport in the colonial period continues to resonate in postcolonial India. In explaining recent failures, the Indian FA published a report arguing that the 'genetic imperfection of Indian footballers concerning physical fitness' was a significant factor leading to India's poor soccer performances (Mills and Dimeo 2003: 121). However, the real reasons for India's football failures lie in the mismanagement and politicking of the Indian FA and not in the bodies of the Indian players. The quote from the Indian FA shows how, long after the departure of the British, the sportsman's body in South Asia remains a politically constructed site.

Dimeo's work in Bengal has recently been followed up by research in what might be called the *Soccer and Society* school. Fostered by its 'Executive Academic Editor', J.A. Mangan, this work suffers from many of the inconsistencies of the latter's output, namely erratic secondary reading and analysis

poorly disguised by a slavish devotion to the work of J.A. Mangan. Kausik
Bandyopadhyay's article 'Race, Nation and Sport: Footballing nationalism in
colonial Calcutta' contains some interesting new information but simply
repeats Dimeo's conclusions in stating that 'cricket and football came to be
utilized by the British as an important means of Anglicizing the indigenous
rulers', but 'football, a British cultural import, became … a cultural weapon
to reassert Bengali masculinity and fight the racist British imperialist'
(Bandyopadhyay 2003). Confirming Dimeo's thesis with fresh research is an
appropriate exercise but the fact that Bandyopadhyay treads the same ground
as Dimeo (the 1911 game for example), reaches the same conclusions and
fails to acknowledge any of the relevant work from Dimeo's publications is
troubling.[11]

Less controversial but no less perplexing are Boria Majumdar's publications
in *Soccer and Society*. Chief among these is 'The Politics of Soccer in Colonial
India, 1930–1937: The Years of Turmoil'. He sets out to argue that 'British
recognition and support were pivotal in shaping the development of Indian
soccer in the 1930s and 1940s' (Majumdar 2002: 22) in order to dispute
research which insists that the British retained only a distant and nominal control over the forces that shaped Indian soccer – which by this time was held
firmly in the hands of local interest groups. Confusingly, however, he tells a
story in which all the actors are Indian and in which the disputes concern
which group of Indians would control the game. Indeed, when the British did
get involved in his story they were dismissed as simply representing European
opinion and therefore of little bearing, while the English FA was dragged
into the dispute only as a makeweight by one group of Indian disputants.
Majumdar's research in this article is excellent and offers a fascinating insight
into how far Indians had wrested control of modern sports from the British in
the decade before the end of the colonial period. It is to be hoped that his
analysis is rather more considered in the future.

Rather less well researched is Majumdar's subsequent offering, although it
does raise some important issues.[12] Quite how *Bend it Like Beckham* 'opens up
an entry point for historians to comment on the nature of women's soccer in
India' (Majumdar 2003: 81) is never made clear or apparent, as the movie was
made in the UK by a British director about an English girl, albeit one born
into a British Asian family, growing up in Hounslow in the 1990s. Rather than
'women's soccer in India' per se, this film concerns the separate but important
issue of sport and the South Asian diaspora. The ways in which sport is implicated in the relationship between the diaspora and South Asia have been
explored in more detail in the *Football Studies* collection (Dimeo 2002b). The
Indian national football team toured the UK in the summers of 2000–3,
during which time the squad was pitched against a series of lower division

English clubs, and finally set up for a two-match series against the national team of Jamaica. All this despite the fact that Indian coaches had stated that they would prefer to play against the Asian teams that were their traditional opposition in FIFA tournaments, and in the face of poor attendances at the games. The involvement of diaspora groups in organizing the tours was crucial. First, there was the determination of Sapphire Enterprises, a private company run by a British Asian, to make a profit from the tours. Also significant was the role played by enthusiasts such as Jas Bains[13] and Arunava Chaudhuri. Both are European-born Asians (the former is British and the latter German) and they shared a conviction that Indian football needed to be improved. Their approach suggested that contact with the West and its professional leagues was the means of lifting Indian football.

It is interesting that these members of the South Asian diaspora, both of whom were born in Europe, seem to have taken it upon themselves to use sport as a means of civilizing postcolonial India. The standards that they wish to impose on Indian football are those of the cultures and countries in which they were born and raised, and their desire to see the national football team succeed in international competition reflects the importance given to successful results by the national teams of England and Germany. In India, where local rivalries and leagues are the most important competitions in the sport, the national team is an afterthought and national pride is instead defended by the cricket team.[14] In fact there has been a growing call from Indians to resist the NRIs and as one journalist noted 'most people in Indian football do not like these changes as they feel these outsiders lack knowledge of the traditions and difficulties of Indian football'.[15]

Subaltern Sports

Taken together then the range of recent studies discussed here and those examined in more detail elsewhere have addressed a number of issues pertinent to this volume. Sport and sporting activities in South Asia have been shaped by exercises in power and resistance and driven by the relationships and forces that have shaped modern India. In turn they have been exercises in power and resistance that have shaped those relationships and forces. This volume seeks to narrow the focus to explicitly concentrate on these issues of power and resistance in sport in south Asia and to explore the ways in which these sporting activities in the region can aid an understanding of subalternity.

The papers in this volume address the issue of subalternity in a variety of ways. The first three chapters by Zarrilli, Alter and Parkes are important reminders that South Asia has its own sporting forms and traditions and that these have survived the introduction of modern, western sports, albeit in transformation. Philip Zarrilli's chapter offers an introduction to his work on *kalarippayattu* a martial art that has its origins in Kerala (1995; 1998). On the one hand the chapter is a study of the ways in which a set of corporal, competitive practices evolve from historical origins in the preparation for warfare into a leisure time lifestyle choice for modern Indians. *Kalarippayattu* emerged in a troubled period of local history as a set of mental and physical exercises designed to produce an accomplished warrior. However its survival in the modern period has partly been ensured by practitioners that have turned to the rigors of the discipline for its health benefits or the boon that it has brought to their dealings with the wider world. Zarrilli's chapter is also a contribution to certain discussions of sport and the body in South Asia. It is certainly the case that modern sports were introduced to South Asia to produce new bodies and new subjectivities suitable for the purposes of the state (Dimeo 2004) but the case of *kalarippayattu* shows historians that it was not exclusively modern sports that had such an objective. Long before football and cricket were introduced to South Asia in order to get Indians to perform and to think in certain ways *kalarippayattu* was being used to fashion a certain type of individual and to create new ways for people to be.

Joseph Alter extends his previous work on wrestling, *kabbadi* and yoga (2004) by examining competitions in *jori*-swinging in Banaras. Arguing that it has roots in similar exercises in the Middle East from which it was transmitted to north India through various waves of Muslim invaders, he suggests that here is a physical regime that reverses the more commonly examined route of transmission from West to East. British officers encountered *jori*-swinging in the eighteenth and nineteenth centuries and practised it as part of their own corporal routines in order to build strength and stamina. Before long *jori*-swinging was a routine of army drill known as 'Indian-clubs'. Later in the nineteenth-century these were popularized in the United States and Alter highlights the fact that there they were linked to the emergence of the women's health movement and eugenicist anxieties about female reproduction. This is an irony that Alter enjoys as his analysis of *jori*-swinging in India suggests that it is in fact a celebration of male fertility and control and acts as an index of masculine power. These meanings are derived from the cultures of rural Uttar Pradesh and have survived the co-option of the *jori* by the British and a transmission into western cultures that has almost reversed their meaning. In *jori*-swinging Alter presents readers with evidence of the ways in which the sports and sporting activities of subaltern groups can be used to trace evidence of the 'autonomous domains' of meaning and action posited by Subaltern Studies theorists.

Some of Peter Parkes' themes complement Alter's concerns. Polo is a sport that probably arrived in the mountains of South Asia during the waves of invasions from Central Asia of the last millennium. Once established it survived the decline of Mughal power in the north-eastern and north-western Himalayas where it became central to rituals of both kingship and kinship. Parkes shows that, much like *jori*-swinging in Alter's account, this was an activity that was enthusiastically adopted by the British for military reasons in the nineteenth-century and that this adoption was to kick-start curious political and cultural processes. The British set about 'civilizing' the game, and the same processes that were acting in Britain to establish formal rules for such games as football seized on polo and set out a code known as the Hurlingham Association Rules. These were then exported back to India where they became the basis for matches that involved colonial officers. There was much to be gained from playing with the British and when locals signed up for a game they were introduced to the rules of the colonial elite. Indeed, after the departure of the British in 1947 the colonial elite was simply replaced by a Pakistani one which continued to use polo as a tool of government and which reshaped the game further with such ostentatious displays of power as airlifting a team of part-Arab horses into the mountains to improve the stock of animals available to polo-players. It was only on the fringes of government control, in isolated or reluctant areas, that traditional polo survives and is now culturally framed as 'inferior' in comparison to the 'superior' games of the Shandu season.

If these three chapters consider sports and activities that emerged from South Asian culture and practice then Ramachandra Guha's work turns to a game that has been thoroughly indigenized since its introduction in the nineteenth-century. Within the story of the cricketing brothers of the Palwankar family Guha traces the complex ways in which sporting prowess disrupted one of India's most enduring systems of subordination. The Palwankars came from the *Chamaar* caste which lies at the bottom of the Hindu social hierarchy. Traditionally discriminated against by elite Hindus the family took advantage of the opportunities provided by the arrival of the British to escape their traditional role and to work for the colonial military. Contact with the army meant familiarity with British sports and eventually a job for the eldest brother at the Europeans' cricket club in Pune. Here his natural talents as a bowler meant that he was quickly employed as practice for British batsmen. Such was his skill that the local Indian elite, desperate to beat the British at the game, began to relax their taboos about contact with *Chamaars* in order to coax Baloo Palwankar on to their team. His earnings and the contacts that he developed through moving in cricketing circles meant that he was able to send his brothers to the prestigious Elphinstone College in Bombay where their cricketing abilities quickly made themselves obvious. The story is not simply one of the ways in which the personal fortunes of a low-caste family were dramatically changed through sporting success or indeed of the way in which the prejudices of the Indian elites were disrupted by the desire to beat the British at cricket.

Instead Guha argues that the Palwankars were in fact intimately linked to the Untouchable movement that emerged in the 1920s and 1930s and that has formed the basis of the Dalit politics of resistance ever since.

Satadru Sen's review of more recent episodes from cricketing history is an exercise in historicizing subject positions. He argues that during the period of British rule in India sporting challenges to the supremacy of the white, colonial elite were safely contained within the discourses of Orientalism. He highlights the ways in which Ranjitsinhji was constructed within the British imagination so that his skills became 'magical' and his prowess 'other-worldly'. In doing this the colonizers emptied his achievements of significance for wider relationships between the British and Indians and denied the threats that the combination of his prowess and his race made to English claims over the ownership of cricket. More recently, however, similar attempts to exclude South Asians using such discursive strategies have been more vigorously challenged. Sen argues that these challenges both reflect and assert the growing power of South Asians in the cricketing sphere as well as in wider relationships in the postcolonial world. The political and discursive perspectives that developed on the Denness Affair of 2001 show how centre and periphery have been reversed in the postcolonial world, at least in the game of cricket. The game which was intended to civilize and to create new subjectivities in the colonized is now claimed by those who were once meant to be its victims, while those who represented the game as peculiarly their own find ownership of its institutions and its ethics disputed.

Paul Dimeo's work examines the way in which sporting spaces are implicated in unequal power relations. He looks at the history of Royal Calcutta Golf Club (RCGC) and shows that golf, with its extensive use of considerable amounts of land, its demand for expensive equipment and its organizational structure based on the 'club', readily lends itself to exercises in social exclusion. The RCGC was founded in the 1830s and was originally situated on the Maidan in the heart of the city around which the other symbols of Britain's presence, such as Fort William and the Esplanade, were grouped. Indians were forbidden to play on the course and were prevented from joining the club which was deliberately constructed as a symbol of Britishness at which 'home' could be experienced even while 'abroad'. As the British elites moved out of the city to the affluent suburb of Tollygunge the club followed them and expanded to offer the luxury of two eighteen-hole courses there. It was only on 15 August 1946 that the first Indian member was admitted to the club and it was not until 1963 that it was first captained by an Indian. As such, Dimeo argues, golf disrupts the simplistic 'muscular Christianity' model used by many historians when examining sport in colonial contexts as he shows that at no time was golf used as a means of disciplining or training Indians, as were football and cricket.

Instead, golf was deliberately denied to locals and the spaces on which it was practiced were at once ostentatious displays of resource domination and theatres in which a performance of social distance was played out. However, in the postcolonial period these displays and this performance have been maintained as a means of constructing class and community divisions by the Indian elite that has gradually assumed control of the club. Dimeo shows, however, how this has been resisted by local residents and by migrants who arrived from Bangladesh. Those around the club's perimeters regularly break down the walls erected around the fairways in order to use the land for housing, recreation and even for their own sporting activities.

Contested sporting spaces are among the concerns of James Heitzman and Smriti Srinivas in examining the preparations in Bangalore for the 1997 National Games. They argue that the form of the pre-modern city was celebrated in the Karaga festival in which key points in the geography of the urban centre were visited by an effigy carried by a priest and accompanied by men from the Tigala community who were specially trained for the task. These men had been sent into training at the local wrestling-houses and their strength and virility was built up through gymnastic exercises, celibacy and a controlled diet. Yet the Karaga festival has been forced to accommodate recent urban changes, especially when lakes around the city which had been among the festival sites were drained to create modern sporting facilities. The first to suffer in such a way was the Sampangi Tank which made way for the Sri Kanteerava stadium and this was followed in the 1990s when the tank in Koramangala was designated as the location for the National Games Village. The tanks had been so important to the Karaga festival and its athletic participants as the Tigala community from which they were drawn had traditionally relied on the water to support the agricultural activities from which they made their livelihood. Heitzman and Srinivas trace the relationship between athletic activities, space and urban change to argue that the fate of the tanks reflect competing visions of the city. The activities of the Karaga festival evoke mobile maps of the urban labyrinth, which allow for playing with constructs of place. On the other hand a the permanent athletic spaces of the National Games complexes impose a static order on the city that emphasizes zones of segregated functioning and that calls to the global norms of the twenty-first century metropolis. Yet both the Karaga festival and the National Games complexes coexist in Bangalore and the chapter argues that the different athletic activities within the city's spaces reflect a 'contemporaneous' world wherein the city becomes a site contested by several histories and cultures.

In looking at women's football in Manipur in the 1990s James Mills begins to explore the place of modern sports in the history and politics of South Asia's margins. The team from the state has a remarkable record as, since the competition between women's state representative teams began, it has won nine of the eleven trophies and the victory in 2003 brought their sixth Championship in a row. At first sight this appears incongruous as Bengal is the traditional football giant of India and it is the team from that state that has lost out to Manipur on each of the nine occasions that the latter have won the Championships. Indeed, Manipur rarely makes the news for positive reasons and is more usually regarded in the national press as a centre of armed resistance to the Indian state. Mills argues that the sporting success of Manipur's women's football team can be seen as resting on conditions of sporting participation and female power that have roots long in the region's past but at the same time their achievements have contemporary resonance in a period when Manipur is a contested region and the Meitei group in particular is struggling to assert an ethnic identity. All of this means that the phenomenon of Manipuri women's football is important for a number of academic discussions. It is a useful reminder that there is more to gender studies in India than marriage, reproduction and widowhood and that the ongoing success of female athletes in India is a neglected sphere of activity by academics. The account given also has significance for debates in sports studies. Many studies in this subject area that have concentrated specifically on women have seen the development of modern sports as a 'liberating' process and yet, in Manipur, Mills argues that the emergence of modern sport in fact reflects female physical autonomy rather than causes it. Finally, the issue of team games is one made much of by other sports studies specialists who argue that modern sports acted as 'tools of empire' in colonial contexts by introducing the ethics of the team to local societies. In Manipur, however, the evidence suggests that the concept and dynamics of teamwork were certainly not alien imports to this particular part of South Asia.

Alex McKay's review of football in Bhutan and in the South Asian Tibetan community similarly explores modern sports on South Asia's geographical margins. Football has very different histories in Bhutan and Tibet. In the latter it was introduced by the British during the period of Empire in South Asia and it was eventually banned by the Buddhist authorities in Tibet who feared that it was proving to be an all too effective tool of western cultural imperialism. Recently, however, football has grown in popularity among the young in the Tibetan exile community in India and on June 30th 2001 that community fielded a 'national' side to play a friendly. This was a self-consciously political move and the organizers of the team christened themselves the Tibetan National Football Association to thumb their nose at the Chinese authorities and their control of Tibet. The aim of the organization is 'through games and sports [to] help create better understanding and awareness of the Tibetan issue in the international scenario'. The 'national' team is now

patronized by key members of the Buddhist elite. Football in Bhutan was not
a British introduction but instead arrived with Indian teachers who worked
there from the 1950s onwards. Its growth in popularity since had a dramatic
outcome in the 1990s when the demand for access to the game lead to the
introduction of television, resisted by the authorities until then, so that the
local population could watch matches from around the world. The nation's
football federation affiliated with FIFA in 2000 and a new stadium is being
constructed in the capital with state support. McKay argues that the history
of football in these communities reflects the changing politics of their relations
with the outside world. The elites of both communities rejected relationships
with modernity earlier in the twentieth century and indeed the Bhutanese
pursued this policy into the 1990s. However, the Tibetans are now stateless
and the Bhutanese find themselves sandwiched between China and India and
McKay argues that, with their political options limited, the peoples of the
High Himalayas are seeking to bolster their claims to the rights of modern
nations by communicating in the global cultural form that is football. Quite
simply, this is a story of minor nations seeking to protect themselves against
mighty neighbours by appealing to the international community through the
language of sport. At the same time the hope remains within the elites of the
Tibetan exile community and Bhutan that football will prove to be a strain of
mass modern culture that can be managed within the parameters of local belief
systems and practices.

The collection ends with a consideration of sport in the history of a
community that is often considered to be on India's social, rather than
geographical, margins. Megan Mills' focus on the Anglo-Indian community
traces the ways in which modern sports have been linked with the complex
processes of identity and definition in their history. During the colonial period
the playing of modern sports partly reflected the sociology of the community
which was divided into units through educational or occupational organizations and which therefore readily lent itself to the formulation of teams. It also
reflected a growing sense of identity with the British colonial establishment,
which had rewarded Anglo-Indians for loyalty in the nineteenth-century,
encouraging the community to maintain a distance from Indians and to
identify with the rulers. In the postcolonial period, however, sports have
allowed the community to overcome this distance from Indians by engaging
in the processes of nation-building. Participation in sporting victories at the
international level and in the more mundane tasks of training and coaching
Indian players and athletes has allowed the Anglo-Indian community to claim
a part in the emergence of the country's global profile. At the same time,
however, the playing of modern games has provided a means of managing
the dislocations of migration for those that have left India and formed the

Anglo-Indian diaspora. Stories range from that of India's first Olympic medalist in 1900 to the current crop of talent that includes the swimmer Nisha Millet. Mills concludes that, through sport, a subaltern group can devise a range of strategies for managing its position in a changing world.

Each chapter is designed to be read independently as a case study that focuses on specific concerns, particular communities, certain cities or individual games or sports. The volume as a whole is not meant to be comprehensive in its coverage of sports, of regions in South Asia, or of methodological and conceptual approaches to the study of sports in the region. Rather, it deliberately casts its net widely across a range of activities with a conviction that to attempt to define terms like 'sport', 'leisure', 'recreation' or 'exercise' too closely is to invite Orientalizing or otherwise essentializing reductionism.

The volume does however seek to assemble in one place a selection of the most active contributors to the debate on sports in South Asia over the last decade or so. It has done this, in the first place, to focus attention on the subject area in order to promote further research, and secondly, to demonstrate the wide range of approaches that have been adopted and the rich results to be had from applying anthropological, historical, sociological, geographical or gender studies perspectives to sports in South Asia. Finally, when viewed as a whole, the volume has attempted to engage with its own title in a variety of challenging ways and to show the route into a whole new field for the archaeology of subalternity.

1

'KALARIPPAYATTU IS EIGHTY PERCENT MENTAL AND ONLY THE REMAINDER IS PHYSICAL': POWER, AGENCY AND SELF IN A SOUTH ASIAN MARTIAL ART

Philip Zarrilli

Introduction

In the well-known Bhagavad Gita section of India's Mahabharata epic, Krishna elaborates a view of duty and action intended to convince Arjuna that, as a member of the warrior caste (*ksatriya*), he must overcome all his doubts and take up arms, even against his relatives. As anyone familiar with either the Mahabharata or India's second great epic, the Ramayana, knows martial techniques have existed on the South Asian subcontinent since antiquity. Both epics are filled with scenes describing how the princely heroes obtain and use their humanly or divinely acquired skills and powers to defeat their enemies: by training in martial techniques under the tutelage of great gurus like the brahmin master Drona, by practicing austerities and meditation techniques which give the martial master access to subtle powers to be used in combat, and/or by receiving a gift or a boon of divine, magical powers from a god. On the one hand, there is Bhima who depends on his brute strength to crush his foes, while on the other, we find the 'unsurpassable' Arjuna making use of his more subtle accomplishments in single point focus or his powers acquired through meditation.

Among practitioners and teachers of *kalarippayattu*, the martial art of Kerala on the southwestern coast of India, some, like Higgins Masters of the P.B. *Kalari* in Trissur, model their practice on Bhima, emphasizing *kalarippayattu's* practical empty hand techniques of attack, defence, locks and throws. Others, like my first and most important teacher Gurukkal[1] Govindankutty Nayar of

Thirovananthapuram's C.V.N. *Kalari*, with whom I have studied since 1977, follow Arjuna and emphasize *kalarippayattu* as an active, energetic means of disciplining and 'harnessing' (*yuj* the root of yoga) both one's body and one's mind as a form of moving meditation. As comparative scholar of religions Mircea Eliade has explained, 'One always finds a form of yoga whenever there is a question of experiencing the sacred or arriving at complete mastery of oneself' (Eliade 1975: 196). Even though there has been great interest in both yoga and *Ayurveda* (the Indian science of health and well-being) in the West, little is known about a number of Indian martial arts still practiced today. These arts are founded on a set of fundamental cultural assumptions about the body-mind relationship and health and well-being that are similar to the assumptions underlying yoga and *Ayurveda*. This essay is an introduction to *kalarippayattu*-a martial/medical/meditation discipline that has been practiced in Kerala since at least the twelfth century A.D. and, more specifically, is an introduction to the assumptions about the body, mind, and practice shared with yoga and *Ayurveda* which inform the way in which some traditional masters still teach *kalarippayattu*.

Some traditional masters (like Drona and Arjuna) foreground yoga in their practice of *kalarippayattu*, while other masters not discussed here follow other paradigms of teaching and practice, like Bhima mentioned above. In an increasingly heteronomous society, in which traditional practitioners must vie for students with karate teachers who often emphasize immediate 'street wise' results, the paradigms, beliefs and practices discussed in this essay are in a constant process of negotiation with competing paradigms and practices, and, therefore, are only more or less observed by teachers today. Some of the concepts and phenomena discussed here such as 'meditation', 'the sacred', 'oneself', 'power' or 'purity' are neither transparent nor self-evident. What is considered 'sacred', 'the self', 'power', 'pure' or 'meditation' is particular to each interpretive community, history and context. What is 'sacred' or 'pure' to a brahmin male Malayali born in 1924 will be different from what is 'sacred' or 'pure' to a male Nayar *kalarippayattu* fighter of the thirteenth century, a male Sufi Muslim of Kannur born in 1965, an American male born in 1947 who has never been to Kerala or India or a European woman born on the continent who has practiced yoga since her youth and eventually turns to a study of *kalarippayattu*. Historical, social, religious, gender and ideological positions constitute quite different frames of reference and interpretative categories through which the 'sacred', 'self' or 'pure' will be read and understood.

Under the influence of 'new age' religious assumptions or other potentially reductionist ways of thinking[2], too often in the United States there is a humanist tendency to erase cultural difference, disregard history, and to participate or otherwise be involved in romantically projecting onto South Asia an Orientalist essentialism (Said 1976; Inden 1986).[3] Too often accounts reify the self and the 'spiritual' as if all experiences that might be appropriately discussed as in some way 'spiritual' were singular and universal. Most problematic is our Western tendency to project our hegemonic notion of the self as unitary and individual onto 'selves' in other cultures (Marriott 1976; 1977; 1990). As anthropologist Clifford Geertz notes:

> The Western concept of the person as a bounded, unique, more or less integrated motivational and cognitive universe, a dynamic center of awareness, emotion, judgment and action organized into a distinctive whole and set contrastively both against other such wholes and against a social and natural background is, however incorrigible it may seem to us, a rather peculiar idea within the context of the world's cultures ... [We need to] set that concept aside and view their experience within the framework of their own idea of what selfhood is (1983: 59).

As cultural theorist Richard Johnson asserts 'subjectivities are produced, not given, and are therefore the objects of inquiry, not the premises or starting points' (1986: 44). Following both Johnson and anthropologist Dorrine Kondo's (1990) thoughtful ethnographic study of the 'crafting' of selves in Japan, I assume here that 'self' as well as the 'agency' and 'power' which might accrue from the practice of a martial art like *kalarippayattu* are context-and paradigm-specific – i.e. that they are variable and provisional. In this view self, agency and power are never 'absolute' but rather are 'nodal points repositioned in different contexts. Selves [agency and power] in this view can be seen as rhetorical figures and performative assertions enacted in specific situations within fields of power, history, and culture' (Kondo 1990: 304). *Kalarippayattu* is a set of techniques of body-mind practice through which particular 'selves' are understood or assumed to gain particular kinds of agency and power within specific contexts. Consequently, a martial practice like *kalarippayattu* becomes one means of 'crafting' a particular self and, therefore, is a 'culturally, historically specific pathway ... to self-realization ... [and/or] domination' (Kondo 1990: 305). The particular self crafted and realized in a Sufi Muslim *kalari* in northern Kerala will be different from the self crafted in a militantly radical Hindu *kalari* or the self crafted by learning *kalarippayattu* in the United States from an American teacher who might emphasize a 'self-actualized self.'

With these caveats in mind I turn to a brief historical overview of *kalarippayattu* and the nature of power for the martial artists of the past and then to a more specific examination of the ways in which some of today's *kalarippayattu* masters understand yoga, *Ayurveda* and power in interpreting their practice and, therefore, in crafting their 'selves'.

History and the *Kalarippayattu* Tradition

Two traditions of martial practice from antiquity have influenced the history, development, subculture and practice of *kalarippayattu*: Tamil (Dravidian) traditions dating from early Sangam culture and the Sanskritic Dhanur Vedic traditions. Although a complete account of South Indian martial arts in antiquity must be left to South Asian historians of the future, this necessarily brief description outlines a few of the salient features of the early Sangam Age fighting arts, focusing in particular on the Dhanur Vedic tradition and its relationship with the yoga paradigm.

From the early Tamil Sangam 'heroic' (puram) poetry we learn that from the fourth century B.C. to 600 A.D. a warlike, martial spirit was predominant across southern India. The importance of the martial hero in the Sangam Age is evident in the deification of fallen heroes through the planting of hero-stones (*virakkal* or *natukal* 'planted stones'), which were inscribed with the name of the hero and his valourous deeds (Kailaspathy 1968: 35) and worshipped by the common people of the locality (Subramanian 1966: 30). Certainly the earliest precursors of *kalarippayattu* were the Sangam Age combat techniques, which fostered the growth of a heroic ideal. However, there can be no doubt that the techniques and heroic ethos, at least of Kerala's *kalarippayattu*, must have been transformed in some way by the merging of indigenous techniques with the martial practices and ethos accompanying brahmin migrations from Saurastra and Konkan, down the west Indian coast into Karnataka and eventually Kerala (Velutat 1976; 1978). Important among early brahmin institutions were the *salad* or *ghatika*, institutions that were:

> Mostly attached to temples where the cattar or cathirar, proficient in Vedas and sastras and also military activities, lived under the patronage of kings who considered their establishment and maintenance a great privilege (Narayanan 1973: 33)

Drawing on inscriptional evidence, M.G.S. Narayanan has established that the students at these schools were *cattar*, who functioned under the direction of the local village brahmin assembly (*sabha*), recited the Vedas, observed *brahmacarya* and served as a 'voluntary force' to defend the temple and school if and when necessary (Narayanan 1973: 25–26).[4] The eighth century Jain Prakrit work, *Kuvalaymala* by Udyotanasuri from Jalur in Rajasthan, records a clear picture of the nature of these educational institutions:[5]

> Entering the city he sees a big matha. He asks a passerby 'Well sire, whose temple is that?' The person replies 'Bhatta, oh Bhatta, this is not a shrine

but it is a matha [monastery, residential quarter] of all the cattas [students]'.
[On entering the matha] … he sees the cattas, who were natives of various
countries, namely Lata Karnata, Dhakka, Srikantha … and Saindhava.
They were learning and practicing archery, fighting with sword and shield,
with daggers, sticks, lances and with fists and in duels (niuddham). Some
were learning painting (alekhya), singing (giya), musical instruments (vaditra),
staging of Bhanaka, Dombiliya, Siggadaiyam and dancing. They looked
like excited elephants from Maha-Vindhya (Shah 1968: 250–252).

Along with other brahmin institutions the *salad* and the *cattar* played a role in
the gradual formation of the distinctive linguistic, social, and cultural heritage
of the southwest coastal region, although the degree of influence was
certainly in direct proportion to the density of brahminical settlement and
local influence. M.G.S. Narayanan dates this period of change between the
founding of a second or new Cera capital at Makotai under Rama
Rajesekhara (c.800–844 A.D.) and its breakup after the rule of Rama
Kulasekhara (1089–1122 A.D.). Before the founding of the Makotai capital
Kerala was 'a region of Tamilakam with the same society and language';
however, in the post-Makotai period Kerala became distinctive in many ways
from the rest of Tamilakam (Narayanan 1976: 28).

Historians have dated the emergence of *kalarippayattu* as a distinct martial
tradition to the extended period of warfare in the eleventh century that saw
the demise of the second Cera kingdom (Pillai 1970: 241). During the war,
some brahmins continued to be trained in arms themselves, trained others,
and actively participated in fighting the Colas (Pillai, 1970: 155, 243–244).
Although the *salads* themselves declined with the end of the Cera Kingdom
and the division of Kerala into principalities, Brahmins in Kerala continued
to engage in the practice of arms in some sub-castes. Known as *cattar* or *yatra*
brahmins and considered degraded or 'half' brahmins because of their voca-
tion in arms, these groups continued to train, teach, fight, and rule through
the martial arts for several centuries.[6] The legendary Kerala brahmin chronicle *Keralopathi* confirms brahminical sub-caste involvement in teaching and
bearing arms. The chronicle tells that Parasurama gave the land to the brahmins to be enjoyed as 'brahmakshatra' (a land where brahmins take the role
of ksatriyas) and adds that:

3600 brahmins belonging to different settlements or gramas accepted the
right to bear arms from Parasurama. They are described as ardhabrah-
mana or half-brahmins and valnampis or armed brahmins and their
functions are mentioned as padu kidakka [restrain offenders], pada
kuduka [military service] and akampadi nadakukkuka [guard service].

They are said to be divided into four kalakams [a colloquial form of ghatika or the organizations of brahmincattarto defend the land] called Perincallur, Payyanur, Parappur and Chengannur respectively. These kalakams nominated four preceptors or rakshapurushas for the duration of three years with the right to collect revenue (Narayanan, 1973: 37–38).

Although the *cattar* continue to be mentioned in Kerala's heavily Sanskritized Manipravalam literature between the thirteenth and fifteenth centuries, these formerly well-respected brahmin scholars and practitioners in arms are depicted as living decadent lives. References find them 'wearing weapons with fresh blood in them' engaging in combat, demonstrating feats with their swords and touting the prowess of cattars in combat (Pillai 1970: 275). Whatever the caste or religion of the medieval practitioners of *kalarippayattu* all practiced their martial art within a socio-political environment which was shaped by a constantly shifting set of alliances and outbreaks of warfare between feuding rulers of petty principalities. Since practitioners had pledged themselves to death on behalf of their rulers, they were obliged to develop both the mental power and battlefield skills that would allow them to sacrifice themselves in order to fulfill their pledges.

Following J. Richardson Freeman's recent research on the nature of *teyyam* worship in North Malabar to which *kalarippayattu* practice and martial heroes are integrally linked, it is clear that for the medieval Malayali practitioners of *kalarippayattu* the 'world' within which they exercised their martial skills was shaped by a religious and socio-political ideology in which 'battle serves as a dominant metaphor for conceptualizing relations of spiritual and socio-political power' (Freeman 1991: 588). Following Hart's research on the early Dravidian notion of power (*ananku*) as capricious and immanent, Freeman convincingly argues that in medieval Kerala 'the locus of divine power is not primarily, or at least usefully, transcendent but immanent and located in human persons and their ritual objects' (Freeman 1991: 130). The martial practitioner was compelled to harness through whatever techniques might be at his disposal those special, local and immanent powers that might be of use to him in fulfilling his pledged duty to a ruler.

Power and Agency in Classical Contests

It seems likely that at least some of the distinctive traits of Kerala's *kalarippayattu* crystallized during the intensive period of warfare between the Cholas and Ceras and that such developments were at least in part attributable to the mingling of indigenous Dravidian martial techniques dating from the Sangam Age with techniques and an ethos imported by brahmins and practiced in their *salai*, especially in the northern and central Kerala region where brahminical culture became dominant and *kalarippayattu* developed. It is not insignificant that some present masters trace their lineages of practice to 'Dhanur Veda' and claim that the texts in which their martial techniques are recorded derive from Dhanur Vedic texts. Although the Dhanur Veda, to which present-day *kalarippayattu* masters refer, is literally translated as the 'science of archery', it encompassed all the traditional fighting arts. The explicit concern in Dhanur Veda texts is not with battlefield strategies, but rather with training in martial techniques.[7] Like the purana as a whole, the Dhanur Veda chapters provide both 'sacred knowledge' (*paravidya*) and 'profane knowledge' (*aparavidya*) on the subject. The Dhanur Veda opens by cataloging the subject, stating that there are five training divisions (for warriors on chariots, elephants, horseback, infantry and wrestling) and five types of weapons to be learned (those projected by machine [arrows or missiles], those thrown by the hands [spears], those cast by hands yet retained [noose], those permanently held in the hands [sword] and the hands themselves [249: 1–5]). Regarding who should teach, we are told that either a brahmin or ksatriya 'should be engaged to teach and drill soldiers in the art and tactics of the Dhanur Veda' because it is their birthright, while shudras can be called upon to take up arms when necessary if they have 'acquired a general proficiency in the art of warfare by regular training and practice'. Finally, 'people of mixed castes' might also be called upon if needed by the king (249: 6–8) (M.N. Dutt Shastri, 1967: 894–5).

Beginning with the noblest of weapons (bow and arrow), the text discusses the specifics of training and practice. It names and describes ten basic lower-body poses to be assumed when practicing with bow and arrow and the specific posture with which the disciple should pay obeisance to his preceptor (249: 9–19). Once the basic positions have been described, there is technical instruction in how to string, draw, raise, aim and release the bow and arrow and a catalogue of types of bows and arrows (249: 20–29). In the second chapter are recorded more advanced and difficult bow-and-arrow techniques. But first are details of how a brahmin should ritually purify weapons before they are used (250: 1). Also within the first seven lines of this chapter appear several phrases which collectively constitute the manual's leitmotif: an intimation of the ideal, subtle state of interior accomplishment which the practitioner must possess to become a consummate martial practitioner. The archer is first described as 'girding up his loins' and tying in place his quiver only after he has 'collected himself'; he places the arrow on the string only after 'his mind [is] divested of all cares and anxieties' (M.N. Dutt Shastra 1967: 897) and finally, when the archer has become so well practiced that he 'knows the procedure' he 'should fix his mind on the target' before releasing the arrow (Gangadharan 1985: 648). Implicit throughout is a clear sense of a systematic progression in training from preliminary lower body postures which provide a psychophysiological foundation for virtuosity, through technical mastery of lifting, placing, drawing and releasing and thence to the interior subtleties of mental discipline necessary to become a consummate archer and, therefore, an accomplished fighter. Having achieved the ability to fix his mind, the archer's training is still not complete. The archer must apply this ability while performing increasingly difficult techniques, such as hitting targets above and below the line of vision and while riding a horse; hitting targets farther and farther away; and finally hitting whirling, moving, or fixed targets one after the other (250:13–19). The chapter concludes with a summary statement of the accomplished abilities of the archer:

> Having learned all these ways, one who knows the system of karma-yoga [associated with this practice] should perform this way of doing things with his mind, eyes, and inner vision since one who knows [this] yoga will conquer even the god of death [Yama] (Dasgupta 1993).

To 'conquer the god of death [Yama]' is to have 'conquered' the 'self' i.e. to have overcome all obstacles (physical, mental and emotional) inasmuch as one has cultivated a self-possessed presence in the face of potential death in combat. Although this quote concludes the second chapter, it does not complete all there is to say about the training and abilities of the archer. The opening verse of the third chapter describes a further stage in the training of the archer:

> Having acquired control of the hands, mind, and vision, and become accomplished in target practice, then [through this] you will achieve disciplined accomplishment (siddhi) after this, practice riding vehicles (Dasgupta 1993).

The remainder of Chapter 251 and most of the final Chapter 252 are brief descriptions of postures and/or techniques for wrestling and the use of a variety of weapons including the noose, sword, armors, iron dart, club, battle axe, discus and the trident. A short passage near the end of the text returns to the larger concerns of warfare and explains the various uses of war elephants and men. The text concludes with a description of how to appropriately send the well-trained fighter off to war:

> The man who goes to war after worshipping his weapons and the Trai/okyamohan Sastra [one which pleases the three worlds] with his own mantra [given to him by his preceptor], will conquer his enemy and protect the world (Dasgupta 1993).

To summarize, the Dhanur Veda paradigm of practice was a highly developed system of training through which the martial practitioner was able to achieve success with combat skills utilized as duty (dharma) demanded. This level of martial accomplishment was circumscribed by ritual practices and achieved by combining technical practice with training in specific forms of yoga and meditation (including repetition of mantra) so that the practitioner might ideally achieve the superior degree of self-control, mental calm and single-point concentration necessary to face combat and possible death and thus attain access to certain aspects of power and agency in the use of weapons in combat. What is implicit in these Dravidian, Sanskritic and medieval Keralan sources and history is the view that combat is not simply a test of strength and will between two human beings like modern sport boxing, but rather a contest between a host of complex contingent, unstable and immanent powers to which each combatant gains access through divine gifts, through magico-ritual means, and by attaining mastery of some aspect of power through practice and training. The first two of these modes of gaining access to power are religio-sacred and the third is more 'rational' in that accomplishment comes through training. Other realms of practiced knowledge in South Asian antiquity, such as Ayurvedic medicine, reflect a similar symbiotic relationship and interaction between the divine and the 'scientifically' explainable. The antique medical authority, Susruta, articulated the existence of both rationally understood causes for systemic imbalance in the body's humours as well as the possibility of divine and/or magical sources of imbalance and/or cure. In fact Susruta identified one of seven kinds of disease as 'the providential type-which includes diseases that are the embodiments of curses, divine wrath or displeasure, or are brought about through the mystic potencies of charms and spells' (Zimmermann 1986; Bhisagratna 1963: 231).

The agency and power of the martial artist in Indian antiquity must be understood as a complex set of interactions between humanly acquired techniques of virtuosity (the human microcosm) and the divine macrocosm. Unlike our modern biomedical and/or scientifically-based notions of power and agency, which assume that any type of power (electricity, gravity etc.) is totally rational and stable, and therefore measurable and quantifiable, 'power' (*ananku* or *sakti*) in Dravidian antiquity, and at least through the medieval period in South India, was considered unstable, capricious and locally immanent. Given this instability the martial practitioner accumulated numerous different powers through any and all means at his disposal, depending not only on his own humanly acquired skills achieved under the guidance of his teachers but also on the acquisition of powers through magical or religious techniques such as the repetition of mantra (Alper 1989: 3, 6).

Sanskrit epic literature reflects this complex interplay between divinely gifted and humanly acquired powers for the martial practitioners of antiquity.

One example is the playwright Bhasa's version of Karna's story, *Karnabhara*, which illustrates the divine gift of power (*sakti*) which requires no attainment on the part of the practitioner. Indra, disguised as a brahmin, has come to Karna on his way to do combat with the Pandavas. As a brahmin Indra begs a gift from Karna. Karna freely offers gift after great gift, all of which are refused. Finally, against the advice of his charioteer he offers that which provides him as a fighter with magical protection, his body armor, which could not be pierced by gods or demons. Indra joyfully takes it. Moments later a divine messenger informs Karna that Indra is filled with remorse for having stripped him of his protection. The messenger asks Karna to 'accept this unfailing weapon whose sakti is named Vimala, to slay one among the Pandavas' (102). At first Karna refuses, saying that he never accepts anything in return for a gift. However, since this gift is offered by a brahmin he agrees to accept it. As he takes the weapon from the messenger he asks, 'When shall I gain its power (sakti)?' and the messenger responds 'When you take it in [your] mind, you will [immediately] gain its power' (105–106).[8] Unlike other powers to which a martial artist gains access through the practice and repetition of exercises and/or austerities here Karna is a vehicle of divine power which requires that he simply 'take [the weapon] in mind' for its full power to be at his disposal.

A more complex set of circumstances are at play in the story of Arjuna and the Pasupata and his mastery of the weapon requires much more of him than simply accepting the weapon as a gift.[9] Yudhisthira knows that, should combat come, the Kauravas have gained access to 'the entire art of archery' including 'Brahmic, Divine and Demoniac use of all types of arrows, along with practices and cures'. The 'entire earth is subject to Duryodhana', due to this extraordinary accumulation of powers. Yudhisthira, therefore, calls upon Arjuna to go and gain access to still higher powers than those possessed by the Kauravas. To do this Arjuna must embark on a quest to find 'the Lord of Beings, three-eyes, trident-bearing Siva'. Setting out on his journey 'with a steady mind' he travels to the peaks of the Himalayas where he settles to practice 'awesome austerities'. Eventually Siva comes to test him in the form of a hunter. After a prolonged fight Siva-the-hunter subdues Arjuna when he 'loses control of his body'. Siva then reveals his true form to Arjuna who lays before him. Siva recognizes that 'no mortal is your equal' and offers to grant him a wish. Arjuna requests the Pasupata, the divine weapon. Siva agrees to give him this unusual weapon, which is so great that 'no one in all the three worlds [the Brahmic, Divine, and Demonic] is invulnerable to it'. In other words, with this weapon he will gain access to powers greater than those possessed by the Kauravas. However, to gain access to the weapon's power Arjuna must first undergo ritual purification, prostrate himself in devotion before Lord Siva and embrace his feet, and then learn its special techniques. Siva instructs him in the specific techniques of the Pasupata, and having become accomplished in these techniques he also learns 'the secrets of its return.'

Among all the martial heroes of the epics Arjuna is the perfect royal sage, possessing the ideal combination of martial and ascetic skills and able to marshal the various powers at his command as and when necessary. Arjuna is able to attain the awesome power of the Pasupata because of his extraordinary 'steadiness of mind', his superior skills at archery, and his ability to undergo 'awesome' austerities. Although Arjuna's skills and accomplishments appear superhuman, the process of attainment of powers follows a pattern we shall find repeated among some traditional masters in the ethnographic present: ritual purification, superior devotion, practice of techniques to gain mastery, access to higher powers through the practice of austerities and/or special meditation, acquiring the secrets of practice, and even the use of magical means to obtain immediate access to a specific power.[10] However, even if this pattern of attainment of powers is still evident in the ethnographic present, as the necessity of gaining access to powers when confronting death in combat has become largely a moot point, the hitherto capricious, unstable, immanent, and local nature of power has been somewhat muted and pacified today – a subject to which I shall return in the concluding discussion.

The *Kalarippayattu* System in the Ethnographic Present

Like their epic and purist counterparts, traditional *kalarippayattu* practitioners attaining power must access a composite, multi-dimensioned set of practices. There is the power to be attained through repetition of mantra, each of which must be individually accomplished; the power inherent in discovery and control of the internal energy/breath (*prana-vayu*); the strength of mental power (*manasakti*) manifest in one-point focus and complete doubtlessness; the elemental discovery and raising of the power per se (*kundalini sakti*); and the powers of the divine gained through worship and rituals (*puja*), meditation, devotion and magic. However, to gain access to the majority of these types of power, one must begin with the body and its training in actualizing particular powers. A Muslim master once told me 'He who wants to become a master must possess complete knowledge of the body'. As assumed in traditional yoga practice, knowledge of the body begins with the physical or gross body (*sthula-sarira*) discovered through exercises and massage. Together they are considered 'body preparation' (*meyyorukkam*). The exercises include a vast array of poses, steps, jumps, kicks and leg movements performed in increasingly complex combinations, back and forth across the *kalari* floor.

Collectively they are considered a 'body art' (*meiabhyasam*). Individual body-exercise sequences (*meippayattu*) are taught one by one and every student masters simple forms before moving on to more complex and difficult sequences. Most important is mastery of basic poses (*vadivu*) named after animals and comparable to the basic postures (*asana*) of yoga and the mastery of the steps (*cuvadu*) by which one moves into and out of poses. Repetitious practice of these outer forms eventually renders the external body flexible (*meivalakkam*) and, as one master said 'flowing (*olukku*) like a river'.

During the most intensive period of training, while the monsoon is active, masters are supposed to require observance of specific behavioral, dietary and devotional practices and restraints, similar to those traditionally practiced in the classic eightfold Patanjali yoga: (1) negative (*yama*, 'do not') restrictions, (2) positive ('do') practices, and (3) the development of a devotional attitude. Students are instructed never to sleep during the day time nor to keep awake at night; to refrain from sex during the most intensive monsoon period of training; never to misuse what one is being taught; to only use *kalarippayattu* to defend oneself (i.e. when dharma demands); and to be of good character (i.e. not to steal, lie, cheat, drink liquor or take drugs). Finally, from the very first day of practice in a traditional Hindu *kalari* students must participate in the devotional life of the *kalari* from the point of ritual entry into the sacred space through the practice of personal devotion to the *kalari* deities and to the master. As Eliade explains these restraints do not produce 'a yogic state but a 'purified' human being ... This purity is essential to the succeeding stages' (1975: 63).

One of the important dimensions of initial training is direction of the student's visual focus. Students are told to 'look at a specific place' on the opposite side of the *kalari* while performing the leg exercises, the initial step in developing one-point focus (*ekagrata*). As master Achuthan Gurukkal told me 'One-point focus is first developed by constant practice of correct form in exercises'. Once the external, physical eye is steadied the student eventually begins to discover the 'inner eye' of practice, a state of inner connection to practice. The body-exercise sequences are linked combinations of basic body movements (*meitolil*) including poses (*vativu*), steps (*cuvat*), kicks (*kaletupp*), a variety of jumps and turns and coordinated hand/arm movements performed in increasingly swift succession, back and forth across the *kalari*. Masters emphasize the importance of poses (*vadivu*) in a student's progression. As Gurukkal P. K. Balan told me, 'Only a person who has learned these eight poses can perform the *kalari* law (*mura*) and go on to empty-hand combat, weapons, massage or *marma* applications'. The poses (*vadivu*), usually numbering eight, are named after animals. They are not static forms but configurations of movements which embody both the external and internal essence of the animal after which they are named. P. K. Balan explained his version of the animal names:

> When any animal fights, it uses its whole body. This must also be true in *kalarippayattu*. The horse is an animal which can concentrate all its powers centrally, and it can run fast by jumping up. The same pause, preparation for jumping, and forward movement [that are in a horse] are in the *asvavadivu*.

> When a peacock is going to attack its enemies, it spreads its feathers, raises its neck, and dances by steadying itself on one leg. Then it shifts to the other leg and attacks by jumping and flying. The capability of doing this attack is known as *mayuravadivu*.

> A snake attacks its enemy by standing up; however, its tail remains on the ground without movement. From this position, it can turn in any direction and bite a person. This ability to turn in any direction and attack by rising up is known as *sarpavadivu*.

> When a cock attacks, he uses all parts of his body: wings, neck, legs, fingernails. He will lift one leg and shake his feathers and neck, fix his gaze on the enemy, and attack. This is *kukkuvadivu*.

Like the leg exercises, the body sequences at first further develop flexibility, balance and control of the body. This most often occurs when the training is rigorous. The oiled bodies begin to sweat and, by the conclusion of a class, the student's entire body should be drenched in sweat. As one teacher said 'The sweat of the students should become the water washing the *kalari* floor'. Chirakkal T. Balakrishnan describes the results of such practice for one sequence, *pakarcakkal* as being like 'a bee circling a flower. While doing *pakarcakkal* a person first moves forward and back and then again forward and back. It should be done like a spider weaving its web'. What is most important is swift and facile changes of direction executed at the transition points between sets of movements, essential for combat in which instantaneous changes of direction are necessary. Only much later are specific martial applications taught.

Behind the fluid grace of the gymnastic forms is the strength and power of movements which can, when necessary, be applied with lightning-fast speed and precision in potentially deadly attacks. 'Hidden' within all the preliminary exercises and basic poses are complex combinations of offensive and defensive applications, which are eventually learned through constant practice. The body-exercise sequences 'just look like exercises' but many applications (*prayogam*) are possible. Correctly executing locks to escape an enemy's grasp, taught as part of the empty-hand techniques (*verumkai*) late in training, can only be completed with full force when a student is able to assume a pose, such as the elephant, deeply and fully. An advanced student should be able to move with fluid spontaneity in any direction and perform any combination of moves from the body exercise sequences for offensive or defensive purposes. As Gurukkal Govindankutty Nayar put it, the student himself will begin to discover these applications 'in due time.' Students advance through the system individually. The teacher keeps a constant and watchful eye on each student's gradual progress i.e. on how well the student masters the forms of practice and on his general demeanor and behavior. The discerning teacher does not simply look at a student's overt, physical progress but also looks 'within at the heart of the student'. Some masters say that they 'know [each student's] mind from the countenance of the face' (*mukhabhavattil ninnu manassilakkam*). Nothing overt is expressed, explained or spoken; the master simply watches, observes and 'reads' each student. Physically embodying the forms of practice, mentally achieving the degree of focus and concentration necessary and personally developing the requisite devotion for deities and master all take considerable time. Only when a master intuitively senses that a student is psychophysiologically, morally and spiritually 'ready' to advance and when the teacher has no doubts about the student's character, is he supposed to teach a new, more difficult exercise. Ideally, each technique is given as a 'gift'. The teacher should take joy in the act of giving, especially as the gifts become more advanced and, therefore, more precious.

Unlike *varmaati*, *kalarippayattu*'s sister martial art indigenous to the Kanyakumari region of the old Travancore kingdom and southern Tamil Nadu, as well as more recent cosmopolitan forms of martial arts oriented toward self-defense and/or street fighting, *kalarippayattu* is similar to its Japanese counterpart, the traditional *bugei* or weapons forms, in which use of weapons was historically the main purpose of practice. Empty- hand fighting has always been important to *kalarippayattu* but more as a means of disarming an armed opponent than as its sole raison d'être. Only when a student is physically, spiritually and ethically 'ready' is he supposed to be allowed to take up the first weapon. If the body and mind have been fully prepared (and therefore integrated) when the student takes up the first weapon, it becomes an extension of the integration of the bodymind in action.[11]

The student first learns wooden weapons: *kolttari* or *kolkayattam payattu*, starting with the long staff and moving on to the short stick and the curved stick. Only after several years does one advance to combat weapons-including the dagger spear, sword and shield and flexible sword (the bow and arrow have died out as part of the *kalarippayattu* tradition). The teacher's instructions are intended to make the weapon an extension of the body. For example, the staff is an extension of the natural line of the spinal column, maintained as one moves into and out of basic poses. The hands are kept in front of the body and the body weight is always kept forward, maximizing the range of the staff to keep the opponent at bay.

For some masters, practice with the curved stick or *otta*, with its deep, wavelike, flowing movements, is considered the culmination and epitome of psychophysiological training. Not only is there superb and beautiful external form, but also a simultaneous internal awakening. When correct spinal alignment is maintained, practice further develops the important region at the root of the navel (*nabhi mula*) region, hips and thighs. Without the student realizing, *otta* also subtly initiates the student in empty-hand combat (*verumkai*), the most advanced part of total *kalarippayattu* training, which eventually culminates when the student learns the location of the body's vital spots (*marmmam*) which are attacked or defended (see Zarrilli 1992). Correct practice of all weapons depends entirely on correct performance of preliminary body exercises. Weapons are never to be manipulated by using overt physical force or trying to make a blow forceful. Gurukkal Govindankutty Nayar said 'Using overt force is the surest way for a blow to 'become nothing' and 'lose its actuality'. Like the body exercises, each blow, thrust, cut or defensive movement must be performed with the entire body and not simply with the hand, arm and/or weapon. While practicing sword and shield, my teacher told me:

> A non-actualized cut originates from the shoulder itself and does not bring the entire body into the execution of the cut, nor does it flow into the next cut in the sequence which follows.

> Just as one movement should flow into the next when one performs the body exercise sequence, so in weapons practice one blow merges naturally with the next as there is a continuous energy flow which should never be broken.

Eventually the student should begin to manifest physical, mental and behavioral signs, resulting from practice. At first the exercises are 'that which is external' (*bahyamayatu*). Like *hatha* yoga, daily practice of the forms leads to extraordinary physical control and eventually should turn the student inward; the exercises eventually become 'that which is internal' (*andarikamayatu*). One master explained the progression: 'First the outer forms, then the inner secrets'. Therefore, exercises and weapon forms are repeated until the student has sufficiently embodied the 'inner life' (*bhava*) of the sequence or until the correct form gets 'inside' the student's body. Once the exercise becomes 'effortless', as one performs the exercise, he should naturally begin to

experience the 'inner action' behind the external movement. As Gurukkal
Govindankutty Nayar discussed in detail with me, simply mimicking correct
external form is not enough:

> Almost all practice you see is partial. It is not complete. Even with
> advanced students practicing, their form may be good and correct in
> [external] form, but it is still lacking something. It is lacking that spark or
> life (jivan) that makes this a real and full practice. They do not yet have
> the soul of the form.

> The external form remains empty, 'lifeless,' and a mere shell if there is
> not simultaneously the correct and appropriate circulation of the internal
> wind or energy.

The Actualization of Power (*sakti*)

Most masters would agree with Achutan Gurukkal's statement that only
through 'correct practice' of poses and steps will the student reap the benefits
of disciplined rehearsal and also begin to discover and eventually manifest
power (*sakti*) in practice. What, precisely, is meant by *sakti* and what are the
signs of its presence? According to those masters who assume the yoga
based paradigm discussed above, three essential features must be realized:
(1) precisely correcting the external physical form and corresponding internal
circulation of the wind or energy (*vayu* or *prana-vayu*) so that alignment and
movement are correct and within the limits of a form (2) ensuring that the
student is breathing properly, coordinating and releasing the breath properly
and therefore circulating the wind or energy correctly (3) ensuring that the
student develops correct external focus and eventually realizes one-point focus
internally. Masters like Achutan Gurukkal stress that 'correct practice also
means breathing naturally and, therefore, having the breath properly coordinated with performing the exercise or pose'. Teachers tell their students to
'breath through the nose; don't open your mouth'. Keeping the mouth closed,
the hands raised and the spinal column firm in its natural alignment during
leg exercises forces the student to begin to develop natural, deep diaphrag-
matic breathing from the navel region and prevents the natural tendency to
take shallow breaths from the chest. In addition to the natural coordination of
breath with exercise some masters, but by no means all, also practice special
breath control techniques understood to help activate and circulate the practitioner's 'internal energy' (*prana vayu*) and, therefore, contribute to the actualization of *sakti* to be used in fighting and/or healing. The emphasis is on
pranayama techniques shared with yoga and taught by either *kalarippayattu* or
yoga masters, which require repetition of the fourfold pattern of inhalation,

retention/pause, exhalation, retention/pause. One Christian master believed that 'breath control exercises are superior to all other forms of exercise. The vital energy (*prana vayu*), mind, intellect and physical strength (*balam*) are all closely related'. Another master claims that practicing *pranayama* leads to 'control over the mind as well as the body's metabolic functions' and therefore to the development of correct form practice in the martial art. Neelakantan Namboodiripad told me that practicing *pranayama* brings 'concentration' and eventually 'air strength' (*vayubalam*) identical with the manifestation of power (*sakti*) itself. One master explained the practical application of pranayama in the martial art:

> In pranayama there are two retentions, one after inhalation and one after exhalation. The one after exhalation is not strong. Therefore, when you give a blow it comes with exhalation. But strong defense comes with inhalation. This is the essence of kalarippayattu, but most people don't know it. Only those who have studied pranayama can understand it.

Other masters have learned special *kalarippayattu* breathing exercises simply called 'swasam.' Their purpose is the same as *pranayama* i.e. 'to gain strength (*balam*) and power (*sakti*).' Master Mohammedunni describes the result as gaining 'wind power' (*vayusakti*) 'so that I will have firm steps and for application [in combat]'. When performing these exercises 'your mind is simply on what you are doing. There is a grip or power in the stomach at the full point of inhalation'.

The third most important feature of 'correct practice' leading to actualization of *sakti* is developing correct or one point, focus (*ekagrata*). There are numerous practical ways in which internal one point focus is practiced in the *kalari*. Visually focusing on the teacher's eyes in weapons training continues the student's development of one-point focus, begun when the student is first instructed to focus when he begins the leg exercises. As Achuttan Gurukkal explained:

> We should never take our eyes from those of our opponent. By ekagrata here I mean kannottam, keeping the eyes on the opponent's. When doing practice you should not see anything else going on around you.

Master Achutan's comments echo the well known example of Arjuna's actualization of one point focus in the archery test which was administered by Drona to all his students and at which only Arjuna was successful. Single-point focus should not be confused with the simple act of focusing the eyes on an external object. One-point focus has both external and internal dimensions, the internal developed as an integral part of the raising and discovery of the internal wind or energy. For a few masters, one point focus is simply the first stage in an ever deepening and more subtle process of interior practice, further developed through special meditational techniques.

Whether Hindu, Christian, or Muslim, those who emphasize the internal aspect of practice teach one or more forms of meditation as a natural extension of this inward progression of practice. Meditation is understood to be a complementary means of controlling the natural state of mental flux which stands in the way of the student's achievement of one point concentration, as well as a path to higher modes of personal accomplishment and actualization. As one master explained:

> Practicing kalarippayattu is conducive to learning both yoga and pranayama; they all come together. Both produce sharpness and steadiness of mind, both also give courage and patience, and both also help to give good health. What eventually results from practicing kalarippayattu is the discovery of the interior subtle body (suksma-sarira) traditionally associated with yoga and meditation, and assumed to be encased within the physical body (Zarrilli 1989).

As Govindankutty Nayar put it '*Kalarippayattu* is 80% percent mental and only the remainder is physical'. The eighty percent mental is further developed through a variety of forms of meditation including everything from simple *vratam* or sitting and focusing one's mind on a deity, name chanting, or focusing on one's own breathing to more complex forms of moving or stationary meditation which cannot be explained in this brief essay. Following the yogic ideal of self-control to its logical extreme, the ultimate mastery of 'mental powers' applied in martial practice is the development of the esoteric, seemingly 'magical' power to attack the body's vital spots (*marmmam*) by simply looking or pointing (Zarrilli 1992). Belief in these subtle powers is simply an extension of pan-Indian assumptions regarding the ability of supremely accomplished individual masters of yoga to accumulate and concentrate their powers internally and then to apply those powers externally. In the ethnographic domain the continued belief in such powers is the closest contemporary reflection of the subtle, esoteric powers attained by epic heroes like Arjuna.[12]

The Fruits of Practice: *Kalarippayattu* and the Ayurvedic Paradigm

For some traditional masters, especially those following the model of epic heroes or teachers like Drona and Arjuna, the training regimen is understood to last a lifetime and, like other yogic disciplines, is intended to lead not only to mastery of the esoteric, subtle powers but also to be, on a much more mundane level, an all encompassing way of life which affects diet, health, moral and ethical behavior, psychophysical development and spiritual wellbeing. Corrections to the psychophysiological exercises are initially given in order to help the student assume the correct external form. With practice, as the form 'becomes more correct', there is assumed to be a corresponding effect on the health, well being, behavior and inner experience of the practitioner, complemented by the forms of meditation and devotion a student may practice. The process of constant repetition eventually leads beyond empty mimicry. At first one must overcome the physical limitations of the gross, physical body, stretching muscles to enable the body to assume correct forms, removing mental distractions and achieving visual focus. Eventually, one begins to experience and reap the first 'fruits' (*phalam*) of practice-assumed to be the 'natural result' of nourishing the seeds planted through correct practice. These fruits cannot be consciously striven for since striving itself is understood to stand in the way of fruition. As Kallada Balakrishnan told me, when forms and breathing are practiced correctly 'you begin to see a change' in the student. The effect of practice on the body of the practitioner is often understood and interpreted according to the traditional humoural concepts of India's classical medical system, *Ayurveda*, which seeks to establish harmony with the environment by maintaining equilibrium in a process of constant fluid exchange. According to South Asian medical anthropologist Francis Zimmermann, the art of medicine is meant to establish:

> yoga or samyoga, 'junctions' or 'articulations' between man and his environment, through the prescription of appropriate diets and regimens … Equality, balance and congruous articulations are meant for the conservation and restoration of these precious fluids … By means of brahmacarya … and various other psychosomatic disciplines, one should establish congruous junctions with the surrounding landscapes and seasons, and thus one should protect one's powers, one should husband one's vital fluids (1983 :17–18).

Kalarippayattu is one such discipline, the daily practice of which is popularly believed to establish congruence among the three humours (*tridosa*): wind (*vata*), phlegm (*kapha*) and fire (*pitta*). The master's understanding of the benefits of training and his treatment of injuries are based on this fundamental notion of the body. The role of exercise and massage in maintaining inner fluidity and articulation among the humors was explained in antiquity in a medical text attributed to Susruta:

> The act born from the effort (ayasa) of the body is called exercise (vyayama). After doing it, one should shampoo the body on all sides until it gives a comfortable sensation.

Growth of the body, radiance, harmonious proportions of the limbs, a kindled [digestive] fire, energy, firmness, lightness, purity (mrja), endurance to fatigue, weariness, thirst, hot and cold, etc., and even a perfect health: this is what is brought by physical exercise.

Nothing comparable to it for reducing obesity. No enemy will attack a man (literally: a mortal, martya) who practices physical exercise, because they all fear his strength.

Senility (or the decay of old age, jara) will not seize him abruptly. The muscles keep firm in one who practices physical exercise; that is, one whose body is sedated by physical exercise and who is massaged with the feet (vyayamasvinnagatrasya padbhyam udvartitasya ca) diseases fly from him, just as small beasts do on seeing a lion.

Physical exercise makes good-looking even the person deprived of youth and beauty. Physical exercise, in one who does it assiduously, digests all food, even the most inappropriate, turned sour or still crude without provoking the humors. For assiduous physical exercise is beneficial to a strong man who eats unctuous foods (snigdhabhojin).

It is especially beneficial to him in the winter and spring. But in all seasons, every day, a man seeking his own good should take physical exercise only to the half limit of his strength, as otherwise it kills.

When the Vayu hitherto properly located in the heart (hrdi) comes to the mouth of the man practicing physical exercise, it is the sign (laksana) of balardha, of his having used half of his strength.

Age, strength, body, place, time, and food: It is only after duly considering these factors, that one should engage in physical exercise, as otherwise it may bring disease (Zimmermann 1986).

Another antique authority, Vagbhata, wrote that a 'harmonious and solid condition of the body results from gymnastics' followed by massage (Vogel 1965: 90). The health benefits of regular exercise and massage are a commonplace of the martial art among today's practitioners. As one student told me 'I practice *kalarippayattu* to maintain health of the body. I can enjoy when I practice. When I exercise and then take a bath, I feel very energetic at work and sleep well … After practicing for three years, I have not had any fever or headache or any other diseases'.

Practice is traditionally regulated by *rtucarya* or 'the art of adapting one's diet and conduct to the cycle of the seasons' (Zimmermann 1979: 13; 1980). The most intensive period of training is the rainy season from June through August which is 'neither too hot nor too cold'. In a discussion about training with Govindankutty Nayar he told me 'During this season it is good for the body to have oil and sweat. This is also the best season for massage (uliccil). It provides protection for the body. If one were to exercise during the hot season (April-May), he would feel weak and lack energy'. Vigorous practice is considered appropriate to monsoon season because more energy is thought to be available at this time. In this cool season the heat produced by vigorous exercise and massage is counterbalanced by the seasonal accumulation of phlegm (*kapha*). By contrast the hot summer season is characterized by accumulation of the wind humor (*vata*) and in this period exercise should be avoided. Exercise and massage also increase the circulation of the wind humor (*vata*) throughout the body and this too counterbalances the accumulation of phlegm during the monsoon. The special restrictions which traditionally circumscribed training maintain balance among the three humors. Since the body is 'heated' by vigorous exercise, other activities must counterbalance this heating effect. For example, sexual activity expends vital energy and increases *vata*. If this accumulation of *vata* is combined with vigorous exercise (also producing *vata* and heat) it would create a humoural imbalance. Therefore, sexual activity was traditionally forbidden during this intense monsoon period of practice.

Exercise should always be within the limits of one's age and basic constitution. Exertion beyond one's normal limits causes an imbalance which can become pathological. Training is, therefore, a long term process in which one's capacity may be enhanced. The daily application of specially prepared oil is thought to add flexibility and strength to muscles, joints and ligaments. Seasonal massage (*uliccil*) and restrictions on behavior and diet are also understood to enhance the ease and fluidity of movement. Specially prepared herbal oils are applied before exercise to produce sweat from internal body heat. The oil keeps the heat from dissipating and its medicinal properties seep into the body through pores opened by sweating. Oil applied after exercise begins introduces a mixture of sweat and oil through the open pores, and this produces a cooling effect leading to a humoural imbalance. The sweating, oiled body should not be exposed to direct sunlight or to outdoor wind; therefore, the place of training is ideally constructed as a pit that protects the practitioner from sun and wind. The flow of air remains above the trainees, keeping the building cool and fresh, with no wind on the trainees' bodies.

The exercise, sweating and oil massage stimulate all forms of the wind humour to course through the body. Long term practice enhances the ability to endure fatigue through balancing the three humors and cultivates a characteristic internal and external ease of movement and body fluidity. The accomplished practitioner's movements flow (*olukku*). These techniques 'clear up the channels and nourish the body fluids and tissues' (Zimmermann 1988: 19) and are centered in the abdomen since the navel region is considered the point from which channels of the body flow.

The benefits of practice are not restricted to the effect on the body of humours. Among some masters, health is viewed as equally dependent on maintaining equanimity among all aspects of one's life including body, mind and behavior. There is a fluid exchange among all three. The same student who told me about the perceived benefits to his physical health gained by practice continued by telling me that 'practice also increases stamina and concentration. Since I joined the *kalari* I have been able to obtain a high degree of concentration in my daily routines. Above all, it has helped me to be calm in the midst of the people with whom I associate. In my experience *kalarippayattu* practice leads both to natural resistance in the body and to better behavior'. Ideally, according to some masters, in addition to physical health, one naturally begins to develop a calm and stable mental state. As Master Govindankutty Nayar told me:

> If you perform the exercises correctly and have the proper grip, then you begin to 'enjoy' practice. By doing this the whole body finds enjoyment. The mind won't be wandering here and there. You can do it with full confidence and courage. Your mind won't be in a 'flurry' (sambhramam). Sometimes, in combat, one might become flustered. If an opponent is powerful, one might become nervous; so, slowly you must develop this ability to be calm, to have mental peace … Only those who follow a strict routine in their lives can have such mental calm.

According to this interpretation, the student who practices forms correctly, coordinates breath with exercise and develops one point focus, should eventually begin to experience a more calm and stable disposition. The mental calm resulting from practice is said to give one 'mental courage' (*manodhairyam*) i.e. 'the power to face anything that is dangerous to my health or mind. If I am confident of my art and health, then only can I have mental power (*manasakti*)'. Mental equilibrium can be 'read' in each person's face. 'If one faces an attack, relaxation of the face reflects mental equilibrium' achieved through daily practice.

In Kerala, there is a folk expression which summarizes the martial practitioner's ideal state of psychophysiological pneumatic accomplishment explored here; it is the state when the 'body becomes all eyes' (*meyyu kannakuka*).

One reading of the 'body as all eyes' is as the yogic/Ayurvedic bodymind which intuitively responds to the sensory environment and which is healthful and fluid in its congruency. It is the animal body in which there is unmediated, uncensored, immediate respondence to stimuli. Like Brahma, the 'thousand eyed', the practitioner who is accomplished can 'see' everywhere around him, intuitively sensing danger in the environment and responding immediately. In a world where power was traditionally assumed to be unstable, capricious, and immanent such immediate reactions would have been essential to counteracting not only a thrust to the stomach but also the possibility of an 'attack' by simply looking or pointing.

Conclusion: Bodily Practice, Morality and Crafting the 'Self'

Although the yogic and Ayurvedic assumptions which inform practice among the masters for whom the 'body becomes all eyes' is relevant to practice today we should not assume that all of the entailments of body, mind, practice, agency and power discussed in the ethnographic present are necessarily the same as those of a *kalarippayattu* practitioner in the middle ages or antiquity. In an era when the necessity of actualizing one's powers in combat have been narrowed from a multitude of forces and powers, locally immanent on the field of battle and the duel platform, to the usually hypothetical arena of application on the streets, the demonstration stage, the training space and/or the treatment room, the powers that might be visited upon one, or those on which one might call, are decidedly more tame and mundane, if no less important, than in the past. *Kalarippayattu* practitioners today no longer pledge themselves to death on behalf of a ruler nor do they form 'suicide squads', which literally sacrifice themselves on the 'glorious' battlefield of death. They do not seek a life or death situation with opponents who may have gained access to esoteric, seemingly magical powers and abilities. Among masters who emphasize the internal development and actualization of *sakti* and its application, however, techniques can still be used with extraordinarily frightening power and force.

With rare exceptions, the practice of *kalarippayattu* today has become more about actualizing and harnessing one's bodymind and powers for use in daily life and in shaping certain kinds of 'selves' rather than about preparing for a fight to the death. As students advance under the guidance of some of today's masters, they are expected to be able to control their feelings and emotions and to develop the ability to resist the 'temptations of modern life'. As one student put it 'You won't go for corruption'. If one practices assiduously and correctly he will 'naturally develop wisdom and not go astray' i.e. he will avoid alcohol and drugs and be of 'good character'. One master, well trained in both *kalarippayattu* and yoga, asserted that if one learns *kalarippayattu* properly then 'he should gain release from unhappiness'. However, he also noted soberly 'many practitioners have turned out to be wasters, drunks, and of bad morals'. He cited the example of Chandu from the northern ballads, an infamous antihero who was bought off by money and a promise of the affection of a beautiful young woman and subsequently betrayed his cousin, Aromar. For this master, Chandu is an example of the type of *kalari* master who possesses a dark (*tamasa*) constitution. The ideal *kalarippayattu* teacher 'has a good or truthful (*satvika*) constitution. If the master has a truthful constitution, it will be a blessing for the student. This master asked me rhetorically as he spoke from bitter personal experience, 'if some masters do possess a dark constitution … there will be a split (sthanabramsam) between student and master. Everything will become confused (alangolappeduka)!'

These examples illustrate two apparently contradictory assumptions: practice is one means of fundamentally altering one's basic, inherent nature (*gunam*) and behavior. However, one's fundamental nature and behavior is understood to be given by one's *gunam*. According to this set of assumptions the proportion of the three *gunam* varies from individual to individual so people are ranked accordingly to their own makeup and the corresponding 'behavioral code (dharma) held appropriate to the disposition of those gun[am]' (Davis 1976: 6). Gunam has been defined as 'property' or 'quality' (Gundert 1982: 332), 'radical material substances' (Davis 1976: 6), or 'subtle qualities, attributes, or strands' (Marriott 1980: 1). The three *gunam* include goodness or truth (*satva*), passion (*rajasa*), and darkness (*tamasa*).[13] It is still usually assumed that all persons belong to specific birth-groups (*jati*) defined by the inhering qualities of one's substance and accompanying behavioral code. As one older master told me, 'the three gunam are according to sastra. Brahmins are satva; ksatriyas are rajasa; and Nayars [as sudras] are usually associated with tamasa'. One's fundamental gunam is determined at birth according to the substances mixed by the parents, the specific time of birth and the influence of the stars and the gods (Marriott 1980: 5).[14] However, as Master Govindan kutty Nayar told me, 'among every person the combination of the three gunam varies'. He goes on to say:

> Arjuna as the Son of Indra is predominantly rajasa, but with all his meditational practices he tended to gain satva. Bhima as the son of Vayu has strength and power. His power is more from his strength than skill. Therefore, he is more tamasa than Arjuna, and there is also an element of the demon in his skill.

Although the fundamental combination of *gunam* is thought to be determined at birth, it is still possible for some persons to change it. Govindankutty Nayar explained further 'it is possible to alter the three gunam. But if a person has a predominance of one of the gunam, he will do all things with that personality. One can alter the three gunam through his karma or through the nature of his actions. *Kalarippayattu* is one way of altering the gunam, but it depends on the involvement of the person practicing. If you watch three different students in the *kalari*, you can see change in some, but in others there will be no change'. He illustrated his point with the following story:

> One man who was hideous was always hurting others while practicing *kalarippayattu*. He was a tamasa type. Others will be gentle and quiet, and some may even be too satva to practice the martial art. Only after a very very long practice the gunam may begin to change. There are reasons for the change: when one gets more self-confidence, he becomes softer and is less prone to anger [associated with tamasa], the mind becomes much calmer. One becomes calmer because of practice, especially through breath control. And when one's behavior changes, his gunam changes. Just as vratam [simple forms of meditation and concentration] brings more of the satva aspect, so in my experience does *kalarippayattu* practice.

Since 'a person's [g]unam attains its mature and relatively permanent state between the ages of three and twelve' (Daniel 1983: 141), students who begin their training at the traditional age of seven are considered more likely to develop more of the *satva* aspect in their basic *gunam* complex i.e. training is assumed to effect the type of person they become since they began so young. However, more students today begin their training at an older age and some teachers are wary and suspicious of these students, since their *gunam* complex is much more solidified and their behavior less open to change. Some teachers put themselves on guard by watching for signs of a *tamasa* type of student:

> In my experience I can usually see a tamasa because he has no patience. Immediately he goes outside [the *kalari*] and tries everything [contrary to instructions]. He's overpolite the first day, trying to please and offer the guru everything. If I find a student who has these [tamasa] qualities I will send him away. It won't go right and won't be right for the art as well.

For these masters, the ideal student of *kalarippayattu* gains control of his emotions and, through the development of mental calm and courage, becomes 'concentrated with a strong will'. The student should develop the intuitive ability to follow the common code of conduct assumed by some *kalarippayattu* practitioners, to use these potentially deadly techniques only when life is in danger, and never to become an unprovoked aggressor. This description of practitioners as having a controlled, fluid physical body and a calm, *satvika* mental state which is doubtless and fearless in the face of death comes from a brahmanically-influenced, idealized discourse of the self and person constituted by practice and actualized when 'the body is all eyes.' However, there are numerous historical and contemporary examples of practitioners who transgress or fail to actualize this experiential and behavioral ideal. Nowhere is this better witnessed than in the example of the infamous figure of one of the medieval practitioners of *kalarippayattu*, the well-known Tacholi Otenan, immortalized in the northern ballads (*vadakkan pattukal*) and most recently in popular Malayalam films and comic books. In one of the many escapades of this Malayali cultural hero, the proud, vain and often hot headed Tacholi was deputed by a local ruler to collect three years' back rent from a landholding family in the Kodumala area where the powerful young woman of the Kunki family was holding sway and refusing to come forward with rent due the ruler. Tacholi used his expertise in attacking the body's vital spots (*marmmam*) to subdue her with a cattle prod. Tacholi's direct action immediately tamed and controlled this rebellious young woman. In this and other instances Tacholi's predominantly *rajasic* type of behavior, characteristic of 'the passionate and impulsive' warrior (*kshatriya*), (Kakar, 1982: 249) was legitimized by his acting in the service to the power of the local ruler.[15]

Tacholi is perhaps the best example of the potentially erratic, *rajasic* personality whose use of the martial practitioner's powers is as capricious as the nature of that constellation of powers itself. What Tacholi and his numerous contemporary counterparts in Kerala today illustrate is the fact that any set of martial techniques and the powers to which practice leads an individual are circumscribed, shaped and actualized by the idiosyncratic temperament of the individual. No matter how esoteric the techniques, no matter how subtle the powers, no matter how apparently controlled the bodymind, all such martial and meditational powers are actualized by persons who are more or less responsible to the moral use or abuse of those powers in particular socio-political circumstances. This is nowhere more evident than in the unfortunate fact that a few masters are even using *kalarippayattu* today to train students for communal violence against Hindus and/or Muslims. To reiterate a point that Kondo makes *kalarippayattu* becomes one means of 'crafting' a particular self and therefore is a 'culturally, historically specific pathway … to self-realization … [and/or] domination' (Kondo 1990: 305).

The 'body as all eyes' as a special, virtuoso body of practice is not separate from the daily body inhabited by the practitioner. Rather, it is one mode of incorporation which is constitutive of the practitioner's horizon of experience (in a sense that Connerton illustrates in his writings). Along with other modes of incorporation and cultural practice, *kalarippayattu* is, as anthropologist Michelle Rosaldo explains 'the very stuff of which our subjectivities are created' (1984: 150). It helps shape one's perceptions, experience and behavior. The *kalarippayattu* student training in self-control and restraint in a *kalari* where Muslims, Christians and Hindus are now welcome to train together will be different from the *kalarippayattu* student secretively trained in an exclusively Muslim or Hindu environment where hate may be bred. Practice itself and the subjectivity it helps create are not static, but rather open to manipulation and interpretation in the interplay between the constantly altering horizons of individual subjectivities; the interplay between the metaphors, images and representations of the body culturally available; the interpretation of the body, experience and practice articulated by individual masters; and the socio political and economic environments. Sometimes the 'self' crafted, and the use to which that self puts its martial powers and practices, are for a larger good. All too often today they are not.

Acknowledgements

This essay is based on six extended trips to Kerala in India, on extensive interviews with over fifty masters and on fifteen years of training, practice, and teaching of the discipline described. The most recent research trips were made possible by a Fulbright Senior Research Fellowship (1993) and by an American Institute of Indian Studies and NEH Senior Research Fellowship (1988–89). In the essay, I restrict myself to *kalarippayattu* and do not address the complex history of the closely related Tamil martial art, *varma ati*. For a brief discussion of the latter see Zarrilli (1992).

2

EMPOWERING YOURSELF: SPORT, SEXUALITY AND AUTOEROTICISM IN NORTH INDIAN *JORI* SWINGING

Joseph S. Alter

The Gymnasium, *Jori*-Clubs, Sexuality and Culture

In *The Mythology of Sex* Sarah Dening argues that the Hebrew prohibition against eating the 'sinew of the hip which is upon the hollow of the thigh' should be understood symbolically as a prohibition against the practice common among neighboring tribes whereby a new king would eat the penis of his predecessor in order to imbibe his power and authority. Dening and others point out that the 'thigh' was a biblical euphemism for the penis and that the penis was clearly associated with the power to rule and proclaim the truth. In the Genesis story God wrestles with Jacob and 'touches the hollow of his thigh'. With this almighty 'goose' God metaphorically 'eats Jacobs penis' thus setting in place the rationale for the dietary prohibition, making himself the King of Kings, the one true God. In this myth sex, sacredness, power and sportive competition are linked together both figuratively and literally. The homoerotics of touching if not actually eating penises is also evident. Homoerotics are most clearly reflected in the classical Greek gymnasium, an institution that can arguably be held accountable for putting 'civilization' in modern Western history. Gymnasiums in Athens were places where men went to become men and develop themselves into citizens of the city state. For Plato and Aristotle they were institutions of embodied knowledge, to an extent that tends to get forgotten in the disembodied philosophical abstractions of the modern intellectual academy, where departments of philosophy and physical education are decidedly separate and unequal.

In the context of the early Greek gymnasium, the embodiment of *arete*, manly virtues of strength, courage, fairness and honesty, was of central importance. As the etymology of the word itself indicates, gymnasiums were places of nakedness and, although many other things went on in gymnasiums, wrestling was very important. So was the intimate relationship between male lovers, as this relationship was integral to the development of manhood and identity. Naked wrestling, and the visibility of the penis, can be understood as charged with homoeroticism particularly in the context of a cultural milieu where the sexual relationship between older men (*erastes*) and young boys (*eromenos*) was understood as central to the embodied development of *arete*. As David Friedman points out in his cultural history of the penis:

> When an *erastes* entered an *eromenos* with his penis, a symbolic, and to these Greeks, real act occurred–the full and final transfer of *arete*. That the vehicle for this transfer was semen accorded with the teachings of Aristotle, who believed that sperm alone provided the soul of the child. With pederasty Greek men trumped nature: with a penis and without women they gave birth to other men. (2001: 24)

The gymnasium was the place where men gave birth to other men. Much more can and should be made of this particular aspect of the history of sexuality. On the one hand it links sport and physical fitness and, on the other hand, gender and sexuality to the development of philosophy, politics, art and most other things in the intellectual history of Western civilization. My expertise, however, is not in this area but in the study of a somewhat different kind of gymnasium: the gymnasium in modern North India. My reason for invoking the image of Jacob getting 'accidentally-on-purpose' goosed by God and of the intimate homoerotics of early Greek philosopher athletes, is not at all to make some universalist point about sex and sport, but rather to use what seems to be a fairly common understanding of the power manifest in homoerotic intimacy, as this intimacy comes into play in some forms of sport more than in others, in order to understand the specific features of an Indian sport that has had a profound impact on the history of Western physical education. Sometime around the end of the 18th century or early in the 19th the British in India learned about the practice of a form of physical exercise known as *jori* or *mugdal ferana*. At this time the British were still engaged in embodying an Anglo-Indian identity, and had not yet become concerned with insulating themselves from contact with the colonized (Collingham 2001). In other words this was a time when questions concerning diet, hygiene and exercise were worked out with a degree of cross-cultural flexibility rather than outright colonial chauvinism. In this light *jori* club swinging came to be recognized as a more superior form of physical training than any other available. Over time *jori* swinging was integrated into existing modes of calisthenic gymnastic drill, in particular Swedish forms, and was included into the routine of the British Army in India and elsewhere. By 1840 *jori* swinging had become an important feature of the physical fitness movement associated with muscular Christianity in England. By 1860 it was popularized by Sim Kehoe in the United States and between 1870 and 1910 it came to define the post-Civil War health reform movement. By this time *jori* were known as 'Indian Clubs' and had been radically transformed in a number of ways. They were lighter, smaller and swung in many different ways, each of which was designed to develop the body in general and the nervous system in particular. Modern civilization was thought to produce a spectrum of maladies that compromised the health of the nervous system, many of which were linked to sex and sexuality. Significantly, soon after it was developed as an exercise for men it became extremely popular as an exercise for women, as women's exercise became increasingly important in the context of eugenicist concerns with the reproduction of a more fit and healthy population. By the turn of the century Indian Club swinging came to define key principles of physical education in American schools. It is ironic, if not something more, since symbolic value can transcend time and place, that the reproductive health of American women should have been developed by swinging a club that in India was so closely linked to sex and sexuality in men.

Rather than analyze the transnational mutation of *jori*s into Indian clubs, and one configuration of sexuality into another, my focus in this chapter is exclusively on *jori*s as they define sexuality in North Indian gymnasiums (*akharas*). It is necessarily a preliminary, partial and somewhat dehistoricized analysis which anticipates a more comprehensive study of the connection between Muscular Christianity and masturbation and homosexuality in the United States, where club swinging was far more popular around the turn of the century than it ever has been in India. My focus here is on homoeroticism, but only somewhat obliquely. As in ancient Greece, homoerotics in the North Indian gymnasium is about turning men into men by means of semen, but only where an 'act of sex' is meaningful on an abstracted symbolic level, and where the sex and fluid substance in question is contained by the self. *Jori* swinging is, thus, a kind of symbolic onanism, where a man turns himself into a man. This does not entail intimate contact between men, or between men and the hand of God. The symbolic onanism of *jori* swinging can, I think, be understood as more directly and explicitly homoerotic, if still purely symbolic, in the context of competitions where men see who can swing the heaviest club the most number of times, thereby 'using' their semen to demonstrate their masculinity to other men.

Jori-Swinging in India

A pair of *Jori* or *Mugdal*, upon which 'Indian Clubs' are modeled, are stylized wooden clubs, themselves ostensibly modeled on ancient war clubs described in some detail in a number of the Sanskrit classics. *Jori*, the Hindi term itself meaning 'pair', are of various sizes and shapes ranging in weight and length from a modest 5 kilograms and 750 cm to those that, at upward of 70 kilograms and 1.5 meters each, are almost but not quite unswingable. Each club is carved of wood and shaped like an inverted cone with a wide, flat base tapering up to a narrow collar. A cylindrical handle with a knob at the end is used to grip and swing the club. Although made of wood, heavy metal rings are often affixed to the base of each club, thus both adding and shifting weight to a lower center of gravity.

It is unlikely that ancient war clubs were shaped in this way so it is difficult to know how the clubs came to be so designed historically. Given the widespread use of very similar clubs throughout the Middle East, and the extent of contact between South Asia and this part of the world at various points in time, it is likely that club swinging emerged as a quasi-martial art that flowed through the trade, military and political networks of Islamic conquest. With reference to war clubs, most of the Sanskrit literature refers to *gadas*, a kind of mace that finds modern gymnastic form in large stone balls affixed to bamboo polls that are swung for exercise. In any event, photographs taken of *jori* in the 1930s show clubs that resemble ones currently in use, and it is reasonable to assume that it was these kinds of clubs that military personnel, police officers and missionaries saw being swung in the late 18th and early 19th century. Although aware of its similarity to an extremely popular and somewhat more recognized tradition throughout the middle-east, *jori* swinging is characterized by enthusiasts from the city of Banaras as a sport that is associated with the area now defined by the state of Uttar Pradesh in North India. Just as *kabaddi* is regionally identified with Maharashtra, and *kalaripayattu* with Kerala, *jori* swinging is regarded, with both pride and a degree of resentment for being thus marginalized, as a manly rural sport of the Gangetic plane. It is closely associated with a tradition of Indian wrestling and is regarded as one of several training exercises for this sport.

Akharas, however recent their specific history of development and popularization, are designed as 'traditional' gymnasiums for the practice of a range of indigenous sports such as wrestling, *jori* and *gada* swinging, boxing, and *nal* lifting. Usually an *akhara* is known as a place for practicing one or the other of these sports but activities are not necessarily exclusive. Although regarded as institutions intimately linked to the rural ethos of North India, most *akharas* are urban institutions. In the city of Banaras, where indigenous sports are still quite popular, there are several hundred. Most of these are associated with particular neighborhoods and although they are public institutions almost all are under the control of a guru or master teacher. *Akharas* are exclusively masculine domains and tend to attract boys and young men between the ages of 8 and 20, as well as older men with grown children of their own. Primarily a form of exercise in the regimen of wrestling, *jori* swinging has also become a competitive sport in its own right. Competitions (*dangals*) tend to be organized on various special occasions, a process that has been facilitated and formalized by the founding of the Banaras Society for *Jori* and *Gada* Swinging in 1985. The competitive season is defined as lasting three months during the monsoon when there are approximately 20 *dangals* organized by several civic groups and a number of the well-known *jori akharas* in the larger metropolitan area of which there are approximately ten. Although there is some very minor variation in how clubs are swung, the standard for competition is called a *hath* or hand. To complete one hand the pair of *jori* are 'stood up' such that they are gripped by both hands and rested upon each shoulder. One at a time each club is lifted off the shoulder and swung back and down in a pendulum arc behind the back and then lifted up to rest on the shoulder again. Each swing counts as a hand, the number of hands decreasing in number as the weight of the *jori* increases. There is a loose ranking of *jori* established by the Banaras Society for *Jori* and Gada Swinging, with small, medium and large pairs weighing 50, 57 and 73 kilograms each. However, since weight is not precisely standardized, competitions revolve around specific named pairs.

The *jori* in *jori akharas* are not simply weighted clubs, they are named, artfully decorated and come to possess an identity of their own. That identity is linked to the place they hold in the local history of swinging. A pair of *jori* is always very clearly associated with a particular gymnasium, and is named either after the person who commissioned its production or the competitor who swung it the most number of times. Alternatively, the pair is named after a distinctive feature, perhaps color, design or the number of weighted rings attached to the base. As a consequence of being named, *jori* take on a life of their own in the minds of local enthusiasts who speak of them in highly personal and intimate terms almost as if they had become personified. I was told by a number of men that at an earlier time when the world was not so corrupt and jaded *jori* were not just personified but were regarded as divine beings. They were bathed, decorated and clothed much the same way as temple deities. Some were kept in seclusion and only brought out for special competitions. To give some indication of these names and the somewhat sacred aura that is still associated with them, the following is a list of the most important *jori* in Banaras as provided by a leading member of Azad Akharda: At Bari Gaivi Vyayamshala there is a pair called 'The White Ones' (*Safeda Wali*); at Karan Ghanta a pair referred to as 'The Tiger' (*Sher Wali*); at Malviya Market Vyayamashala a pair called 'Hanuman

Ones' honoring the patron deity of almost all gymnasiums who embodies the principles of strength; at Choti Gaivi Akharda is a pair called 'Punwasi Wali' named after the man who swung them the most number of hands; and at Sant Ram *Akhara* there are two famous pairs, known as 'The Mountainous Ones' (*Pahar Wali*) and 'The Glass Spiked Ones' (*Shishe Wali*), the former on account of their large size and a painted design at the base and the latter because of pieces of glass which make swinging these clubs more difficult and dangerous. Indicating the extent to which size and weight really matters, at Shyam Bazaar Vyayamshala there is a pair called 'Sakra Wali' which, I was told, 'no one has ever been able to lift and swing.' *Jori* swinging enthusiasts often spend hours talking about the unique features of each pair and debating finer points of history and discussing the most recent competition in which each was featured. Thus, there is very little abstract technical discourse on the art of swinging. Almost everything is couched in terms of the particular history of first-person, pronominal local practice or what might be called intimate history. It is ironic that the transnational global history of Indian Clubs, where connections are forgotten almost faster than they are made, is in many ways the antithesis of this kind of history.

Aside from its modern sportive form in Banaras, *jori* swinging is done by wrestlers as part of their exercise routine. As both an exercise and a sport it is designed as a kind of 'weight swinging' to the extent that the idea is to swing a pair until one no longer has the strength to do so, thus building both muscle strength and stamina as well as one's reserve of semen and the ability to digest more food to produce more semen. Although there are certainly some men, mostly those who are older, who swing relatively light clubs as a kind of calisthenic regimen, the very idea of *jori* swinging in contemporary Banaras is associated with the impress of extremity and a kind of over-the-top, maximized masculinity where the power of sex and sexuality is only just barely internalized. As might be expected, therefore, everything hinges on the strength and skill of the individual *jori* swingers who compete with one another. This strength and skill is directly and unambiguously embodied, to the extent that I was told and came to recognize that the physical features of the *jori* swinger are somewhat different from those of a wrestler. *Jori* swingers possess tremendously strong forearms, wrists, shoulders and necks and their chests are even more expanded than wrestlers. However, as with wrestlers, what is ultimately important is over-all 'tone' and a kind of balanced development reflected in the ideal of a smooth, thick, solid 'body of one color.'

Competitive swinging in Banaras involves high-drama, as on display is the *jori* swingers' strength, stamina, and self-confidence, reflecting other features of masculinity. As Daya Ram puts it, writing for the Banaras Society of *Jori* and Gada Swingers:

> Those who participate in this sport must practice as hard and be as self-disciplined as wrestlers. They must be celibate, honor and respect their guru, and along with having enough strength to digest a rich diet, they must engage regularly in daily practice (1985: 5).

A successful swinger embodies these qualities. During a *dangal* his body is on display. I watched a number of *jori* swinging *dangals* in the Banaras area, and they were all spectacles involving high drama and the investment of a tremendous amount of emotional energy. As I have indicated elsewhere, tournaments are somewhat problematic in the context of wrestling insofar as the contained and channeled sexual energy that is integral to training and self-development is dangerously destabilized in the context of aggressive competition (Alter 1995). The term *dangal* itself denotes competition but has the connotation of chaos. As with wrestling *dangals, jori* swinging *dangals* often end in contentious, potentially violent conflict between the members of rival *akharas* and the relationship between competition and chaotic violent conflict is very much the same as between contained sexuality and the threat of unrestrained passionate eroticism. Wrestling involves physical contact wherein the focus of attention is skill and technique. In *jori* swinging however it is the swinger's strength that is the focus of attention. Although there is no physical contact between *jori* swinging competitors, overt embodied sexuality is more of an issue than it is for wrestlers, since *jori* swinging is simply a contest of strength and strength is a reflection of celibacy.

The Choti Gaivi *dangal*

All *dangals* revolve around the swinging of the heaviest clubs, usually around 70 kilograms, and the top contenders weigh close to 90 or 100 kilograms. In the 1988 season there were two men vieing for the formal rank of regional champion, Baccha from Ragunath Maharaj *Akhara* and Ghansu from Murchalibir *Akhara*. A relatively small *dangal* at Choti Gaivi *Akhara* was organized to demonstrate a claim of rightful property ownership to the municipal authorities. A brief description of it will serve to set the stage for an analysis of sexual symbolism.

Starting at 5:30 in the evening a crowd started to gather on the plain in front of the *akhara* dias, upon which were placed an array of *jori*, some freshly painted and all rendered auspicious through the ritual anointment of ochre coloured swastikas. As the crowd swelled to over 500 the preparation of the *jori* began. This involved members of the host gymnasium lifting and dropping the clubs to ensure their stability and hammering the iron bands to make them secure. After the lighter weight *jori* had been swung by junior members of various gymnasiums, Baccha made his entry with an entourage of six '*akhara* brothers'. With what appeared to be clearly affected pomp, they began to prepare the *jori* themselves, again pounding the rings and wiping them clean. As some of the entourage worked with the *jori*, others began to prepare a platform of bricks upon which Baccha would position himself to 'stand the *jori* up' prior to swinging them behind his back. Ensuring that the platform is secure and stable is important, since if the bricks slip the swinger can fall and put himself at considerable risk. Nevertheless, organizers of regional competitions have voiced their frustration at the amount of time, often as much as half an hour, that goes into this relatively simple task. It is obvious that the whole thing is intended to serve, at least in part, as a spectacle. Once the platform was in place several members of Baccha's entourage worked carefully on the handle grip of each club, vigorously scraping it clean and smooth. Then resin crystals were crushed in a pestle and, again with greatly affected pomp, rubbed onto the handles. While the *jori* were being prepared, Baccha was engaged in doing *dands* and *bethaks* (pushups and squats) as warm-up exercises for the competition. It was early July, the temperature close to 36 degrees and Baccha was sweating profusely. One member of the entourage kept wiping him dry with a towel. At last, the *jori* were positioned one on each side of the platform, although in doing so care was taken not to touch the handle. Baccha carefully placed his feet on the platform, right foot on three bricks in front and left foot behind on a single brick. He took some time to get his balance and then leaned forward to grip the handles from the front with his weight on his right leg. He grabbed, twisted and released the grip several times until feeling it to be secure. All of this took a considerable length of time, but once Baccha was on the platform, the crowed grew hushed. Finally, shifting all of his weight to his front leg and foot, Baccha lifted the *jori*. He swung them once forward, once back and then, leaping off of the bricks, tried but failed to flip them up into an inverted perpendicular position. The clubs crashed to the ground as Baccha leaped out of the way. The crowd, absolutely silent up until this point, gasped and exclaimed with empathy. Baccha then tried again, preparing himself and the *jori* with as much affected pomp as the first time, but again failed to stand the *jori* up. At this point men around me began to exchange opinions such as 'His swinging is no good. His balance is off. His grip is not firm'. Baccha tried a third time and failed again. With this, people began to say that he had lost his courage and that the next competitor should be given a chance. As if on cue Ghansu made his entrance. If any thing, he took even longer than Baccha to prepare himself and the clubs, rubbing the handles, having his body dried off repeatedly and arranging and rearranging his *gamcha* (loincloth). Finally, turning to the moon and the arch lights, both of which were brightly lit by this time, he offered a short prayer to each and one toward a nearby Choti Gaivi temple. He then positioned himself fifteen feet behind the platform. Striding up he quickly steadied himself, got his grip and balance and swung the clubs back once, and then jerked them forward flipping them into a perpendicular position. At this the crowed went wild, cheering madly as Ghansu swung the clubs five hands, 'just to warm up' according to the man next to me.

After Ghansu's success, Baccha followed suit, and neither one had to 'stand the *jori* up' before trying to swing them as many times as possible. This does not mean however that the preamble to a swing is any less dramatic. Members of Ghansu's entourage rubbed fresh resin on the handles, wiped the sweat covered clubs dry and then, as two stalwarts lifted each club high above their heads, taking care not to touch the handles, another dried Ghansu's body with particular attention to his neck, back and underarms. Once the clubs were lowered onto his shoulders and he had gripped them to his satisfaction Ghansu began to swing them back and forth in pendulum arcs, at the end of each swing lifting the club onto his shoulder. He completed eleven hands. Next Baccha swung the clubs eleven hands. Each had another turn and Ghansu won swinging 12 ½ hands to Baccha's 12. By the end of the *dangal* the crowed had grown to about 700 and had encroached on the *dias* such that there was very little room left for the swingers to prepare themselves. Local Choti Gaivi *akhara* members, officials and the hired police guard tried, with little effect, to get the crowd to move back. Most deemed the Choti Gaivi *dangal* a success. For several days afterward there was talk about Baccha's and Ghansu's relative strength, with a number of remarks made about Ghansu's 'body of one color.' The dangal was what is called a '*nam ka dangal*' rather than an '*inam ka dangal*' meaning, as the dramatic and affected nature of the performance might indicate, that it was simply for name recognition rather than to win any sort of prize or money. Even an '*inam ka dangal*' however, is more about prestige than about winning something of material value. Needless to say name recognition is linked to a very specific representation of masculinity.

Jori-Swinging as Intersexual Autoerotics

I have described this *dangal* trying not to use overly 'sexualized' terminology. Yet I hope to have communicated the intimate, affected, highly sensual link between the *jori* and the *jori* swinger's body as that link is facilitated by the men who scrape, rub, lift and clean both body and club. If this were all there was to it an interpretation focusing on homoerotics would probably not be justified. But given the broader symbolic grammar associated with *jori* swinging, I think the intimate sensuality (and the mine-is-bigger-than-yours competitiveness), of the *dangals* makes sense. As I hope to show, climax is controlled by the regimented hand of onistic self-development wherein 'ejaculation' is internalized. Here the dangerous risk of erotic stimulation is what engenders power: chaos is necessary, and not, as I have indicated elsewhere (1992, 1995) something to be categorically contained and avoided.

Jori are self-supporting and stand erect. Although it helps, one need not be a Freudian to appreciate their phallic nature. The exercise is designed to enhance the kind of strength reflected in and produced by the associated practice of *brahmacharya* (celibacy). Even though they have obvious phallic connotations clubs, as I have illustrated elsewhere (Alter 1992), are more con-sciously associated with teats. Apart from the fact that they are cone shaped with a nipple like grip on the end, and that they come in pairs, *Jori* swingers in Banaras are often Yadav dairy farmers many of whom explain that the grip needed to swing a hand is very much like the grip needed to milk a buffalo. Milking buffalos, particularly a large herd, is regarded as hard work and a sign of physical prowess, if not also a kind of exercise. One man with whom I spoke counted the number of buffalos he had milked in a manner very similar to the number of hands he had swung a pair of *jori*. In any case, through asso-ciation with milking and churning, another important analogy, *jori* swinging is consciously associated with milk and what in general might be regarded as female symbolism. Polysimically, however, milk is an androgynous substance. It is linked directly and unambiguously to semen through the milk based diet of wrestlers and *jori* swingers as this diet is associated with celibacy and the power derived thereby. Furthermore, just as the earth from wrestling pits is often used to anoint new brides and thereby ensure fertility, *jori* are swung by members of the groom's party in competition with the bride's party when the two groups meet for the first time. It would seem that, under these circum-stances, *jori* swinging is as much a reflection of virility as it is linked to generic, non-sex specific fertility, and not simply to a kind of virility that unambigu-ously reflects male bravado. To swing *jori* is to produce semen, but unlike other forms of exercise that also produce semen, jor (wrestling practice), *dands*, *bethaks*, for example, *jori* swinging exhibits a kind of masculinity that is some-what more intimately linked to sex as an act. While the question of represen-tation is always interpretive, and thereby neither here nor there, I was struck by the extent to which *jori* swingers in Banaras wear *gamchas* around their waists. Although worn by many as very casual attire, the swinger's loin cloth is distinctively folded in such a way that a thick wad of pleats hangs down between his legs to his knees. This contrasts sharply with the *langot* he wears underneath, which both literally and figuratively 'binds' and firmly contains his genitals.

Jori swinging fits into the symbolic logic of the *akhara* in general and the regimen of physical fitness that is common to both wrestlers and *jori* swingers. This logic is most clearly reflected in the ritual of Nag Panchami, a minor festival marking the onset of the monsoon season when snakes are given milk to drink. It is celebrated as a major event in North Indian *akharas*. In the context of Nag Panchami the consumption of semen-milk by androgenous snakes symbolizes contained virility insofar as the power of sexuality is invoked but then turned back on itself. Significantly, it is milk that is fed to snakes, even though *ghi* (clarified butter) is regarded as the most semen-like of all substances in the wrestler's diet. Ghi is produced when churned butter is cooked and both the churning and the cooking render *ghi* the symbolic equivalent of a snake drinking milk. As I have argued in my analysis of wrestling:

> Churning symbolism is crucial to understanding what *ghi* means as an androgenous symbol. Whereas to a certain extent milking refers to sexual union and the drawing out of essence, churning, more often than not refers to unilateral creation wherein a male or female brings forth life by churning their own fluids (O'Flaherty 1976: 333-334). Even in instances where churning is taken as a metaphor for coitus, the image is of mixing together not milking out or taking essence away. Significantly, the metaphor of milking implies only a transfer of substance, whereas churning clearly demands a change of substance, but without addition or subtraction. In this respect, then, milk symbolizes either male or female seed, whereas ghi represents a kind of mutated androgynous fluid that is potent but asexual in the sense of already having been churned (1992: 152).

In my analysis of wrestling I focused on 'thigh slapping', one of the most common actions in the symbolic grammar of the *akhara*, as well as thigh rubbing, concluding that these actions symbolized the androgynous agency of churning and were not directly concerned with the penis or its manipulation. In this context I wrote:

> [T]he manipulation of one's thigh is an act of androgynous agency while the manipulation of one's penis is, even in the instance of masturbation, a directed act of sexuality which is, by definition, only half of a whole: either heterosexual or homosexual but never androgynous (1992: 153).

In arriving at this conclusion I think I was too eager to make a sharp distinction between celibacy and eroticism in general, and androgynous churning and masturbation in particular. While it is true that thigh slapping, when it is performed as a provocative challenge made by one wrestler to another, is not necessarily homoerotic, in the sense that it is a self-directed act, it is also true that its power as a symbolic statement derives from indirect association with the power of directed, externalized sex and sexuality. A thigh is not a penis, but without the penis being where it is and doing what it does, a thigh would only ever be a thigh. Beyond the realm of North Indian *akharas* this interdependent ambiguity is, after all, precisely how the biblical euphemism works. In other words thigh slapping and rubbing would be meaningless as symbols of the churning transmutation of semen into power unless they invoked sex as a directed act involving the flow of fluids. Eroticism in general, and homoeroticism in particular, is thus what enables the discourse and practice of contained sexuality. Although erotic sex and masturbation are anathema in and of themselves, when invoked in conjunction with symbolic statements that redirect the flow of substance and meaning, and redirect it most directly to the embodied person himself, the power that would have been egregiously wasted is maximized and internalized by 'flirting,' so to speak, with the risk of flow that is integral to transubstantiation.

Jori swinging, probably even more than thigh slapping or rubbing, flirts with the risk of flow most directly and therefore can be understood both as the most erotic expression of sexuality in the *akhara* as well as the most purely self-contained expression of celibate power. This was graphically illustrated at one *jori akhara*. On one wall of a room in which *jori* were kept there was a mural painting of Lord Shiva dancing. In one hand was a flame and in the other a *jori* made of peacock feathers resting on one shoulder. Significantly Hanuman, the purely celibate and extremely powerful devotee of Lord Ram, is the usual subject of *akhara* art. In these representations he is celibacy incarnate. Shiva, on the other hand is closely associated with androgynous power and the intimate and often graphic dialectics of eroticism and asceticism in Hindu mythology and iconography. Shiva 'spills his seed' as often, if not more often, than he contains it. Hanuman is almost always depicted with a *gada*, but never with *jori*. For Shiva to be represented with a *jori*, erotically enhanced with peacock plumage, would seem to suggest an important convergence of meaning. This striking contrast between contained and expressed sexuality as well as the androgynous symbolism of the clubs and their manipulation leads me to speculate, in a provisional and partial way, that *jori* swinging may be understood as a kind of intersexual autoerotics. Here the categorical distinction between male and female becomes ambiguous. And this ambiguity further complicates the already complex nature of autoeroticism as asocial, if not anti-social, sexuality. Finally, the intersexual autoerotics of *jori* swinging confuses the otherwise fairly clear distinction between celibacy as an act of containing sexual fluids on the one hand and the erotics of ejaculation on the other. The *jori* swinger swings his phallic-breasts to produce semen-milk that is never wasted. It is used only to produce more of itself rather than reproduce anything or anyone else. Thus the containment of semen-milk is dependent on its manipulation, and in this sense I think *jori* swinging can be understood as a kind of mastrabatory self-reproduction.

The problem with the term mastrabatory, of course, is that it is almost impossible to divest of negative connotations. Unlike sex, there is not even a putatively 'normal' or good way to masturbate. Certainly in the context of the *akhara* the very idea of masturbation is anathema, just as celibacy is regarded as the embodiment of virtue; but perhaps this is precisely what makes *jori* swinging such an index of masculine power. Just as power cannot exist without resistance, celibacy does not make sense apart from sex but only in direct and intimate relation to the act of sex itself. The meaningfulness of *jori* swinging is inextricably linked to the extremely intimate relationship between celibacy and masturbation as categorically opposed, consubstantiating acts that are equally anti-social and self indulgent.

3

INDIGENOUS POLO IN NORTHERN PAKISTAN: GAME AND POWER ON THE PERIPHERY

Peter Parkes

Introduction

G. Whitney Azoy's *Buzkashi: Game and Power in Afghanistan* (1982) is an exemplary ethnography of Asian sport. Focusing on the social and political mobilization of this dramatic equestrian game, Azoy moved well beyond a conventional hermeneutic interpretation of sport as ritual display, and highlighted the broader social and performative functions of *buzkashi* tournaments. These were force-fields of national and regional ethnicity: they enacted a distinctive ethnic identity among minority Uzbeks of northern Afghanistan, conveying their own regional aspirations of rugged autonomy from the alien hegemony of Pashtun officials in Kabul, who were attempting to appropriate this prestigious tribal game as a national Afghan sport. The patronage of Uzbek *khans* sponsoring the game was thereby reduced to brokerage with the regional Afghan Governor and his bureaucratic entourage of Pashtun athletic officials. By the 1970s these had already imposed their own disciplinary apparatus of civilizing rules and penalties on the game, together with national (Pashtunist) civilizing discourses of government propaganda. Azoy's historical ethnography of successive Afghan appropriations of the tribal Uzbek game from the 1950s thus exemplified societal changes of Weberian magnitude: a political transition from 'traditional, patrimonial' to 'national-bureaucratic' modes of authority and ideology which occurred within a single generation in mid-twentieth century Afghanistan and the repercussions of which, in terms of regional, ethnic and sectarian strife, remain unresolved.

This essay outlines a comparable historical ethnography of the similar equestrian sport of indigenous polo in neighbouring regions of northern Pakistan. I examine comparable political processes concerning nationalist appropriations of a regionally localized game over much the same period as that treated by Azoy in northern Afghanistan, but under different historical circumstances in adjacent Pakistan. It is possible to observe a parallel transformation of indigenous polo from a rough local game, once emblematic of regal authority and nobility within formerly independent mountain principalities, into an organized athletic sport under national government and paramilitary patronage. But a crucial difference here was the political legacy of British colonial government in Pakistan.

The Game of Kings, and of Colonial Officers

Like Afghan *buzkashi*, the game of polo probably derived from the equestrian sports of mounted Turkic and Iranian nomads of Central Asia, whence it was adopted as a symbol of 'arena state' ceremony in Saljuq Persia (Diem 1942; cf. Geertz 1980).[1] The sixteenth century Safavid ruler Shah Abbas even designed his new capital at Isphahan to focus on its central 'royal arena' (*maidan-i-shah*) for polo-playing, his palace and mosque displaced to the edge of the imperial sportsfield. This Persian game was then incorporated into court rituals of Timurid and Mughal rulers of Central and South Asia and was noted in a curious account of this 'football on horseback' by the Elizabethan Sherley brothers visiting the court of Akbar the Great (Watson 1989: 51). The indigenous game played in the Hindu Kush may have been influenced by Mughal Indian forms of Persian *chaughán-bazi*, the 'game of squared mallets', for it had similar ritual functions in traditional state ceremonies persisting into the 1960s and early 70s, when the princely states of northern Pakistan were finally dissolved.

It was from just two peripheral Himalayan enclaves on India's north-western and north-eastern frontiers that all extant forms of modern polo derive, for the Mughal sport was abandoned elsewhere in the subcontinent by the eighteenth century. Although this essay concerns the indigenous game of the north-western enclave in present day Pakistan, its other north-eastern Himalayan survivor is of thematic pertinence. For it was from Manipur that the game was ingeniously reconstructed as a British regimental sport and subsequently re-introduced to colonial India in the mid-nineteenth century. It was through the reinvented British sport that modern polo evolved as a Pakistani regimental recreation whose civilizing rules have since encroached upon the sporting customs of its indigenous mountain heartland.

The curious story of polo's imperial reinvention and metropolitan reprocessing, its raw retrieval from Manipur to Hurlingham and its re-export as a finished product to the subcontinent, offers an instructive paradigm for the historical anthropology of other colonially appropriated sports (Watson 1986). We witness the trans-cultural regenesis of a regionally localized game transfigured through an imperial world system, which thereby accumulated a sophisticated canon of civilizing rules that were ultimately re-imposed upon a now primitivized and peripheralized indigenous game. In the case of native Indian polo, both its north-eastern and north-western Himalayan forms were discovered and described more or less simultaneously by British officers who were penetrating the northern frontiers of the subcontinent in the mid-nineteenth century (cf. Vigne 1842). But it was the Manipuri game that was famously adopted by Joseph Scherer, commandant of the Kuki Levy at Cachar in Assam, who arranged for the first British team of tea-planters to play against the Raja of Manipur. He established the Calcutta Polo Club in 1863 and thereby instigated polo's contagious adoption by cavalry regiments throughout Bengal (Watson 1989: 50, 59). Accounts of this Manipuri game are identical in most respects with that witnessed in the same decade by Frederik Drew (1875: 380, 92) in Baltistan and Gilgit i.e. the indigenous game still played in villages throughout northern Pakistan. There were seven or more players per side with games lasting up to an hour without break until a winning team had scored nine goals. There were minimal rules beyond polite injunctions against, for example, 'using teeth' in riding-off.

The modern sport of polo however stemmed from a written report of the Manipuri game in *The Field* which inspired officers of the 10th Hussars, on home leave at Aldershot, to reconstruct their own 'hockey on horseback' with the aid of walking-sticks and a billiard ball. Devising their own basic rules, adapted from British hockey and regimental equestrian sports, they defined criteria of duration and foul-play and moves to safeguard their Irish ponies. The Hussars' imaginative reconstruction of the Manipuri game laid the foundations of regimental polo which were ultimately enshrined in the Hurlingham Association Rules of 1876. It was this regimental game that was then carried back to the subcontinent.[2] Embraced by British Indian army officers and then readopted by Indian princes, this modern game outlived the Raj as a disciplined sport of both Indian and Pakistani cavalry regiments and was also incorporated into the recreational drill and display of Indian civil service departments. There are now over a score of clubs in the Pakistan Polo Association (PPA), including regimental stations throughout the northern Punjab and North-West Frontier Province, together with such government service teams as the Pakistan Railway Club and the Punjab Police Club. Yet the more numerous indigenous polo associations of the northern Pakistani districts of Chitral and Gilgit have only 'affiliation status' within the PPA.

The Traditional Game

Frederik Drew's extensive early account of polo in Baltistan and Gilgit is a primary source on the traditional form and tactics of the indigenous game

(Drew 1875: 380, 92; cf. Leitner 1889: App. IV.1; Frembgen 1988). Drew was an enthusiastic participant-observer of polo when serving as a mining engineer seconded to the Maharaja of Kashmir in the 1860s and he noted that polo grounds were found in virtually every large village throughout Baltistan, Gilgit and Chitral (Figure 1). Unlike the roughly square regulation grounds of Hurlingham Association standards (200 × 300 yards), the equally long *shawaran* or *maidan* field was rarely over 40 yards wide, usually contained by a rough stone wall with drystone pillars set four to eight yards apart at either end as goal-posts. In some large settlements, such as Aiun in southern Chitral, the game was even played between shop-fronts along the bazaar. In most villages the polo-ground was carefully irrigated to maintain a fine turf and usually situated beside the local ruler's fort, where it would serve as the site for other festivals too. A raised stone dais or 'throne' (*takht*) on the perimeter wall would accommodate such lords and attendant nobility, nowadays replaced or accompanied by local government officials and distinguished visitors (Balneaves 1972: 48). Opposite this regal dais was the place for low-caste musicians (*dombericho*) who were employed to orchestrate games with stirring melodies played on a barrel-drum and two kettle drums accompanied by *surnai* reed flutes (cf. Schmid 1997). Each noble player had an inherited or assigned personal tune, often a uniquely composed melody awarded as a royal boon to outstanding players and their lineal descendants, specially played on the occasion of their triumphal 'taking off' (*tampok*) after scoring a goal (Drew 1875: 383, 385; cf. Frembgen 1988: 208, 9). The musicians also performed these honorific tunes for dances of victory and of forfeiture at the conclusion of each game (Drew 1875: 385, 86; Biddulph 1880: 85, 86; cf. Tahir Ali 1981).

Frederik Drew further noted that there was no fixed number of players per side, observing teams with as many as 15 participants in Baltistan, although tournaments are nowadays limited to teams of five or six. He also saw little evidence of any tactical 'positions' in the traditional game comparable with the numbered team positions of what would become Hurlingham Association Polo (i.e. numbers 1, 2, 3 and back; Watson 1989: 15, 41, 43). Rather, Drew described an anarchic and tactically individualized game, reminiscent of Whitney Azoy's (1982: 3) account of Uzbek *buzkashi*:

> The players do not take up their station at their respective goals, but all congregate at one end. Then from here one player begins the game by taking the ball in his hand, starting off at full gallop, and, when he comes to the middle of the ground, throwing it up and striking it as best he can towards the enemy's goal [i.e. *tampok*] ... But the leader is followed not only by his own side, but by all his opponents, galloping close behind, and the struggle comes for the second blow, if the ball has not reached the

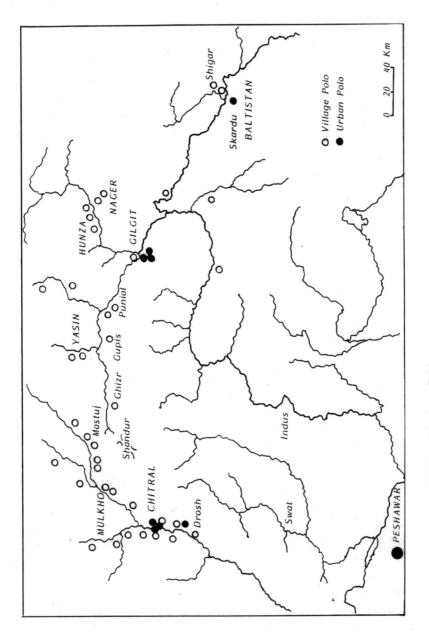

Figure 1. Distribution of Polo in Northern Pakistan.

goal. Now when one of the other party gets the chance, he does not strike it back in the direction he wishes it ultimately to go, but carries it on towards his own base, for the sake of making the ball miss the goal and pass behind. If this happens, the practice is for a bystander to take up the ball and throw it as hard as he can in the other direction, so that now the second side have the advantage due to the impetus. And it is the rule that the game is not considered as again started until one of that side has touched the ball, this being done without interruption from the other side. Now probably will come the time when the ball gets checked and entangled among the horses' legs; then comes a melée, often amusing enough, when crowding of horses, pushing, hooking of sticks–intentionally as well as by accident, for it is an allowed thing–the ball remains for long confined and often invisible; till by some chance it gets clear and is carried away by some nimble, handed one; when a race again begins, to make or save the goal. (Drew 1875: 383, 4)

Drew further notes that goals (*hal*) were confirmed only when one of the winning players dismounted and picked the ball up, prior to which any opponent could still strike the ball out. Goals would then be reversed with the scorer galloping out in triumph to throw and strike the ball in the opposite direction. Unlike Hurlingham polo, there were thus no short 'chukkas' of seven-minute play, nor any changing of ponies. Traditional games could persist for an hour or more until one side had scored nine goals, as was the case in Manipur. Nowadays local tournament games are divided into halves of 30 minutes duration with a stipulated rest break of ten minutes to ensure that horses are not over-exerted.

Drew and other mid-nineteenth century British observers also detailed the ceremonial functions of polo within mountain principalities of this region, which persisted until their dissolution barely twenty-five years ago. In Chitral the spring polo season was inaugurated with state rituals conducted by the ruling Mehtar during the New Year festival of Nauroz held at the vernal equinox (Lentz 1939: 148f.). In Hunza, more elaborate rites of inauguration were held during the spring barley-sowing festival (*bóphao*). After the king had been invited by his vizier to inaugurate ploughing, the latter initiated the first *tampok* strike on the royal polo-ground and then galloped through the goal with a cry that 'Many sons will be born!' (Lorimer 1979: 75). It was subsequently explained by Lorimer that 'if the horse and ball go through the goal, there will be a favourable year and sons will be born. On the other hand, if the ball goes out, they say that there will be a difficult year and daughters will be born' (ibid.: 255).[3]

Polo games were also expressive of regal authority and patronage in the mountain principalities of this region, where it was expected that fit rulers should be seen to participate in demonstration games, if not in competitive tournaments. Sponsorship of new polo-grounds, together with the hosting of communal feasts at sporting festivals, were essential policies of populist legitimation for tyrannous princes, some of whom were prone to sell their subjects into slavery to subsidize their polo expenses (Müller-Stellrecht 1981). There were also substantial royal grants (*meherbani* benefices) of horses or landed estates awarded to favoured players. Yet polo had seemingly ambivalent connotations of both courtly hierarchy and populist democracy where princes, courtiers and commoners might all be seen playing and competing together on an athletically equal footing: 'All people are passionately fond of the game; those of rank look upon the playing of it as one of the chief objects for which they were sent into the world; but not to them is the pursuit confined; all who can get a pony to mount join in it, and the poorest enter thoroughly into the spirit of it' (Drew 1875: 380, 81). Another colonial traveller, witnessing the game in the small principality of Yasin in the 1930s, similarly commented on indigenous polo's 'real democracy ... where the raja, the headman and all the ragbag and bobtail of the countryside–in fact everyone who possessed a horse– played together in perfect good, fellowship and complete indifference to person' (Schomberg 1935: 51). Again in Gilgit, 'it is a wonderful democratic game; it is a curious paradox in a land of autocracy to see the Raja, his sons and wazir all jostling and crashing together with any peasant who has a pony and cares to play. There is no respect for persons whatever' (Schomberg 1935: 192).

Contrasted with an elaborate court etiquette that surrounded the ranking of caste-like tributary estates in these mountain principalities (Biddulph 1880: 61, 68; Schomberg 1938: 213, 18; cf. Barth 1956: 81, 83; Eggert 1990; Parkes 2001a), the public competition of teams of mixed rank might well be represented as a 'democratic' spectacle, subordinating court distinctions of rank to merits of athletic skill. Yet participation was perforce restricted to those who could afford the upkeep of horses, a knightly nobility of 'true human beings' (*adamzada* literally 'offspring of Adam') who formed a minority in comparison with the predominantly pedestrian population of 'miserable poor' (*fakir mishkin*) in such arid states as Chitral. Polo was thus essentially a fraternizing ceremony of this equestrian elite, itself internally stratified by rank and hypergamy yet interrelated by ties of foster allegiance or 'milk kinship' (Biddulph 1880: 82; Schomberg 1938: 225, 26), further allying petty nobility with commoners throughout the district (Schomberg 1935: 90, 92; see Parkes 2001b). The competitive performance of polo by the powerful, irrespective of court rank, thus played out wider coalitions that transcended caste, ethnicity and locality, whereby the lowliest spectator could identify with the sporting fortunes or mishaps of 'his' prince and adoptive kinsman. In view of the perpetual internecine struggles of princes over rulership of these petty states, such coalitional identification of spectators with players on the polo-ground signified more than mystified fanship. These allegiances were ever ready to erupt in violent support of princely pretenders to the throne, as they did notoriously in Chitral at the end of the nineteenth century (Robertson 1898: ch. 4; Alder 1963: 287, 99; Parkes 2001b: 21, 23).

Polo tournaments were also traditionally employed to consolidate the fragile regional alliances of these rulers who seasonally travelled from one district to another in order to reactivate local allegiances of their own dependent foster-kin and supporters. But sponsorship of such games, together with other expenses of these royal peripatetic tours, was largely borne by a hereditary gentry of 'food-providers' (*ashimadek*, Biddulph 1880: 64, 65) and a yeoman 'yoke' (*yuft*). The latter were the substantial 'middle classes' of smallholders that had long resented their enforced subsidies of such royal largesse (Schomberg 1938: 217, 18). These resentful sponsors of the traditional game would ultimately rally against their obligatory services through political mobilization within the anti-royalist Muslim League in the troubled years following Partition, when the northern principalities were incorporated into the new nation of Pakistan (Ghufran 1962: ch. 15).

The Colonial and Postcolonial Game

As the formerly autonomous mountain principalities of the Hindu Kush and Karakorum became subject to imperial annexation from the 1890s there was a gradual appropriation of princely polo patronage by British Political Agents. These foreign patrons also enthusiastically suggested various 'improvements' upon the local game in which their officers were now regularly participating. One should note, however, that an earlier generation of civilian explorers in the 1870s such as Gottlieb Leitner and Frederik Drew were less inclined to fiddle with the local game:

> One cannot help allowing considerable weight to the fact of three, if nor four, Englishmen having lost their lives at this game within the first ten years of its introduction into Upper India... [But] in Baltistan, fatal accidents at polo are hardly known, and it behoves us to examine whether this may not be due to their different way of conducting the game. I have little doubt that this freedom from accident arises from the galloping being done in the same direction at one time; there is no meeting; both sides start together and ride together after the ball. This is a very different thing from two sides being drawn up opposing each other, as in a tournament, and galloping towards each other ... As to the commencing,

the Balti plan of striking the ball in the air at a gallop is much more workmanlike– requiring as it does some considerable skill– than any other. (Drew 1875: 390)

Such suggestions for apprenticeship of the indigenous game were scarcely heeded by Hurlingham, nor by Drew's political successors in Gilgit and Chitral. Within two decades, such professional soldiers as E.F. Knight had 'no doubt that, though this game is native to the country, we have much improved upon it, and polo as played by British officers in India is a far superior sport' (1897: 185). Bringing lowland regimental ponies to their outposts in the Karakorum, these officers' concern for damage to their horses encouraged further modifications of indigenous rules and penalties along Hurlingham guidelines, at least in regulating matches with native teams. As Colonal Reginald Schomberg noted, 'To anyone used to Indian polo, the roughness of the game is remarkable. There is "crossing" of an outrageous nature, hitting your opponents pony very hard with a polo stick, catching the ball with the hand, putting the arm round a man's waist, and a number of customs that would not be tolerated down country' (1935: 193). Padded flags therefore now replaced the stone goal-posts; the rule of dismounting to seize the ball after making a goal, similar to grappling the goat carcass in *buzkashi*, was waived as a criterion of scoring; a rest period was introduced; and intentional hooking of sticks above shoulders or across a pony was discouraged as foul-play.[4] These imposed regulations, applicable only in matches with the foreign *sarkar* officers, were no doubt considered a small accommodation to otherwise generous sponsorship of the indigenous game by such popular Political Agents as Major Cobb, who exceeded local rulers in founding polo-grounds in virtually every village within Gilgit Agency by the late 1930s (Frembgen 1988: 198). In Gilgit, Cobb's vigour for the game is even still enshrined in a traditional saying: 'Better to be a donkey and carry wood from [distant] Harelli than play number one on Cobb Sahib's polo team' (Staley 1982: 256). Such Political Agents also helped support the game and its princely patrons against the occasional rebellions of hereditary service estates which escalated with Muslim League agitation in the 1940s. Famously, Major Cobb broke a strike of *dom* musicians who had refused to perform for polo matches in Gilgit (Staley 1982: 264). After Partition in 1947, British Political Agents were replaced by their Pakistani counterparts.[5] These civil administrators were also mainly regimental officers, often from the Punjab, who continued the tradition of military sponsorship of the still popular local game despite occasional mullahs' protests against polo's frivolity and profanity with its 'un-Islamic' music and dance. By the 1960s polo-playing Punjabi and Pakhtun officers were beginning to introduce their own thoroughbred lowland ponies to the game and were therefore encouraging further regulations and 'improvements' of tactics according to the Hurlingham conventions of their lowland regimental practice.

The Modern Game

We arrive at the era of my own fieldwork and amateur experience of polo-playing in Chitral in the 1970s. The feudal principality of Chitral State was dissolved by presidential decree in 1969, followed by the local rajaships of Gilgit and Baltistan Agencies in 1972 and finally the Mirdom of Hunza in September 1974. Polo-playing Deputy Commissioners (DCs) now keenly encouraged a safer and tactically more sophisticated training for the game. Although resisted by an older generation of courtly players, and having little impact on the village game in remote regions, these innovations were eagerly adopted by a younger generation of players stemming from the old noble families of the court, as well as by officers of the old state militias, such as the Chitral Scouts (Trench 1985). These elite players had already embraced mod-ifications to the game introduced at Chitrali tournaments a generation earlier. This was explained to me in 1995 by a champion player who was an English-speaking advocate of courtier descent:

> The only small difference between the way we play here, and how they still play in Gilgit, is over what we call 'catch tampok' (*tamphok dosik*): when the ball is hooked up in the air and you catch it, and take it to the goal, and throw it through; or you take your horse with the ball in your hand through the goal; or else you give it to a companion who can do this. This 'catch tampok' is still played in Gilgit. But not in Shandur or anywhere much in Chitral now. We stopped this in '56 or '57. There was too much quarrelling on those occasions, too much hitting of the horses, and of each other.

The same player, currently a leading member of Chitral's civil A-team, further explained how fouls and tactical 'positions', similar to those of Hurlingham Association polo, might have naturally developed:

> The game has perhaps developed a bit, but without any *real* changes. That would affect the charm of the game. But even our rule-less (*bekanun*) game has conventions or 'unwritten laws' you might say. You cannot hit someone intentionally or hit his horse's legs if there is no ball there; and you should be calm and quiet in defence. So we have a judge [umpire] there but he has no work at all to do in most games. If rules were intro-duced, well there would be no end of introducing new rules then, to make it a 'gentleman's game'. But the people would lose interest in it,

because the people are interested in too much courage, too much danger. These are the circumstances: some techniques and positions have developed, because our horses are more trained than in the past, and we now practise too much. More sweetness is also coming into the game, because our horses are Punjabi 'first breed'. But there were positions in the past too: that number one guards number six; and number six keeps the goal, although sometimes carrying the ball even to the other goal if there is an open space; while numbers three and four stay in the middle. In the past there were those numbers too ...

Confronted with Drew's account of a positionless and seemingly individualistic game, this champion player further speculated that strategic 'positions' might have emerged with improved breeds of ponies:

The old Badakshani horses were not trained, not expert, nor as sensual as Punjabi horses. Those horses are 'sweet' by nature, they are quick to your heart [? to start], even if they lack stamina. But in twenty-minute games it's more the quickness of the horse, his response to orders, his handiness in turning that really counts. Maybe with Badakshani horses the game then depended on just one or two good horses, so there could be no fixed positions. But some tactics have always been there. It's the same as what they call 'collective defense', that German way of thinking, even in war. I have gone through an article of Henry Kissinger [a former President of World Polo] and I definitely agree with him: not only in football, not only in war games, but in polo also, everywhere there are the *same* tactics. So changes may take place, but not very much. The game itself has *not* changed.

Chitrali polo-playing has, however, noticeably changed since the introduction of Punjabi (part Arab) horses around 1974, when an enthusiastic Deputy Commissioner had a string of regimental ponies flown into Chitral. I well remember this friendly DC's proudly confided ambitions of 'uplifting' the primitive local game, which was then a subject of bemused mockery by elite polo-players, including my informant's now deceased father who was a former court counsellor of the last Mehtar. With the teaching of new tactics appropriate for foreign horses came a new anglophone code with calls such as 'Leave it!' or 'Turn!' in place of the old argot of Khowar phrases (cf. Frembgen 1988: 206; also Azoy 1982: 95). By the end of my doctoral fieldwork in spring 1977 all militia and civil teams in Lower Chitral had converted to Punjabi horses, so only remote village teams in the Upper District retained the old Badakshani ponies. Apart from discrepancies of cost, there were insurmountable differences of size (12-13 hand Badakshanis against 15-hand or higher Punjabis). This resulted in a consequent lengthening of polo-sticks which now rendered tournament play between village and elite teams a handicapped exercise. The once homogeneous and 'democratic' indigenous game had thus ruptured into separate class and regional fractions largely as a result of tournament sponsorship.

Direct government subsidies of polo-playing in Chitral had long been limited to performing officers of the Chitral Scouts, who received free horses and rations as well as training as professional players. Those of the Chitral Police Team still receive an ordinary constable's wages of Rupees 3,000 per month and otherwise have to purchase and maintain their own ponies. All other teams are self-financed and with estimated annual costs of Rs. 25–30,000 for maintaining Punjabi ponies only hereditary rentier landlords can usually afford the game.[6] The Pakistan Tourism Development Corporation, succeeded by the provincial Sarhad Tourism Corporation in 1996, awards selected tournament players a small bursary of Rs. 1–2000 for the season. As another civilian A-team player of elite descent, but lesser means, explained:

> It is very difficult for people who are not big landowners, but who just have an enthusiasm (*shauk*) for polo. Their life becomes miserable, spending everything they have at home on horses. When Chitral was a State, perhaps not everyone played polo; but those who did considered it a service (*khesmat*) to the Mehtar; and they were rewarded with horses, or given good dinners; they were 'patronised' by the Mehtar. Now we really need such sponsorship, either from the government or from semi-agencies [NGOs]. But it should be given to those players at least according to their standard: A-category, B-type or C-type. These players *must* be helped; for it is important for tourism; it supports Kho [Chitrali] culture, which the government is bound to preserve; it contributes to health; it increases the competitiveness of the region.

Despite the escalating costs of maintaining horses, Chitral still has an estimated 50 village teams although barely half are selected to participate in regional tournaments. As my A-team friends concurred 'it is not that those teams are discriminated against, in any way, by the Chitral Polo Association; those teams are simply not of that calibre'. Those teams of course were of remote villages in Mulkho and Mastuj districts of Upper Chitral, who were still playing the anarchic traditional game on Badakshani ponies. Village teams in Gilgit Agency and Baltistan suffered more devastating setbacks of modernization. Polo-playing in these regions, as in Upper Chitral, had always been associated with the necessity of horse transport for conveying trade and tribute. With the building of jeep and truck roads in recent decades, the always costly maintenance of horses has become a needless extravagance. After the completion in 1978 of the Karakorum Highway, a metalled road linking Islamabad with Kashgar in China through the gorges of the upper Indus and along Hunza valley (Kreutzman 1991), polo-playing has virtually disappeared along its entire length. Of the six teams in the Ghujal District of upper Hunza that arranged spring and autumn tournaments in the 1970s just two horses survived by 1990 (Kassam p.c.).[7] Two teams from the renowned polo centre of Nager persist, their carefully selected players still dominating tournaments in Gilgit (Frembgen 1988: 198, 204), while rural teams from the still poorly accessible villages of Ishkoman, Punial and Ghizr still flourish although they are rarely invited to tournaments at the prestigious Agha Shahi Stadium in Gilgit town. Here, as in Chitral, the dominant A-teams are comprised of professionally salaried and equipped players of the old Gilgit Scouts milita, renamed the Northern Light Infantry (NLI), together with the Northern Areas Working Organization (NAWO) and the Public Works Team (PWT). All notoriously poach their star *Nager* players from each other, with ever inflated transfer bids for these prima donna 'Imran Khans of the Northern Areas' before major tournaments (Kassam p.c.). The NLI team is thus rather rudely acronymed as the 'Nakedly Lucrative Infantry' (Urdu *Nanga Luch Infantri*) by civil players.

District and regional polo tournaments in Chitral and Gilgit stem from the enthusiastic administrative arrangements of British Political Agents like Major Cobb, who regularized the more informally orchestrated tournaments of princes as these waned in the 1930s and 40s. In Chitral the polo spring season is now inaugurated by the Deputy Commissioner during government celebrations of Pakistan Day on the 23rd March, coinciding with the Mehtar's ancient equinoctial rites of Nauroz (around 21 March). Heading a Selection Committee of polo veterans predominantly of princely descent, the DC supervises the 'Commisioner's Cup' tournament in May, comprising separate games for the elite military or civil A-teams and some 20 rural village teams invited from Upper Chitral, with small cash prizes informally financed from District Council development funds. A second 'Chief Minister's Cup' is presided over by North-West Frontier Province officials who come up from Peshawar to celebrate Pakistan Independence Day on August 14. These events act as convenient occasions for government propaganda and opportunities for election promises to be delivered to spectators. An 'Inspector-General Frontier Corps Cup' tournament used to be held in June but it was withdrawn in the early 1990s, as was a spring tournament once sponsored by Pakistan International Airlines (PIA).

PIA indeed once flew in their own prestigious Hurlingham Association team for a demonstration match at their sponsored tournament in 1990, but this was not a happy experiment. As Chitrali players politely remember 'our game did not really suit their big Arab horses; they could not turn in our little *junali* ground, and they seemed worried about hurting these horses. This 'free-style' was just not *their* game: it was too costly, their chances of winning were dim, and there was no thrill, even for the people'. The same year also witnessed a brief adoption of the bad poaching habits of the Gilgit Northern Light Infantry, when the Chitral Scouts at Drosh began offering lucrative transfer bids to civil players. This malpractice was promptly debarred on the advice of the DC's Committee in autumn 1994. Similar regional tournaments in Gilgit were formerly sponsored by PIA but have since been replaced by stipends and horse allowances awarded by the Pakistan Tourism Development Corporation (PTDC) which hosts its own tournament in April. A second autumn tournament is sponsored by the Commisioner for Northern Areas to commemorate the patriotic 'Gilgit Freedom Struggle' (*Jashni Azadi Gilgit*) against Indian Kashmir in November 1947.[8] Local District Council Tournaments are also held in some remote areas such as Ghizr just before the Commissioner's Cup, when civil and military B-teams occasionally compete with rural players. But as in Chitral, such local teams with their 'rough and ready' (*andarun*) approach and little Wakhi ponies are no real match for even second-grade professional teams with their sophisticated regimental 'techniques' (*nafarsat*) of blocking and backhand passing. The spectacular culmination of all these district matches is the inter-regional Shandur Tournament, sponsored annually by the Central Government Ministry of Tourism and Culture in late June or early July.

Shandur: the Post-Modern Game?

Located on an otherwise deserted high mountain pass between Chitral District and the Northern Areas of Gilgit Agency (see Figure 1) over 12000 feet above sea level, the Shandur Tournament is justly touted as the supreme tourist attraction of Pakistan: 'Polo on the Roof of the World' (with an appended 'World's Highest Golf Tournament' and an 'All-Pakistan Trout Fishing Competition'). This inter-regional tournament has its own contested local histories. It was supposedly initiated in 1938, when local polo teams from Rajaships in Gilgit Agency first visited Chitral, with sporadic return matches of these village teams played in 1958 in Gilgit and at Shandur in 1966 (Shahzad 1995: 40). However, there is a less exalted reference in the official history of Chitral to an unexpected arrival, on 24 May 1938, of a composite polo team from three minor Rajaships of Gilgit Agency at the Mehtar's Darbar and District Tournament in Chitral: 'It was led by the three brothers of the Governors [or Rajas] of these areas ... some interesting matches were held ... the Chitral team distinguished themselves in the game ... they were, however, beaten by the Punial team'. (Ghufran 1962: Ch. 14). A more alluring account was entrusted to me by Advocate Wali Rakhman of Chitral:

> The tournament really started when Major White or Kirkbride [P.A. Gilgit 1934, 37] came to Shandur Pass in the case of some elopement or abduction of a noble girl from this area [Chitral] by men of Ghizr at Yasin. The party from Chitral went on horseback to settle this dispute there, and then they played polo. English gentlemen were playing on both sides with the local gentry [as respective adjudicators from Chitral and Gilgit]: they did not know that there would be any competition, but all of a sudden they started playing at *mahuran*... This was all recorded by Babar Jan, Governor of Gupis, in his Diaries, which I have in my possession. There he mentions that Major Kirkbride was actually captain of our [Chitral] team, so *we* really won that first match.

Chitral has since won just three Shandur tournaments against Gilgit's enviable and notorious NLI team (in 1986, 1993 and 2000). From 1989 however, the Shandur Tournament was reinvented as a traditionalized annual contest between 'Gilgit Agency' and 'Chitral District' teams through the effective promotional efforts of the Pakistan Tourism Development Corporation. As they put it, 'The ancient game of polo was born in Central Asia, grew up in Persia ... and reached maturity at Shandur, in the majestic Northern Areas of Pakistan' (PTDC brochure, Gilgit 1990). Its local history has since been elaborated by PTDC copyeditors into a venerable sporting tradition of inter-regional integration (between Chitral's North-West Frontier Province and the federally administered Northern Areas of Gilgit, still contested with India) further associated with the legendary Cobb Sahib, now immortalized in a dramatic feature film *Halfway To Heaven* (dir. Terence Bulley 2001) which is screened at international polo events:

> During the 1920s, the ruler of Mastuj, the Hindu Kush highland between Chitral and Gilgit, was told by his *Mir* or king to promote integration within his realm through a polo tournament with the best players. The British resident at the time, Col. Evelyn Hey Cobb, a keen polo player himself, came up with the idea of holding the tournament in the Shandur Pass... The site is described dramatically as being on the ridge between Heaven and the descent to Hell. Col. Cobb felt that, because the moon seemed so close to earth, his dream of playing polo in the light of a full moon could be realised. It was agreed that the games should be held between the best teams from Chitral and Gilgit, and played following the centuries old rules of Ali Sher Khan, a descendant of Ghengis Khan (Bulley 2001: 1)

The Shandur Tournament is a truly national event, well covered by the Pakistan Television Corporation, whose highlights can be almost simultaneously viewed through satellite dishes sprouting on the mud roofs of remote villages of Upper Chitral and Gilgit. It is also a vast government function, regularly attended by Presidents and Prime Ministers (both Nawaz Sharif and Benazir Bhutto in recent years), by the Chief of Army Staff and by the Ministries of Culture and Sport from both Central and Provincial Governments. Many such VIPs are flown in by military helicopter and accommodated in elaborate marquees erected around the high-pasture *mahuran bagh* (fairy-garden) stadium. Here they are regally entertained by Colonel Khushwaqt, ex-prince of nearby Mastuj and an outstanding former polo-player of Chitral, who manages an international Karakorum trekking company from his crumbling royal fort.

The Shandur tournament already costs hundreds of thousands of Rupees specially allocated in 1995 to the NWFP Provincial Government, no doubt to sooth regional factions within the Pakistan People's Party. But such funds are wholly accounted for in 'VIP and VVIP budgeting', providing security and support staff for government officials and diplomats and meeting their transport and accommodation costs. Lowlier prize money for A-team and B-team polo-players (Rs. 100,000) is sponsored by Red and White Cigarettes, Coca-Cola (Pakistan) or PIA, while the meagre subsistence of civil teams can only be partly covered from District development funds. Local polo-playing is indeed becoming a barely noticed backdrop for the Shandur Season, Islamabad's Royal Ascot. As described by an American travel-writer in July 2000:

> On the third morning of the tournament, the start of the match was postponed in anticipation of President Musharraf's arrival. Helicopters had been circling about and disappearing all day, and three finally landed, creating a dust storm that choked thousands of patiently waiting spectators. Musharraf's retinue of six SUVs wound its way along the dirt road that led to the back of the VIP building at the top of the south bleachers ... At the half-time break, the crackle of loud speakers was heard, and the voice of Pakistan's new dictator filled the thin mountain air. How he knew that there were exactly 116 western tourists there that day is something that I am quite comfortable not knowing. His speech was welcoming, however, praising the westerners for their courage to ignore cultural stereotypes and media stigmas and travel in remote and beautiful North Pakistan ... The applause was uproarious. I was patted on the back, congratulated and then thanked for being present at one of Pakistan's most unique and culturally significant festivals (Mabey 2002).

The writer finally noted that 'Chitral was victorious in the A-division final in a stunning 7 to 6 win (i.e. the third or fourth such victory since Major White or

Newsletter
PAKISTAN TOURISM
An information bank of Pakistan Tourism Development Corporation

Monthly

July 1998, Vol. Number 007

SHANDUR POLO SPECIAL

SHANDUR FESTIVAL

World's famous Shandur Polo festival is being celebrated from July 7 to July 9 at a height of 12,200 feet above sea level in Chitral valley.
In order to facilitate the domestic and international polo enthusiasts and adventure lovers their overnight accommodation requirements during the event, a tourist tent village has been set up at Shandur pass which includes shops, medical stores and restaurants.
A large number of foreign travel writers, local journalists and nature lovers have confirmed their programme to visit the place during the event. Tourists are advised to contact Pakistan Tours Limited (PTL), a subsidiary of PTDC at Flashman's Hotel, the Mall, Rawalpindi for group handling of this event.

PTDC is tourism.
Pakistan is tourism - friendly.
PAKISTAN-
far from ordinary

SHANDUR: POLO FINAL ON ROOF-TOP OF WORLD

Shandur has been a thrilling destination for polo lovers for decades attracting a large number of foreign tourists, travel writers and adventurers. Polo which is regarded as King of Games is played at a height of more than 12000 feet above sea level.
A German writer was right to say when he said: "in Shandur playing polo is like playing this game at Moon". Those who visit to see the final polo match between traditional arch rivals Gilgit and Chitral, term it as playing polo on roof-top of the world.
In fact, the entire journey from Islamabad to Chitral, crossing over Lowari Top is fascinating and from Chitral to Shandur it is a real adventure of lifetime.
Polo is very popular game in the valleys of Skardu, Gilgit and Chitral. Although the exact origin of the game of polo is now known, yet the game is not properly documented.

There is enough evidences that it was played by Kings and members of royal families. The history bears evidence to it. For more than 20 centuries polo remained a popular sport of the rulers of Asia.

An in-house publication of Pakistan Tourism Development Corporation

Figure 2. The high profile marketing of the Shandur tournament.

Kirkbride or Cobb's legendary foundation of this usually predictable contest). Ecstatic Chitralis rushed the field and were met by baton-wielding soldiers, striking randomly and without mercy. Musharraf departed before the chaos erupted. [But] the soldiers could not control the victorious. They ran en

masse onto the field to dance their joy' (ibid.). Indeed, Shandur was the last
forlorn hope of Pakistan's once grandiose ambitions of massively developing
international tourism along a slightly deviated 'Silk Road' in the Hindu Kush
and Karakorum mountains, foiled by events in neighbouring Afghanistan, and
then dashed in its Year of International Mountain Tourism on September 11th
2001.[9] The revamped Shandur Tournament has had further widespread
effects on the nature and reception of polo-playing in Chitral and Gilgit. Prior
to its annual institutionalization from 1989, all Chitrali teams traditionally had
five players. But in order to compete with the six-player teams of the champion
Northern Light Infantry of Gilgit Agency, Chitral A-Teams needed to practice
with an additional player. Now six-player teams are conventional in regional
Chitrali tournaments and this has required a reconfiguration of all positional
tactics according to Gilgiti techniques that further alienated the elite and
professional game from that persisting in rural villages.

The entanglement of Deputy Commissioners in the extravagant ambitions
of the Pakistan Tourism Development Corporation also caused unintended
political reactions that echoed the social protests mobilized by Muslim League
agitators against the princely games of the 1940s. One of the great polo-
sponsoring DCs of contemporay Chitral was obliged to seek a transfer as a
consequence of his all too visible support for the game, which he had partly
provided from his own pocket according to his own account. After rebuilding
and widening the main *junali* polo ground of Chitral in 1989 and furnishing
its tourist spectators with a splendid tin-roofed pavilion, Islamist agitators of
the opposition Jamaati Islami party began disseminating scandalous rumours
of his misappropriation of Chitral Area Development Project funds. In their
account, the allocated money was intended for productive projects and was
being lavished upon the un-Islamic pastimes of the old courtly elite. The
accusations were spiced with allegations of indecent impropriety with the
young English school-teachers at the new college who attended the game.
Piously outraged demonstrations against the DC's supposed profligacy were
soon interrupting tourist polo-games throughout summer and autumn 1990
and Chitrali polo's briefly powerful patron was transferred to another District
before the end of the year.

Conclusion

Sporting activities have been used to diagnostically reflect historical processes
of societal differentiation (Bourdieu 1990) and of colonial and postcolonial
power (Armstrong and Bates 2001; Mills 2001) and as such it is useful to draw
further on some of the relationships identified in this paper. Following the sim-
plest episodic narrative of observed transformations in the indigenous polo of

northern Pakistan, we have witnessed this game's subtly shifting practices and discourses, as it accommodated itself to successive alien administrations. I have particularly examined the ambivalent legacy of British colonial patronage, whose devolution through a similarly elite anglophone administration of Punjabi officers perpetuated an alternative lowland tradition of regimental Hurlingham Association polo. Yet this lent recognizable affinities between the sporting habits of rulers and ruled that could be fruitfully grafted onto the stem of princely patronage. Improving the indigenous game according to their own regimentally instilled dispositions of sporting excellence and fair-play, neither British nor Punjabi administrators ever intended to 'change' it. They rather wished to nurture what they perceived as its intrinsic qualities, albeit sensed through their own civilized sporting habits. Polo-playing administrators indeed boasted of daringly demotic participation in a 'wild' (*jangali*) game that would shock fellow civil servants and regimental colleagues posted to tamer lowland districts. They therefore regarded themselves as participant caretakers of an indigenous and endangered local tradition whose authentic preservation, although for foreign consumption, was equally an objective of the Pakistan Tourism Development Corporation. Justification for each slight modification introduced by these foreign benefactors peculiarly concerned the welfare of horses, which again stems from the sporting sensibilities of an originally British regimental equestrian tradition. To the fine feelings of a foreign spectator the anarchic traditional game may well appear unnecessarily cruel at times, as the little Badakshani ponies get bloodily gouged with spurs and whips as well as struck by the sticks in the chaotic frenzy of a massed challenge (Balneaves 1972: 46, 53). Yet one might reconsider Frederik Drew's vigorous defence of the traditional game against its original animal welfare detractors:

> I must try to efface an impression that has lately got abroad, that polo is a cause of cruelty to the ponies. It can only be so if racing be cruel to race-horses, and hunting to hunters. The truth is that the game brings out a horse's capabilities, exercises his faculties, and so makes him fulfil the object of his life, in the highest degree. In the heat of the game a blow from the ball on his shin or his knee (a joint by no means so tender as our own knee, with which it does not correspond in structure) is hardly felt ... If one exposes the ponies to no greater risk of injury than we do ourselves at polo, and I cannot think their greater, then the best friends of animals should be satisfied (Drew 1875: 391, 92).

As we know from the historiography of animal welfare (e.g. Turner 1980), the contemporary liberal concerns that Drew was addressing here implicated broader moralizing sensibilities of a modernizing civility (cf. Elias 1978).

Similar civilizing instincts still evidently inform the sporting motives of polo-playing Deputy Commissioners in their attempts to correct what they cannot help but experience in recreational practice as an occasionally brutal and bru-talizing local game. Hence the successive and seemingly endless reforms of local polo in northern Pakistan.

A second theme of our chronicle has been the gradual, almost impercepti-ble division of a once socially coherent indigenous game into separate elite and rural village factions, belying a still widely upheld belief in indigenous polo's epitomization of 'participatory democracy'. DCs and ex-princes may still be seen playing with ordinary locals irrespective of their administrative rank. But tournament play has inevitably introduced a distinctly competitive grading of military and elite civil teams. Their incremental evolution, under the influence of regimental Hurlingham Association conventions, has further resulted in the speciation of a technically hybrid polo that can no longer fruitfully interact with the original game: there are now physical incompatabilities (of height or team numbers) redefining the mutual tactics of consensual play that mark a saltatory divide from former differences of relative skill. This irreversible evo-lution into a separate, quasi-professional species of competing civil A-team and Scouts players in Chitral may be precisely dated to the onset of major tourna-ment promotion in the early 1970s. In Gilgit it seems to have occurred slightly earlier under the predatorial pressures of the competitive Northern Light Infantry who still dominate all indigenous polo teams in northern Pakistan.

The courtly fathers and grandfathers of my champion polo-playing friends in Chitral were still regularly playing the indigenous game with commoners from local village teams twenty-five years ago. But their A-team descendants and inheritors are understandably more anxious nowadays that their well-practised skills should be recognizably differentiated from those of their 'back-ward' country cousins (and local village teams typically include ex-nobility who are related and intermarried with Chitral's young urban professionals) in their desperate lobbies for government or corporate subsidies. We witness, in plaintive English voices, a further rupturing of moral sensibilities concerning the former solidarity of Chitrali players, irrespective of merit, in resisting the civilizing pretensions of DCs and Scouts officers which I well remember being discussed with disrespectful mirth at their family homes in the 1970s. This necessary compliance with the authoritative tournament game, always with a hopeful if sceptical ear to long heard promises of further PTDC, Sarhad or Provincial Government subsidies, seems indicative of a broader quasi-class division isolating this educated and increasingly professionalized urban elite of former nobility.

Differences in sporting practice may thus be emblematic of a wider recreational culture that now irrevocably divides this elite from their barely literate relatives as well as their old social inferiors (other manifestations of this include language (Urdu and English) and musical tastes (a conversely conservative connoisseurship of Chitrali court melodies elsewhere swamped by popular Hindi film music)). These amateur players, whether professionally employed or idle gentry in what little spare time is left from strenuous daily polo practice, are also typically private contractors (*tikadar*) for the many lucrative development projects flooding into northern Pakistan over the past decade (Parkes 2000). Their fortunes and lifestyles are thus becoming more intimately associated with outside (Punjabi, Pakhtun or European) project administrators than with their seemingly backward compatriots. Their detachment from the indigenous village game thus accompanies a more general disinterest in hereditary, and now distastefully 'paternalist', obligations to dependants and former foster-kin which once welded these mountain principalities into socially interlinked although hierarchically ranked sodalities. Rifts in the tactical playing of polo are again tokens of a more general type of 'cultural speciation' occurring throughout northern Pakistan, which has been exacerbated with the injection of foreign financed development projects.[10]

However, we should note that polo is still a hugely popular spectator sport in Chitral and Gilgit. Just as Frederik Drew noted long ago: '[all] the children of an early age get their eye and hand in accord by practising it on foot–playing indeed the ordinary hockey of our country' (1875: 381). Such juvenile polo, played on foot or on bicycle, still beats football while the bazaars of Chitral and Gilgit still invariably close shop whenever a tournament match begins. Rural village players continue to flock to the regional tournaments of Chitral, Gilgit and Shandur, deprecating their own 'wild' (*jangali*) game at home, in contrast to the properly 'regulated' (*kanuni*) sport of their civil and army superiors. Indeed, they employ just the same terms of ironic and yet resistant self-mockery as those used by elite champions reflecting on the relative 'barbarism' of *their* indigenous game in relation to the lowland regimental sport. A shared discourse of collective self-deprecation from an imagined national perspective verbally papers over the class fissures of polo that I have diagnosed here, which were indeed mirthfully denied or scorned by my Chitrali friends on reading this essay.

I should finally state that I quizzically respect these differing opinions of Chitrali polo players and I share their hopes for sponsorship of the elite game from wherever it may come, as it may prove vital if indigenous polo is to survive at all in modern Pakistan. The fate of *buzkashi* in contemporary Afghanistan, whose stadia were re-employed for the public execution of adulterers by Pakistan (CIS) supported Taliban, is a sobering reminder that athletic sport in this part of South Asia faces threats that make it an increasingly endangered communitarian activity.

Acknowledgements

This is a revised and updated version of an article originally published in J. McClancy (ed.) *Sport, Ethnicity and Identity* (Oxford: Berg 1996). I am grateful to the ESRC for the award of a travel grant (R000 22 1087) for research in Chitral and Gilgit in 1989. The Department of Anthropology at the University of Kent also generously supported my attendance, at short notice, of the 3rd International Hindu Kush Cultural Conference in Chitral, in August, September 1995, when I was able to update a hitherto casual knowledge of polo, playing. I further benefited there from discussion of the game with its erudite ethnographer in Nager, Dr Jürgen Frembgen, and especially from interviews with the Chitrali polo champions, Nasir and Wali Rakhman. My knowledge of contemporay polo in Gilgit and Hunza is largely derived from answers to enquiries kindly conducted on my behalf by Dr Sabrina Kassam.

4

'THE MORAL THAT CAN BE SAFELY DRAWN FROM THE HINDUS' MAGNIFICENT VICTORY': CRICKET, CASTE AND THE PALWANKAR BROTHERS[1]

Ramachandra Guha

Introduction

V. S. Naipaul once wrote of his native Trinidad that 'we were a society with no heroes, except cricketers'. In other times and other places too it is sportsmen who have often most fully embodied the hopes of the lowly and dispossessed. Naipaul's sentiments would be recognized by blacks in the Chicago ghetto, who honour no hero other than Michael Jordan, and by mulattos in the slums of Buenos Aires who are devotees of the deity Diego Maradona. They would also have been appreciated by an Indian not generally known for his interest in sport, Dr B. R. Ambedkar. As an Untouchable boy placed by the accident of birth at the bottom of the Hindu hierarchy Ambedkar, the future draughtsman of the Indian Constitution, took as his hero a slow left-arm bowler named Palwankar Baloo. Year after year Baloo dominated the Bombay Quadrangular which was the showcase cricketing tournament of India at that time. He was one of the first great Indian cricketers and among the earliest public figures to emerge from the ranks of the Untouchables. Now almost wholly forgotten, Palwankar Baloo commanded enormous respect inside and outside his community during his lifetime. Consider thus a little, thirty-page biography published in Poona in 1959 as part of a series of Marathi tracts with the running title 'Kahintari Navech Kara!' or 'Do Something Distinctive!' Priced at half-a-rupee these booklets were aimed at school and college kids presumed to be in search of role models. The subjects were chosen for having 'gone outside the rut of normal life' by making a name through courage and innovativeness.

The tracts were short enough to be read within thirty minutes. Of the forty titles listed in the series twenty were about Maharashtrians and twenty featuring people from other parts of India or the world. The publishers did not, of course, commission tracts on men like Shivaji or Tilak or Gandhi or Einstein whom one could worship but certainly not emulate. The subjects chosen included Marathi pioneers of theatre, printing, education, history and the cinema. They included a progressive Marathi poet, a wealthy and successful Marathi lawyer and the first circus promoter in Maharashtra. From elsewhere in the sub-continent came the hockey player Dhyan Chand, architect of India's Olympic victories in 1928, 1932 and 1936; the first of our great modern painters Raja Ravi Varma of Kerala; and the myriad-minded Bengali Rabindranath Tagore. More interesting perhaps was the choice of foreigners. There was Spartacus of Rome described simply as 'A Slave who Revolted'. There was Michaelangelo, the 'Unequalled Sculptor', and Benjamin Franklin, the diplomat and scientist remembered also for 'The Art of Cultivating Good Qualities'. There was a pamphlet on Captain Cook, 'Girdling the Oceans for his Country', and another on Lawrence of Arabia, that 'Great Organizer of Military Campaigns'. From the world of technology came the builder of the Suez Canal, the 'Monumental Architect', Ferdinand Lesseps and finally, moving from the heroic to the pragmatic there was a study of Woolworth, the founder of the supermarket, with the title 'Buy Anything Here'. In this exalted company was to be found the name of Palwankar Baloo. The pamphlet on him, written by the Poona cricketer and broadcaster Bal J. Pandit, was titled 'Khada Kheladu' or 'True Sportsman'.

Palwankar Baloo

Palwankar Baloo was born in July 1875 in the town of Dharwad which is deep in the Deccan Plateau. His father worked there but soon after his birth appears to have taken a job in Poona. The family were Chamaars from a caste that lies almost at the bottom of the Hindu social hierarchy. The caste's name comes from the Sanskrit word for leather, 'charman', and the people of the caste work with leather as tanners and dyers and as the makers of shoes, bottles, tents and saddles.

The Chamaars, wrote one authority, 'are by birth doomed to illiteracy' and to 'lamentable and abject poverty'. They undertook tasks vital to the clean castes yet were despised by them. 'Economically the Chamar is a most valuable element in the population and his function is the rough toil and drudgery of the community'. In the 'traditional' Indian village the Chamaar is:

> Regarded with loathing and disgust by the higher castes … Except when
> it is absolutely necessary, a clean-living Hindu will not visit his part of the

village. The author of *Hindu Castes and Sects* says that the very touch of a Chamar renders it necessary for a good Hindu to bathe with all his clothes on. The Chamar's very name connects him with the carcasses of cattle. Besides, he not only removes the skins from the cattle that have died, but also he eats the flesh. The defilement and degradation resulting from these acts is insurmountable (Briggs 1920: 241, 228, 58, 20).

For the Chamaars, as for other Untouchable castes, the advent of British rule allowed a means of escape. The adventurous and skilled among them could abandon the village to seek employment in the towns and cities of the Raj. In some professions, indeed, their past was an advantage. Caste Hindus would not work in ammunition depots and gun factories as it was feared that the bullets might use the grease of the sacred cow. But the Chamaars had no such inhibition. They would, when they could, flock to the cantonments and factories set up by the British in western and southern India after their defeat of the Peshwas in 1818.

Baloo's own father was employed in the army. One account suggests that he worked in the ammunition factory in the suburb of Kirkee, while another claims that he was a sepoy in the 112th Infantry Regiment.[2] It was in Poona that Baloo and his younger brother Shivram learnt to play cricket with equipment discarded by army officers. The boys also went, briefly, to school but were soon withdrawn to help augment the family income. Baloo's first job was at a cricket club run by Parsis. Here he swept and rolled the pitch and occasionally bowled to the members at the nets. For this work he took home three rupees a month (Vithal 1948: 11–12; Pandit 1959: 11; Palwankar 1996). After this and around 1892, Baloo moved from his job with the Parsi cricketers of the city to their European counterparts. These congregated in the Poona Club which had been founded a few years previously in a wooded estate known as the Edwardes Gardens. Baloo was now paid 4 rupees a month and his duties included rolling and marking the pitch, erecting the nets and, when required, marking out the tennis courts as well. To these routine tasks was later added an altogether more pleasurable one: bowling to the members after a Mr Tross first encouraged Baloo to bowl to him. Baloo took as his model a Captain Barton, a left-arm bowler with a smooth, flowing action. Soon Baloo was bowling on a more-or-less regular basis to the members of the Club to provide valuable practice for the matches they would play against other teams of expatriates (Pandit 11–12).

At this time the leading English cricketer of Poona was Captain J. G. Greig. He was known as 'Jungly' because that was how his forenames 'John Glennie' sounded if spoken quickly (Green 1986: 354; Raiji 1986: 61). Greig was a small man with supple wrists and quick feet. A master of the square cut he was regarded for years as the best white batsman in India. Every day Greig would arrive at the Poona Club an hour before anybody else and command Baloo to bowl to him. There is a nice story, undocumented but therefore all the more appealing, that Greig paid Baloo eight *annas* for every time he got him out. At this rate if the bowler was successful once a week he would have doubled his salary every month. Baloo once told his son that although he had bowled for hundreds of hours at the Poona Club he was not once given a chance to bat (Palwankar 1999). In India, as in England, batting was the pre-serve of the aristocratic élite. One consolation was that by adding bowling to his other duties Baloo had his salary tripled. And his control of spin and flight was honed to perfection by the thousands of balls bowled to Jungly Greig and his less gifted colleagues. Like his ancestors Palwankar Baloo had come to make a living working with skill and care upon a piece of leather. Slowly, word of his talents with the cricket ball reached the 'native' part of the city. There was a pioneering Hindu club which was seeking to challenge the Europeans of Poona and they faced the dilemma of whether or not they should call upon the services of a low-caste bowler. The question divided the Hindu cricketers. Some Telugu members were keen to include Baloo whereas the local Marathi-speaking Brahmins were not. At this stage J. G. Greig jumped into the fray. He gave an interview to the press suggesting that the Hindus would be fools to deprive themselves of Baloo's services. It was not that Greig had the instincts of a social reformer, his commitment to his race was scarcely less strict than the Poona Brahmin's commitment to his caste, but rather he wished to test his skills against Baloo in the fierce heat of match competition.

In the event Baloo was invited to play for the Poona Hindus, but at a price. On the field the upper caste cricketers touched the same ball as him but off it they observed the ritual taboos. At the tea interval, that ceremony sacred to cricket, Baloo was served the liquid outside the pavilion and in a disposable clay *matka* while his colleagues drank in white porcelain cups inside. If he wished to wash his hands and face an 'untouchable' servant of the club took a kettle out into a corner of the field and poured water from it. Baloo also ate his lunch off a separate plate and on a separate table (Vithal 10–13; Pandit 1999). He took plenty of wickets all the same. Due chiefly to Baloo's bowling the Poona Hindus defeated the Poona Europeans and other local sides as well. On a celebrated occasion they visited the inland town of Satara, to play against its white-only Gymkhana. The hosts had instructed their groundsman to roll the wicket for a week so that it would blunt Baloo's spin. Baloo still took seven wickets and his team won easily. In one account the bowler was then serenaded on an elephant through the streets of Satara. In another account he was garlanded at a public function on his return to Poona by the great scholar and reformer Mahadev Govind Ranade. It was also Ranade who told his fellow Brahmins that if they could play with Baloo they must drink tea and break bread with him too (Pandit: 16–17; Vithal: 14; Palwankar 1996). Later, Baloo was praised at a public meeting by a Brahmin nationalist even more celebrated than Ranade, Bal Gangadhar Tilak. This, writes one chronicler, created 'a stir, because in those days a person from the backward community did not have a honourable place in society' (Pandit: 17).

Just as the orthodoxies of Poona were relenting for him, Baloo chose to move with his family to Bombay. One reason for this was the plague of 1896, which was especially severe in Poona; another was the attractions of cricket at the centre. By the 1890s there were dozens of active cricket teams in Bombay and while Parsi clubs were generally demarcated by locality, Hindu cricketers sorted themselves out on the lines of caste and region: as such there were the Gowd Saraswat Cricket Club, Kshatriya Cricket Club, Gujarati Union Cricket Club, Maratha Cricket Club or the Telugu Young Cricketers. The smaller communities in this city of migrants also formed their own clubs so that there were the Mangalorian Catholic Cricket Club (for émigres from the southern port town of Mangalore), the Instituto Luso Cricket Club (for those coming to the city from Portuguese-ruled Goa) and the Bombay Jewish Cricket Club. A different category of clubs was those sponsored by companies and banks. Cricket teams were run by Thomas Cook, Forbes, Forbes and Campbell, the Bombay Gas Company, the Bank of Bombay and the Army and Navy Stores. These were heterogeneous in their membership with employees of various Hindu castes playing on the same side as Muslims and Christians under the leadership of a senior manager who was almost always an Englishman. One active club of this kind was run by the Bombay Berar and Central Indian Railway. It was this company that gave Palwankar Baloo a job, at the suggestion of its manager and cricket captain, a Mr Lucas (Palwankar 1996).

Cricket, Caste and Colonialism in Bombay

Baloo played for the B. B. C. I. Railway in inter-office matches but more significantly he was poached for the newly commissioned P. J. Hindu Gymkhana team. This institution had been in two minds about whether to admit him even though the cricket captain Kirtikar wanted to augment his bowling attack. He got his way only after 'pacifying a few Gujerati members as regards his [Baloo's] admission' (Anon. 1906). By the turn of the century the most terrific excitement attended contests between the Hindu Gymkhana and leading Parsi teams such as the Baronet Cricket Club. There were large crowds ringing the ground, five or ten rows deep, with the overspill accommodated on the railway bridge that linked the Gymkhana to the nearby Churnee Road station. The scene was made more vivid by the nearness of the sea.

There was no Marine Drive then and, as a participant in those games recalled, 'the waves often used to beat over the rocks and enter the cricket ground' (Mehta 1954).

The statistics of those matches are lost to history but one may safely assume that Palwankar Baloo took plenty of wickets as from a very early stage he was regarded as the bulwark of the Hindu Gymkhana. One of his opponents, Dr M. E. Pavri (1901) of the Baronet C. C., described him as 'one of the best native bowlers. A left-handed medium-pace bowler with an easy action. Has both breaks and a curl in the air and has a lot of spin on the ball. The most deadly bowler on a sticky wicket. May be called [Wilfred] 'Rhodes' of India. A sound bat and an active field' (Pavri 1901: 164). Baloo's control was phenomenal and his variations subtle. 'His pace was medium', recalled a Bombay journalist J.C. Maitra 'but he could bowl from a very slow to a really fast one and send them by round to full over-arm action. He manipulated an amazing change of flight in the ball and set the batsman always guessing in each delivery, which was always different' (Sportsman 30/11/1929). From across India, a Calcutta cricketer H.C. Muckerjee who had observed Baloo at close quarters remarked that he was:

> A fine left-hand bowler, who possesses marvellous stamina. Breaks from both sides. Has the easiest of deliveries. Seldom tires. Can bowl all day long. Keeps an excellent length. Never sends down a loose delivery. Understands the game thoroughly. Places the field to a nicety, catches come [to the fielders], they have not to go in for them. Decidedly a 'head' bowler (Muckerjee 1911: 20).

By the early years of the twentieth century Baloo's skills with the cricket ball were known as far away as Calcutta. In that city lived a cricketing patron, the Maharajah of Natore, who had an overwhelming ambition to defeat the all-European Calcutta Cricket Club. One year he put together a side of top-class Hindus that included the wicket-keeper K. Seshachari from Madras, the fast bowler H. L. Sempre from Karachi and Palwankar Baloo and his brother Shivram from Bombay. His side won but the colonists took their defeat without grace. After the match the captain of the Calcutta Cricket Club asked Natore how many 'gentlemen' there were in his side, insinuating there was no honour in Indian professionals defeating a side of English amateurs (Langrana 1956).

Seven years younger than Baloo, Shivram was a hard-hitting batsman, a useful medium-pace bowler and an outstanding field. Taller than his brother and powerfully built, his trademark was a black belt that he wore around his waist. We know far less of his early years in the game, but we do know that by

1906 he was regarded as one of the eleven best cricketers of his religion because in February of that year he was chosen with his brother to play for the Hindus against the Europeans of the Bombay Presidency. The match inevitably carried nationalist overtones for in 1905–6 the Indian National Congress was renewing itself under two leaders from Western India, Gopalkrishna Gokhale and Bal Gangadhar Tilak. Meanwhile, in Bengal the *swadeshi* movement had just been launched and was presenting the British with the best organized challenge to their rule of the last half century. Patriotic entrepreneurs had set up factories to compete with British capital. Radicals urged the boycott of foreign goods. Bonfires were being made of cloth manufactured in the mills of Manchester (Sarkar 1973). In the last week of 1905 the Congress had met in the holy city of Benares where the Bengali delegates urged a countrywide spread of their campaign. Tilak's paper, *Kesari*, agreed with the Bengalis. 'It is not so manly to resign onself to one's degraded position' it remarked 'or to sit weeping in the house like women but it is our duty to strive strenuously to remove the causes of our misfortune' (Kesari 02/01/1906). Another Marathi paper asked for India to be granted Home Rule. Indians, it said, 'should fearlessly speak out their minds to their rulers without mincing words' (Bhala 01/01/1906).

It was against this backdrop that the three-day match was played at the Bombay Gymkhana ground from 8th to 10th February 1906. In its assessment of the two teams the *Bombay Gazette* praised Baloo and said of Shivram that 'he is Mr Baloo's brother and that is enough. He must keep up the reputation of the first bowler of India, his brother. Much is expected of his smartness in the field' (Bombay Gazette 08/01/1906). The Hindus batted first and posted a decent score of 242 with Baloo contributing 25 and his brother 24. Much to the disappointment of his admirers the 'Little Man' (Greig) was bowled by Erasha for 11 and the Europeans were all out for 191. After the next Indian innings the British needed 212 to win. The final day of the match was finely poised and 'marked with a deal of excitement and enthusiasm. Large throngs of people of every denomination—even larger than the previous two days—lined the ropes and greeted every stroke with loud ovation'. The European challenge relied heavily on Greig, but with 'a superb piece of stumping worth going miles to see' he was quickly out, and his colleagues crumbled to 102 all out (Bombay Gazette 10 and 12/02/1906; The Madras Mail 15/02/1906). The Indian triumph was celebrated as a nationalist victory. The victorious cricketers had behaved 'with the noble self–restraint which characterized the Japanese over the fall of Port Arthur and all the subsequent victories which attended their arms, victories the like of which history has never recorded'. Had the result been reversed, the report went on, then the English cricketers would have been vulgar and ostentatious in victory, mimicking 'the perfect pandemonium into which hoary England had been converted by modern Britons over the relief of Mafeking'[3] (The Tribune 23/01/1906).

While *The Tribune* interpreted the cricketing victory as another sign that a subdued and suppressed Asia was shaking off its shackles, other papers welcomed it as a victory over caste prejudice. During the three days of the match, the players of both sides dined together, the European with the Hindu and the Brahmin with the Chamaar. The way to this unprecedented inter-mingling had been previously cleared by the decision of the Hindu Gymkhana to allow Baloo and Shivram entry not only into its cricket field but into its café as well. Now, the course of the match and the contribution to the Hindu victory of the Baloo brothers provoked a long leading article in that respected voice of Hindu liberalism *The Indian Social Reformer*. By 'openly interdining' with low-castes the Hindu Gymkhana would 'destroy for good' the 'silly barrier of pollution by touch'. The 'history of the admission of these chamar brothers in the Hindu Gymkhana' continued the *Indian Social Reformer* 'is a credit to all and has done far more to liberalize the minds of thousands of young Hindus than all other attempts in other spheres'. Indeed, the triumph of cricket over caste was:

> a landmark in the nation's emancipation from the old disuniting and denationalizing customs. This is a conscious voluntary change, a manly moral regulated liberty, not, as in [the] railways [where members of different castes had willy–nilly to sit with each other], a compulsory change … Hindu sportsmen of Poona and Bombay have shown in different degrees that, where national interest required, equal opportunity must be given to all of any caste, even though the offer of such oppor-tunity involved the trampling of some old prejudices … Let the lesson learnt in sport be repeated in political, social and educational walks of life. Let all disuniting and denationalizing customs in all high, low or lowest Hindus disappear and let India cease to be the laughing–stock of the whole world (Anon. 1906).

Education, England, the Carnival and Captaincy

In 1907 the Hindus, Parsis and Europeans began playing an annual cricket tournament known as the Triangular. Both Baloo and Shivram played for the Hindus and they were joined in 1910 by a third brother, Palwankar Vithal, who was born in 1886 and sent by Baloo to the cricket-minded Elphinstone High School. Vithal was a graceful right-hand batsman with a penchant for the cover drive.

After leaving school Vithal accepted a job with the Greater Indian Peninsular Railway where Shivram already worked. The youngster scored a sheaf of centuries in club cricket and was chosen to play for the Hindus in the 1910 Triangular. In the next year an All India Team was due to tour England. From January 1911 trial matches were held in Bombay for aspirants from all over the country. The selectors were seven in all, two Muslim, two Hindu, and two Parsi with the venerable Jungly Greig in the chair. This ecumenism was reflected in the team finally chosen. They included six Parsis, three Muslims and five Hindus. The captain however was a Sikh, the twenty-year-old Maharaja Bhupendra Singh of Patiala, freshly installed onto his *gaddi* by the Viceroy Lord Minto (Polishwalla 1919: 64–7). All three Palwankar brothers made the trip.

In England the Indian captain was not often to be found with his team. Patiala played a match at Lord's, and one or two more, but for the most part he was active on the London social circuit (there were many parties to attend that summer as a new King had just ascended the throne). His absence was a blow in purely cricketing terms for this particular prince was a first-class batsman and, while he was away, the side divided into Parsi and Hindu factions. Patiala also took with him wherever he went his five servants who included his secretary Keki Mistry, perhaps the best of all Indian batsmen at the time. Without Patiala and Mistry, the tourists' batting was desperately ill-equipped to handle English wickets and English professional bowling. This showed in the results. Fourteen matches were played against the recognized English counties, of which two were won, ten lost and two drawn. The singular success, from the Indian point of view, was the bowling of Palwankar Baloo. He took 114 wickets at an average of 18. 84 runs per wicket and would easily have claimed 150 wickets had he found more support in the field. Baloo enjoyed success against all the top county sides, including seven wickets against Lancashire and six against Somerset. The real match-winner against Somerset was younger brother Shivram who scored 113 not out as the visitors scraped home with one wicket standing. He was, said one observer, 'the most promising of Hindu batsmen' (S. K. Roy 1946). The respected English critic E. H. D. Sewell meanwhile commented that Baloo 'is a bowler most of our counties would be very glad to have in their eleven' (Muckerjee 1911: 109). In the ninety years since Baloo returned home, only one other Indian bowler, Vinoo Mankad in 1946, has claimed more than a hundred first-class wickets on a tour of England.

The Palwankars were celebrated upon their return to India and there was a function organized by the Depressed Classes of Bombay to felicitate Baloo. The community's pride was well-earned for this erstwhile Untouchable had far exceeded the Brahmins and Muslims and Parsis and Princes who accompanied him to England. At this function the *manpatra*, or welcome address, for Baloo was written and presented by Bhimrao Ambedkar. This, according to

Eleanor Zelliot, was the first public appearance of the man who was to become the greatest of all lower-caste politicians and reformers, and a figure of surpassing importance in modern Indian history (Zelliott 1969). Within a year of their return it became clear that the family was set to produce another fine player. The youngest brother, Ganpat, was studying for a bachelor's degree at Elphinstone College, with fees paid by brother Baloo. In January 1912 he was the undoubted star of the college cricket tour of Northern India. When the visitors defeated the famous Mohammedan College in Aligarh he top-scored in both innings and in a drawn match against the Maharaja of Patiala's XI Ganpat claimed two wickets, effected two catches and scored a brilliant hundred besides. Ganpat Palwankar played 'cricket of the highest class' remarked the college cricket historian: 'It was not the sum of his runs that was so much appreciated as the style in which they were obtained, for he employed a variety of strokes and his batting was perfect and true' (Antia 1913: 194ff.).[4]

That same year the Muslims were admitted into the annual Bombay tournament, which thus became a Quadrangular. The Quadrangular was generally referred to as the 'Bombay Cricket Carnival' but there is also a reference to it as 'a sort of a Roman forum' (Bombay Chronicle (BC) 05/09/1923). Sport was both spectacle and contest, an outing with friends and family but also a vehicle for suppressed social ambitions. Spectators sung songs, shone mirrors, flew kites and garlanded cricketers as each team came to represent their community's pride.

In 1913 Baloo was joined in the Hindu team by Shivram, Vithal and Ganpat. The captain, however, was the batsman M. D. Pai. Pai was lauded by his caste association, the Gowd Saraswat Brahmin Mitra Mandal, for achieving the 'highest honour to which a cricketer can aspire'. In his reply Pai thanked his community for the reception they had hosted for him but made clear that he was uneasy with the politics of his position. He stated baldly that 'the honour of captainship should have been given to his friend Mr Balu, he being the senior and experienced player in the team' (Bombay Chronicle 01/11/1913). Pai had been on that 1911 tour and struggled with the bat while Baloo shone with the ball. Nonetheless his remarks were an extraordinary gesture. For in 1913 Mahatma Gandhi was still in South Africa and the Hindu political élite was, by and large, still bound to the Laws of Manu. An Untouchable cricketer of courage and skill could be chosen to play for the Hindus but it was unthinkable that he could be captain. The leader of a cricket team has to exercise his mind more often and more innovatively than a football or basketball captain. In this slow paced sport it is the captain and not the coach or manager who decides the order of batsmen, the order of bowlers and changes in the field. Intelligence and foresight were commonly held to be the preserve of the high castes and Pai was a Brahmin while Baloo was a Chamaar. To suggest the appointment of the latter as captain of the Hindus was to suggest the symbolic inversion of the hierarchy of caste. But to judge the issue on purely sporting grounds it was clear that the talent and experience of Baloo should long ago have qualified him to act as captain of the Hindus. Pai's speech to his caste group suggests that his team-mates would have found his elevation quite acceptable and that it was sporting rather than cultural criteria that should prevail. But the merchants and lawyers who ran the Hindu Gymkhana evidently did not agree.

In June 1914 the *Bombay Chronicle* commented in an editorial that 'the services rendered by Baloo to Hindu cricket are worth their weight in gold and it speaks volumes for the wonderful vitality of the man that after the lapse of more than two decades he is still their foremost bowler' (Bombay Chronicle 02/02/1914). The next month the paper carried an angry letter by one 'C. S. T.' The angry fan argued that the Hindus had been robbed of a win by 'bad management and worse fielding'. To remedy this, 'the choice of a captain should be a free one and that onerous post should be in the hands of the best and most competent man on the field'. The letter writer was plainly hinting at Baloo whom he elsewhere called a 'sure thing' and a 'crack bowler who can always do some work of outstanding merit' (BC 07/06/1914). One can only imagine C.S.T.'s response when the events of the following season unfolded. In 1915 the Quadrangular was played at Poona, apparently on the insistence of the Europeans. They had lobbied hard for this, because, as one Indian critic sarcastically commented, in a Poona September 'the [social] season is in full swing with all its gaieties, the pitch is more like Home and the climate is less exhausting' (BC 29/05/1913). The matches were played at the Poona Club, that old haunt of Baloo. An early report suggested that all four Palwankar brothers were certainties. But when the side was chosen a week ahead of the Hindu–Parsi match Baloo was not in it. Apparently a selector had asked Baloo how he was and the bowler, out of modesty, answered 'that he was not in his usual form but added that if he were selected he would gladly lend his services in the interests of Hindu cricket'. This diffidence was likely used as an excuse to drop him. The *Bombay Chronicle* now received numerous angry letters of protest. These suggested that the Hindu selection committee had conspired to throw Baloo out. 'Now nobody will say that Baloo is quite the demon bowler he once was' said one writer 'but it cannot be denied that he is still a fine bowler, who is worth his place in any representative eleven'. The decision to dump him remarked this correspondent:

has been received with great and justifiable surprise by the supporters of Hindu cricket. Baloo has been the mainstay of Hindu cricket for more than a decade and a half and his services in the cause of Hindu cricket have been invaluable. By every right of ability, of seniority, and of the services rendered to his side, he should long ago have been appointed captain of the team. He has not only been denied that right but now he has been excluded from the team itself (BC 03/09/1915).

Significantly, the day after the appearance of this letter the *Chronicle* carried an explanatory letter from the Hindu captain M. D. Pai. 'I was strongly in favour of Mr Baloo's inclusion' he wrote 'but the hesitating reply of Mr Baloo showing his inability to keep up for three days forced the Committee to give him up'. The captain had urged that 'preference should be given to Mr Baloo on whom I much rely as a bowler of sound and mature judgement' (BC 04/09/1915). But his words were disregarded. That a captain should openly participate in a selection controversy was most unusual. Perhaps Pai deeply felt Baloo's omission or perhaps he wished to forestall criticism in case his team performed poorly in the tournament. What is noticeable about the exchanges on the issue is that Untouchability was never publicly mentioned. Gandhi had yet to elevate the issue to national prominence and, even those who had the suspicion that Baloo's caste was part of the reason for his being dropped from the team, did not dare to voice it.

Baloo returned to the team and, indeed annually until 1919, there was a concerted annual campaign to have him made captain of the Hindu cricket team. Every year it met with failure. However, in the months leading up to the 1920 Quadrangular Mahatma Gandhi began speaking out against the practice of Untouchability, which he called 'a crime against God and humanity' in May. He expanded on the issue, 'My conscience tells me that untouchability can never be a part of Hinduism. I do not think it too much to dedicate my whole life to removing the thick crust of sin with which Hindu society has covered itself for so long by stupidly regarding these people as untouchables' (Gandhi v. 17: 471, 534). Upper caste Hindus, thought Gandhi, 'must realize that if they wish to offer successful non-co-operation against the Government, they must make common cause with the *Panchammas* [Untouchables], even as they have made common cause with the Mussulmans' (Gandhi v. 18: 377). When he spoke millions listened, among them a growing number of Hindu cricket fans in Bombay.

That year, as usual, there was a slow and stately build-up to the Quandrangular. In mid November the *Bombay Chronicle* ran a full page feature on the preparations of the different teams, their chances, and the likely response of the crowd. Speaking of the Hindus, the anonymous feature writer tastefully put the case for a long overdue elevation. 'It would not be out of place' he suggested:

> to give expression to the very widespread desire that exists among the Hindu public that the captaincy of the team should at least for once be offered to P. Baloo … No Hindu bowler could claim such a distinguished and sustained record of achievement in first-class cricket extending over a large number of years as he … [S]heer justice demands that his long and splendid cricket career should be crowned with the leadership of the Hindu representative team before he finally retires from first-class cricket …
> The desire given expression to above is not the result of any doubt as to the capacity of M. D. Pai (BC 15/11/1920).

A week later, and ten days before the start of the tournament, the Hindu team was announced. M. D. Pai was named as captain, Vithal and Shivram had been included in the eleven and Baloo was dropped. However, before the first game Pai fell ill and withdrew from the fixture, which was against the Muslims. The Hindu selectors now appointed D. B. Deodhar as captain. Deodhar was a fine player, and also a Brahmin and a batsman. The Gymkhana's decision was a subject of furious controversy amongst its rank-and-file. There 'was much discontent prevailing among the members of the [Hindu] Gymkhana over the repeated exclusion of Mr Baloo' reported one scribe: 'The trend of opinion among the bulk of the members who were present in the Gymkhana in the evening was that Mr Baloo should now be taken in the team and asked to captain it' (BC 03/12/20).

To the Palwankars, already bowed by Ganpat's death[5] and Baloo's exclusion, Deodhar's appointment was a final blow. Both Vithal and Shivram were at least the equal in talent of the Poona cricketer and they had preceded him into the team. Vithal recalled in his memoirs that when Pai fell ill, 'amongst the players of the team myself and Shivram were the most senior and considering our ability and skill it was our rightful expectation that one of us should have been chosen captain. Many members of the Hindu Gymkhana also expected the same' (Vithal: 88). In disgust they decided to stand down from the Hindu team. Their explanation, published in the papers the day the Hindu-Muslim match began, still makes compelling reading:

> It need hardly be said [wrote Vithal and Shivram] that the claims of one of us are superior to those of Mr Deodhar, and the [Hindu Selection] Committee's decision can only be characterised as unsportsmanlike in the extreme, inasmuch as they have apparently been influenced by the

caste and social and educational status of their selection rather than his achievements or seniority in the field of cricket, and as such the Committee's decision can only be taken as partial with a bias in favour of caste. Social or educational status has no place in sport, when the claims of a cricketer of lesser social status are admittedly superior. In the decision the Committee arrived at, this vital principle of all sport appears to have been lightly passed over, with the result that the claims of one of us have been brushed aside as beneath contempt. This sort of shuffling of claims by the Hindu Selection Committee has compelled us to withdraw from the Hindu Representative Team this year, much against our desire to add our quota to the achievements of the Hindu Cricket Team. In arriving at this decision [not to play] be it remembered that we feel very strongly the covert or overt insult levelled at us as belonging to the so–called depressed class as it amounts to a nullification of our claims for recognition for all time. That such matters as caste should be the determining factor in Cricket is more than we can quietly bow down to, hence our decision to stand down from the Hindu Team this year. The impartial cricket–loving public, we feel sure, will at once understand our position and exonerate us from all blame for the step we have thus deliberately taken as it was on a question of principle and self–respect (BC 04/12/1920).

The sentiments were unquestionably their own, although the statement itself might have been drafted by a better-educated member of the impartial cricket-loving public.[6] A small section of this public regarded the withdrawal as a 'revolt against authority' but numerous others approved of the action and believed that as 'self-respecting men [Vithal and Shivram] could not have done otherwise'. Among the strikers' supporters were those who approved of Gandhi's wider struggle against Untouchability. A movement was started to collect funds for a purse to be presented to Vithal and Shivram. Contributions were to be sent to 'Mr Govindji Vasanji, the National Confectioner, either at Chira Bazar, Girgaum or at the Grant Road Terminus'.[7] Five hundred rupees, then a considerable sum, was collected in the first twenty-hours itself (BC 04/12/1920).

The Hindus won their match against the Muslims. The formidable Parsis were to be encountered next. Hectic parleys now commenced within the Hindu Gymkhana. Their outcome was summarized in a banner headline printed the day the final began: 'PAI CAPTAINING THE TEAM: BALOO BROTHERS PLAYING'. M. D. Pai, now fit, was to captain and Vithal, Shivram and Baloo were all to play. The decision to reinstate the strikers and to call upon their brother remarked one journalist 'though belated, is a sensible one and is undoubtedly a concession to public opinion'. Baloo, wrote the scribe, was at first inclined to reject the call and it was only 'on the urgent intervention of friends whose love of Hindu cricket surpasses their love for the Committee and its ways, that Mr Baloo consented to play in today's match'. In fact, the Hindu Selection Committee was suitably conciliatory as in this letter written by its Secretary, S. A. Shethe:

Dear Mr Baloo,
I understand that you are hesitating to play though selected in the match against Parsis. I shall be obliged if you will kindly reconsider your decision and play. The interest of cricket will appeal to you as in the past (BC 07/12/1920).

Honour was restored more fully when Baloo was appointed vice-captain. In what must certainly have been a pre-arranged move, Pai left the field while the Parsis were batting in the second innings. A sympathetic reporter commented on the 'excellent leadership' of Baloo, adding that 'he displayed fine judgement in the management of his side's bowling' (BC 09/12/1920). The match itself had a suitably dramatic *denouement*. The Hindus amassed a score of 428 and then dismissed the Parsis for 214. They followed on and early in the Parsi second innings their captain, Dr H. D. Kanga, was injured and taken to hospital. The ninth Parsi wicket fell after lunch on the final day and the Hindu fans streamed into the ground with garlands. As they reached the pitch the umpire drew their attention to Dr Kanga, who had returned from hospital and was slowly emerging from the pavilion. The crowd reluctantly withdrew to the boundary's edge, where they stayed in frustration for the next two hours, as the last wicket pair of Kanga and Elavia played out time to draw the match (Deodhar 1966: 33).

The struggle over the Hindu captaincy anticipated, by nearly forty years, the campaign to have a black man chosen as captain of the West Indies cricket team. The West Indies played its first Test matches in 1928 and for the next three decades it was axiomatic that a white man, and a white man alone, could be the team's captain. Such remarkable cricketers as Learie Constantine and George Headley had to be content with being 'led' by fair-skinned sportsmen of demonstrably inferior skill. In his playing days Constantine had protested against this discrimination. He continued to speak out after he retired, joined by such men as the great historian and revolutionary C. L. R. James. It was James who was in the forefront of the campaign which, in 1960, resulted in Frank Worrell's appointment as the first black captain of the West Indies (James 1963). The career of Palwankar Baloo also anticipated, by half-a-century and more, the much memorialized breakthrough into major league football of Jackie Robinson. Only in 1947 would the American public accept racially mixed teams in sport but already, in 1896–7, the Hindus of Poonā and Bombay were made to accept an Untouchable cricketer. Like Robinson after him, Baloo broke through a previously impenetrable social barrier as much by force of personality as by sporting skill alone.

In 1922 the Quadrangular was played in Poona, Palwankar Baloo's old home town. The captain and players were to be chosen by the local sponsors, the Poona Hindu Gymkhana. The city was a conservative one and its Hindus, by and large, never had time for Gandhi. Unlike the members of the P. J. Hindu Gymkhana the Brahmins of Poona were not convinced that Untouchability was altogether a bad thing. The Poona Hindus chose S. M. Dalvi as captain and Vithal and Shivram went on strike again. The Hindus won their first match, narrowly, and had now to play the Parsis in the final. A compromise was attempted whereby M. D. Pai would be appointed captain and Vithal and Shivram would agree to return. But Pai refused to play ball and the brothers stuck to their stand. A complete nonentity, Dr Prabhakar, was asked to lead the Hindus. The Parsis, by contrast, were at full strength. Expectedly they won by a handsome margin (Deodhar 1966: 41; Roy 1945: 100). The press comment on the Hindu defeat was curious. Before the final the *Chronicle* said that the 'Hindu team will hardly be representative without a trio [the Baloo brothers] whom everybody will miss'. Afterwards it suggested that if the defeat 'will only serve to shed more light on this *faux pas*, real or imaginary, the moral which distills out of this year's tournament will have been sufficiently emphasised' (BC 10 and 21/09/1922). The *Mahratta* of Puné appears to have drawn a different moral from disunity and defeat. 'We do not know what exactly was the apple of discord' it remarked:

> but it is more than probable that it must have been the captainship …
> [We] do not mean to put one caste against one another, but our idea is
> that the healthy spirit of rivalry kindled by such inter-communal games
> must be maintained at a high level. We congratulate the Parsis on their
> deserved success and wish that the Hindus will make up their deficiency
> and will not allow their private grudges to hamper their efficiency
> (Mahratta 24/09/1922).

This reads like a back-handed criticism of Vithal and Shivram. The *Mahratta* wanted them to suppress their 'private' grudges in the interests of the community. Someone who saw the Hindu failure in a different light was the radical playwright B. V. ('Mama') Varerkar. The sidelining of Vithal and Shivram in the 1922 Quadrangular inspired him to write a remarkable play on the bloody intersection where the politics of cricket met the politics of caste. Entitled *Turungachya Darat* (At the Gate of a Prison) the play was written in the weeks following the Quadrangular and first preformed at the New Imperial Theatre in Bombay on the 1st of February 1923. Its climax comes when a Brahmin owner of a bank moves his operations from Poona to Bombay and decides to make an Untouchable his manager. As he puts it, 'Yesterday we made the very serious mistake of leaving out Vithal and Shivram Chambhar and lost in the Quadrangular cricket tournament. I do not want to lose in the battleground of life by leaving you out' (Varerkar 1923). Varerkar was inspired by the cricket field to make a more general statement on behalf of social reform. It is not clear how his play was received but it might very well have played a part in what was to follow. At the next Annual General Meeting of the Hindu Gymkhana a vote of censure was passed against the selectors of the previous year's team. When the tournament came back to Bombay in 1923 the selectors there set against the claims of tradition the call of the Mahatma and the fact that in both 1921 and 1922 their team had lost heavily. Now the management of Hindu cricket in Bombay was dominated by *banias*, or merchants, who were perhaps more pragmatic and certainly less ideological than the Poona Brahmins. Crucially, for the case at hand, Gandhi was himself a *bania*. The concerns of the members reached the selectors who appointed P. Vithal as captain (BC 17/10/1937).[8]

A ten year campaign on behalf of the Chamaar cricketers had finally succeeded. In the early matches the Hindus defeated the Muslims by an innings while the Europeans prevailed over the Parsis. The Final was on and the Europeans batted first and posted an impressive total of 481. The Hindu reply was built around a composed and assured hundred by captain Vithal and they reached 475 all out. Three full days of cricket had passed watched by a large and appreciative crowd. 'Every inch of space was occupied and the crowd at the tree end was at least ten deep. Every pavilion was full and hundreds were watching the game from house-tops, while some were perched on trees'. During the partnership between Vithal and Nayudu, wrote one reporter, the crowd clapped so much that the sound 'was similar to the sound of sea-waves dashing to the floor' (BC 13/12/1923). The captain's century brought forth a surge of 'maddening joy' (Navakal (Bombay) 13/12/1923). One day's play remained. The European captain now suggested that since a result was impossible they might as well call it a draw. Vithal answered that since twenty thousand fans had come to watch the match they must play it out. The Europeans went in again and this time found S. M. Joshi in his best form. As he handed him the ball Vithal told Joshi, in Marathi, that it was time to 'start Bhairavi'. The bowler was a fine classical singer and Bhairavi is the last *raga* sung or played in a concert. Thus inspired, Joshi took 7 for 39

as the Europeans crumbled to 153 all out (Vithal 1948: 90–98). After this
magnificent spell of bowling the Hindus required 162 runs to win. Two hours
of play remained. Vithal played another master stroke. Instead of the wicket-
keeper-batsman J. G. Navle, a careful and orthodox player, he sent in the
big-hitting C. K. Nayudu to open with K. G. Pardeshi. Nayudu smashed the
bowling all over, and outside, the park. One six landed on the Bombay
Gymkhana pavilion and another on the Waudby Road. Pardeshi also scored
at a brisk pace. When Nayudu was dismissed twenty runs were left to get. The
captain promoted himself and hit three slashing boundaries to win the game
(Nayudu 1953). With his final stroke:

> groups of spectators one after another jumped up from the tents and ran
> towards the wicket. A few among them carried both of us (Pardeshi and
> myself) on their shoulders to the pavilion, shouting joyously. On reaching
> the pavilion everyone rushed to shake hands with me. Many European
> ladies congratulated me saying 'O Vithal, well played, congratulations
> Vithal'. The reason for these congratulations (as I came to know after-
> wards) was that they had taken a bet on the result of the match and had
> won against their own menfolk (Vithal 1948: 98–9).

This description is confirmed by the *Bombay Chronicle* report which speaks of
how 'at the end of the game a seething mass of humanity invaded the pavilion and expended their enthusiasm and exuberance of hilarity near the players'. Three thousand rupees were immediately subscribed for a Prize Fund.
The donors, in these last days of the Khilafat movement, included Hindus as
well as Muslims.

In an editorial on the tournament the *Chronicle* noted that 'the success of the
Hindu team was largely due to the confidence which its captain inspired. The
heartiest congratulations of all lovers of cricket are due to him and to his team
and no less to the Hindu Selection Committee which did not allow a perni-
cious caste prejudice to come in the way of selecting the right man to lead the
team'. The same issue contained the same sentiments expressed more evoca-
tively by a letter writer. 'The Hindus' brilliant victory' said Vijayashram was
'due more to the judicious and bold step of the Hindu Gymkhana in appoint-
ing Mr Vithal, brother of Mr Baloo—premier bowler of India—who is a
member of the Untouchable Class to captain the Hindu team. The moral
that can be safely drawn from the Hindus' magnificent victory is that removal
of Untouchability would lead to Swaraj—which is the prophecy of the
Mahatma' (BC 15/12/1923). Another letter three days later noted that 'The
happiest event' he said 'the most agreeable upshot of the set of matches was
the carrying of Captain Vithal on the shoulders of Hindus belonging to the

so-called higher castes. Hurrah! Captain Vithal! Hurrah! Hindus who forget caste prejudice! Mahatma Gandhi Maharaj ki jai!' (BC 18/12/1923).

In four years Palwankar Vithal lead the Hindus to three victories. The last win might have given him the most pleasure for it was a desperately close-fought match, a match played in reactionary Poona and at the ground where his beloved elder brother had slaved and bowled. Baloo was never allowed to enter the pavilion of the Poona Club but it was in that pavilion that Vithal received the Quadrangular trophy. At the ground and afterwards he received tributes aplenty. He and his men were fêted with 'at homes' and 'pan suparis' and even congratulated by the now conservative *Mahratta* for coming out 'with flying colours against the Europeans in a game native to them' (Mahratta 26/11/1926). Vithal was compelled to insert a collective acknowledgement in the newspapers, 'I have received a number of telegrams and letters congratulating the Hindu Team for their victory in the Quadrangular Tournament. It is not possible for me to write to each of them separately. I therefore hereby thank them for all their kindness and sympathy and hope they will kindly accept it' (BC 04/12/1926).

Vithal always underlined his debt to the eldest of the Palwankars. 'I must mention with respect and gratitude my brother Shri P. Baloo' he once wrote 'his advice and instruction were very useful and his deep knowledge about the game was always helpful to me' (Vithal 1948: 156). But he was a real hero in his own right. Once, when he was playing in Rajkot for a team sponsored by the Jam Saheb of Nawanagar a crowd gathered round the players' tent asking: 'Where is Vithal? What does he look like?' At this Ranji himself asked him to stand on a table and announced to the assembled fans 'See! This is Vithal!'. In Calcutta the rush of fans screaming 'esho', 'esho' (come! come!) so unnerved him that he had to escape through the back door of his host Gymkhana (Ibid.: 162). The years of Vithal's greatest triumphs, 1923 to 1926, coincided with the arrival on the political stage of Dr B. R. Ambedkar. Ambedkar had returned to India in 1923 with a doctoral degree from London and another from Columbia University in New York. He had previously qualified for the bar from Grays' Inn. While Vithal was leading the Hindu cricket team Ambedkar was making a name at the Bombay Bar and, when the court was in recess, in politics. He travelled through the villages of the Deccan seeking to build a base among the depressed classes. In his speeches Ambedkar was careful to recall his own association with the first and greatest of the Palwankars. As a student and teacher in Bombay he had 'looked at the solid fame of the Untouchable bowler with pride'. As a little-known lecturer in Sydenham College, he had organized meetings to felicitate the bowler and worked for his elevation to the city's Municipal Corporation. Now as he sought to establish his credentials with the Untouchables of Western India

Ambedkar would tell his audiences of his early efforts as champion of Baloo's achievements (Keer 1971: 39–40, 86).

From Player to Politician

In 1929 the youngest of the Palwankar brotherhood retired from first-class cricket but by now the oldest of the brothers was taking a more active role in politics. In September 1932 Mahatma Gandhi embarked on a fast until death in Poona's Yeravada jail. Gandhi was protesting the decision to award separate electorates to the Untouchables, a move he thought would take them away from the Hindu fold. B. R. Ambedkar was adamant however that the separate electorates must stay because he saw a future for his people only outside the stifling social structure of Hinduism. Gandhi's fast continued for several weeks and ended only after a pact was forged between the two men which gave Untouchables more seats in the legislatures in exchange for the abandonment of their claim for separate electorates. The two key intermediaries in the construction of the Poona pact were the South Indian social worker M. C. Rajah and Palwankar Baloo (Pyarelal 1932). The Poona Pact broke down and Ambedkar established his own party to represent the interests of the Untouchables in explicit opposition to the Congress. In the elections of 1937, the first with an extended franchise, Baloo was persuaded by the Congress to stand in a Bombay constituency. The key rival for the seat was Ambedkar. Thus, a quarter-of-a-century after the young Ambedkar had presented the welcome address to Baloo after his epic 1911 tour of England, the two men came to fight an electoral battle in the city of Bombay.

The decision to select Baloo was made by Congress strongman Sardar Vallabhbhai Patel. Baloo was chosen as a sporting hero, who had once been a hero of his opponent as well. More to the point he was a Chamaar and Patel knew from the Census of India that these city wards had a fair contingent from that particular caste. Sardar calculated that Baloo would split the low caste vote for Ambedkar, and that by giving Ambedkar a fight for his seat it would prevent him from campaigning elsewhere. The Congress High Command sent out its stars to bat for Baloo. Consider the report of a packed election meeting held at Matunga on Saturday 9th January 1937. The Congress candidate was introduced by Patel's own right-hand man, K. M. Munshi, shortly to become Home Minister in the Bombay Government. Baloo, said Munshi, 'had been a great cricketer in his younger days and had once scored [off] many an opponent. Hence, let the opponents take heed that they had to face a first-class bowler'. 'A vote for Baloo' continued Munshi:

> is a vote for the Poona Pact. That seat for the 'E' and 'F' Ward should be fought for tooth and nail. It is a seat which is of an all-India importance.

Dr B. R. Ambedkar, who went to the Round Table Conference, entered into the historical Poona Pact, and even before the ink was dry on the paper, he tried to secede from the Hindu faith. Every vote for Mr Baloo was a vote for the Poona Pact. If Baloo falls, the Poona Pact falls, and with it all of us fall.

After Munshi came Baloo. The cricketer told the voters that:

he personally was not interested in contesting the elections. Though he had not taken [a] very prominent part in politics, he had always come forward to help and take part when necessity demanded. Otherwise, he preferred to remain in the background. The call of the Congress came. At the last moment he agreed to stand on behalf of the Congress, and he did not even know from what constituency he would be asked to contest the seat in the assembly.

After the nominations were filed, he came to know that he was contesting for the same seat as Dr B. R. Ambedkar. It was providential coincidence. As he said before he did not want to go to the Legislature, but what were they to do when seats were reserved for them in the House ? They had to be occupied. He was sure the voters would cast their vote for him, the Congress candidate as against Ambedkar (BC 10/01/1937).

Other reports suggest that Ambedkar had filed his nomination before Baloo. Whatever was the case, Baloo's son and nephew both state that he was very reluctant to fight Ambedkar in the elections of 1937 (Palwankar 1996; Palwankar 1999). The Marathi-language Congress paper *Navakal* forcefully campaigned on Baloo's behalf. It reminded its readers of how Ambedkar 'had himself accepted Baloo's greatness many times'. The lawyer had often expressed his 'great respect and regard' for the cricketer. It offered, in illustration, the story of how Ambedkar was once felicitated at the hands of Baloo at a function organized by the Cobblers Union. This, in truth, actually showed the remarkable emergence of Ambedkar as an Untouchable leader. For once, as in 1911, Ambedkar had felicitated Baloo and now it was the other way around. The paper seems to have recognized this, for immediately after recounting the incident it asked its readers 'to vote for Baloo and not be hypnotized by Ambedkar's personality' (Navakal (Bombay) 11/01/1937, 17/02/1937).

On polling day it was reported that Ambedkar's supporters came to vote in trucks and the Congressmen in cars. In the end, Ambedkar won with 13245 votes against Baloo's 11225. It had been a close-run thing and the *Bombay Chronicle* suggested that Baloo's defeat was due to a 'spoiler', the labour leader

Joglekar who had stood as an independent and garnered 10, 000 votes. If Joglekar had not been in the race complained the paper then 'Dr Ambedkar would have been positively swamped' (BC 28/02/1937). Whatever was the case, Baloo's decision to fight an election was a 'world-first' for a professional cricketer and anticipated the much later moves in the same direction of Guyana's Roy Fredericks and Pakistan's Imran Khan. Baloo had provided Dalits with a hero and a model of progress through his achievements on and off the field and by his great personal dignity at all times. He had demonstrated that the low castes could be the equals of the elites. Yet the election result showed that Baloo had served his purpose by preparing the way for Ambedkar. With the higher expectations and greater confidence that the Palwankars had inspired among the lower castes, Dalits came to regard scholars and lawyers as more likely leaders than sportsmen.

Conclusion

The last word goes to a now forgotten newspaper columnist in an article called 'Hindu Cricket and Baloo Brothers' (BC 30/11/1929). In 1929 Vithal was dropped from the Hindu team to make way for rising young talent. With this demotion the 'last of the Baloo family after years of meritorious service has been unceremoniously driven from first class cricket'. Thus wrote one 'R. V. M.' in a moving tribute to the brothers, a tribute marked by deep knowledge of the game of cricket and a subtle understanding of its sometimes brutal social context. The Hindu team's announcement, he remarked, 'abruptly ends a thirty years' unbroken connection of the Baloo brothers with Hindu cricket. Nowhere else does the history of cricket supply such a glorious page'. The individual brothers were recalled, one by one. First the patriarch:

> And what a proud record to contemplate! It was Baloo who began Hindu bowling as such. With what wonderful wiles did he accomplish single-handed the herculean task of putting the Parsi and European veterans out, only those knew who intelligently watched him doing it. Bowlers on the other side might come and go but Baloo plodded on for ever.

Then the younger siblings:

> Baloo brought Shivram into the field and the best fieldsman he became, with considerable bowling and batting powers in addition. Then came Vithal. He made his first appearance at the Marine Lines Parade Ground, when the Parsi Parekh had a hat-trick and Warden a century against the Hindus. Vithal, however, was not one of the 'tricked' ones.

He played with the sweeping forward style that alone could withstand the fast swerving left-handers of the Parsis. He wielded this weapon with considerable effect and gradually stayed the rot year after year, with centuries against the Mahomedans and the Europeans. To his help then came Gunpat with his pretty style and quick movements. There was thus a time when the Hindu team included all the four brothers at one and the same time, and people fondly called the Hindu side as 'Baloo brothers plus 7'.

R. V. M.'s point was that theirs were not just cricketing achievements:

Did ever a family establish such a record? Could a Hindu lover of cricket having the least culture within him ever dream of breathing against such pillars of Hindu cricket any ignoble reference to their caste? Could a Hindu cricketer think of them with anything but respect? The late Pandharinath Telang, the Hindu Jessop, noble-minded as he was, could never think of Baloo as other than a dear comrade. Sir Chunilal [Mehta] never entertained any ugly thought of the Baloo brothers 'depressed' class.

But society, it seems, sometimes moved more slowly than the cricketers. The final steps to the summit were the hardest:

Baloo though senior was deprived of the captainship. He soon retired and the matter was hushed up. Shivram retired before such a question could crop up in his case. Then it came to the turn of Vithal. But time and again he was put down. His juniors were thrust over his head. No wonder the Hindus failed—miserably failed—yet the die-hards would not listen to justice and reason. But the force of circumstances was too great and after a lot of higgling, at long last, they 'liberalized' themselves enough to throw the captainship at Vithal.

The history of cricket does in fact have pages filled with the deeds of brothers such as the Graces of England, the Waughs of Australia and above all the Mohammeds of Pakistan. In cricketing skill and achievements the Palwankars of India were comfortably the equal of them all. These other families, moreover, had to fight their demons on the field alone whereas the Palwankars were sinned against most grievously by the society into which they were born. Why then are they so wholly forgotten? One reason is that they played before India became an 'official' Test playing nation. Another is the unconscionable ahistoricism of Indians, with their disregard for documents, records, remembrances and past heroes. While the Palwankars lived and played it was all too different. Men like 'R. V. M.' knew what they were worth. Men like Dr B. R. Ambedkar knew it too. It is past time that they were restored to their rightful place in the history of Indian cricket and indeed in the history of Indian social emancipation.

5

THE PEASANTS ARE REVOLTING: RACE, CULTURE AND OWNERSHIP IN CRICKET

Satadru Sen

Introduction: Centres and Subjects

Cricket is no longer England's national game. It might be argued that the sport now belongs to India, Pakistan and Sri Lanka and to the South Asian diaspora in the Persian Gulf, Canada and elsewhere. England's status as a cricketing periphery has been accompanied by its fading reputation as a strong side and by its declining influence in regulatory bodies such as the International Cricket Council (ICC). Some observers have attributed this shift at the centre of the sport to the innate 'Indian-ness' of cricket (Nandy 1989). Whatever the merits of this supposition, international cricket today reflects a series of fundamental changes in the ability of old elites to claim and defend 'their' culture. As Appadurai (1996: 23–48) has noted, cricket in the decolonizing world provides marginal populations with the means of overcoming their marginality in global popular culture. What I intend to do in this essay is examine the tensions that are generated in the process of this reconfiguration of centre and margin and make a broad observation. The primary rivalry in cricket today is not between India and Pakistan or England and Australia. It is a moral, economic and political clash between the colony and the metropole both of which have outgrown those labels. The sport functions both as a mirror of the disjunctures between 'how things stand' and 'how things should be' and as an instrument that continuously widens the gap. Even as the game provides a stage for the assertion (and defence) of white/elite/male models of authority, the colonized and the decolonizing attempt to subvert this authority by conquering the stage. In every instance, these attempts are resisted by the defenders of the old centre, by co-option if possible but also if necessary by casting aspersions on the morality, the masculinity or the centrality of the challenger.

Referring to those who are pained by any mention of racism in cricket C.L.R. James (1963: 59) wrote: 'They are a dying race and they will not be missed. They are a source of discomfort to their children and embarrassment to their grandchildren'. Nearly forty years later it is difficult to escape the conclusion that the dying race is still breathing and the grandchildren are not embarrassed in the least. To fully grasp the political significance of cricket in the modern world we need to understand that the sport has generally been played within a system of extraordinary political barriers which have included not only class, but also race, gender and national identity. Various groups on the wrong side of the barriers, non-whites, working-class whites, marginal non-whites, women and men who did not fit the masculine profile, have historically been forced to extraordinary lengths to gain access to the privileged spaces of the playing field and the dressing room. Broadly speaking the price of admission has been the acknowledgment of ownership i.e. the acceptance of a particular form of subordination that gives the 'owner' the right to delineate not only the terms of proprietorship but also its moral significance, as well as the defining features of the owner and the owned. The demand for this subordination marks the career of Kumar Shri Ranjitsinhji, the first Indian to become a celebrity athlete in England, who played for over a decade as a star batsman for Sussex and England. Ranjitsinhji was himself a superb judge of the opportunities that cricket could generate for him in England and in India (Sen 2001). Nevertheless, his career reveals two major patterns in the history of colonial cricket. I use the term 'colonial' deliberately because, although Ranjitsinhji played nearly all his cricket in England and much of it for England, he always played as a colonial subject. The first pattern is that, in order to breach the racial codes of cricket and play the game at the highest levels, Ranjitsinhji had to overcome formidable opposition. Lord Harris, who as governor of Bombay did more than any other colonial administrator to promote Indian cricket, disliked the idea of an Indian playing for England and did his best to scupper the prospect that Ranjitsinhji might feature against Australia in 1896 (Wild 1934: 36–37). When Ranjitsinhji was finally included in the England team the Australians were given a veto over his selection. Unlike the South Africans of 1968 who refused to accept the English selection of Basil D'Oliveira, the Australians of 1896 agreed to play against Ranjitsinhji. The significance of this story is that the England selectors were far from comfortable with the political implications of fielding a coloured player against a white opponent. Ranjitsinhji may have represented England but ultimately the Australians were closer to the racial core of Englishness than any Indian immigrant.

Even as England admitted Ranjitsinhji into its closed inner circle, it insisted on marking him with the signs of the colonized Other by invoking the discourses of black magic and black bodies to explain his athletic skill (Sen 2001). Eventually this tension generated a perceptible anger on both sides. Ranjitsinhji was far from being 'the ultimate brown Englishman' as Appadurai rather casually labels him (Appadurai 1996: 31). Ranjitsinhji's inclusion in the England team reflected not so much the success of his trans-formation into an Englishman as the failure of that effort. At the precise time when Kipling reminded white colonizers about their 'fluttered folk and wild', Ranjitsinhji was England's living imperial exhibit. His blackness was seen to shine through his white clothes and made him a magical trophy of colonialism. Ultimately, this was the source of his appeal: he was not an Englishman but an exotic that belonged to the English.

Contesting the Postcolonial Centre

Ranji was carefully constructed in this way because the combination of his prowess and his race threatened English claims over the ownership of cricket. A more recent cricket story shows how these clashes over the ownership of the game have intensified in the post-colonial period. In the winter of 2000 the Delhi police announced that it had tape-recorded telephone conversations between South African cricket captain Hansie Cronje and an Indian book-maker. On these tapes Cronje agreed to 'underperform' in games between the Indian and the South African sides and promised to persuade several of his players to do the same. The announcement triggered an instant firestorm of surprise, disbelief and recriminations. For weeks and months the Cronje Affair dominated newspaper headlines and airwaves, not only in India and South Africa but also in the rest of the cricket-playing world. As the scandal spread and other players from other countries became caught up in the rumours and revelations, some very interesting patterns emerged in the responses of fans, players, sports administrators and the media in the various countries. Without going into the details of the scandal, these responses can be grouped into three broad categories.

In the first place, there was a reflexive denial on the part of the South Africans, the English, and the Australians, that 'they' – and I use the collective pronoun deliberately – could have been involved in anything so heinous (Magazine 1999: xvi–xvii). This denial was accompanied by more or less naked racist innuendo aimed at the source of the allegations which included both India in particular and south Asia in general. The implication was that heroic, patriotic Christian athletes like Cronje could never be guilty of such chicanery and that Indian investigators were incompetent and malicious.

When it became impossible to evade the conclusion that Cronje was in fact guilty and that other celebrity cricketers, such as Australia's Mark Waugh and Dean Jones, New Zealand's Martin Crowe and England's Alec Stewart, may also have been involved in 'match fixing' blame was subtly shifted. It was taken away from the Indian investigators, away from the athletes themselves and moved towards what might be described as the Indian milieu. 'We all know that these things happen on the subcontinent' became a common refrain, implying that it was the innate immorality of the subcontinent that had ensnared, seduced and corrupted the erstwhile icons of white moral purity.

Secondly, however, the reaction on the Indian side was marked by a mixture of quiet satisfaction and morbid fascination. The aspersions that were cast on Indian investigators were perceived as a national affront and, for once, the Delhi police actually found themselves basking in the glow of public support. When Cronje finally confessed, there was a discernible sense of vindication and a visible pleasure at the humiliation of those who had assumed an air of moral (and implicitly racial) superiority. Then the attention of the press and the public turned inwards as one Indian icon after another was flushed from the closet by investigators and each other. These exposés came with their own politics of communal animosity: Mohammed Azharuddin's protestations of his innocence were initially met with considerably greater skepticism than the idea that Kapil Dev may have sold out the national side. '*Azhar ne pukka khaya*' ('Azhar has definitely had some') declared advertisements for Amul butter before the Central Bureau of Investigation had even begun its inquiry into the allegations.

Finally, the responses in the 'white nations' and in India both showed a certain bewilderment that bribery, gambling, match-fixing etc. could possibly have happened in cricket. After India's Central Bureau of Investigation named former England captain Alec Stewart in the bribery scandal, Paul Condon (the head of the ICC's anti-corruption cell and former police chief of London) expressed his chagrin with the following remark: 'People want to believe it (cricket) is all about skill, courage and heroic endeavor and not about some seedy conversation in dingy hotel rooms or on mobile phones (Times of India 2/11/00)'. The fact that the ICC has an anti-corruption unit in the first place would seem to indicate certain problems with the image of the sport but that irony was lost on Condon and others who expressed a similar surprize. Clearly, in spite of Bodyline[1] and Packer[2] the dominant image of the sport has changed little since the Victorian era when, as Sandiford (1994: 2–6, 26–29) has noted, cricket was regarded as being above greed and corruption and as a triumph over the moral laxity of Georgians and lesser peoples. In reality the enormous flows of money that surround cricket in India, which includes an illegal gambling industry that handles bets totalling nearly nine billion dollars annually (Magazine 1999: xxiv), threaten not only to revive the corruption of Georgian cricket and overturn the 'Victorian' ownership of the sport but also to expose the modern-day would-be Victorians as being Georgians under their (mostly white) skins. No wonder then that 'Cronjegate' has triggered a desire to reassert the idea that cricket represents, or should represent, a cultural island of innocence in a world of globalized greed.

All three of these responses flared again during the controversy over the Mike Denness decisions in the 2001 series between India and South Africa. During the second game of the series Denness, the match referee, whose job it is to oversee the general conduct of the game, penalized an unprecedented six Indian players for various improprieties ranging from ball-tampering, in the case of Sachin Tendulkar to excessive appealing in the case of Virender Sehwag, and included 'failure to control his players' on the part of Indian captain Saurav Ganguly for good measure. Sehwag was banned from the next game of the series which catapulted the newcomer to international cricket into the center of a snowballing crisis. The Indian players, media and public were more or less unanimous in their anger. The Indians threatened to abandon the tour if Denness was not removed and the South Africans gave in and acceded to their request. In response the ICC, which had refused either to fire Denness or to set up a panel to review his decisions, declared that the third game of the series would lose its 'official' status and therefore the ban on Sehwag would carry over to the first game in the impending series between India and England. The Indians insisted that Sehwag was eligible to play against England and the ICC and England insisted that if Sehwag was selected the series would be called off. Finally, a last-minute compromise was reached. The ICC decided to review the Denness decisions. Denness qualified his verdict on Tendulkar by announcing that the star Indian batsman had only committed a technical offence and not actually tampered with the ball, and the Indian board agreed that Sehwag would sit out the game.[3] However, emotions on both sides had been rubbed raw, diplomatic feathers had been ruffled and international cricket had come close to splitting along the lines of race. To understand the politics of the Denness affair it is important to keep in mind that Denness is a former England captain and is white, as is most of the South African team. The Indian media placed that fact at the very centre of its response to the referee's decisions. Initially, the attention of Indian reporters who covered the episode was focused on the fact that no South African player was cited by Denness for any offence, despite the fact that video replays showed the home captain Shaun Pollock appealing as dramatically as Sehwag. It was now pointed out in the Indian media that in several recent series Indian, Pakistani and Sri Lankan players had been penalized for offences that had been overlooked in the cases of white cricketers.[4] What took the anger to a different level of intensity was the ICC's refusal to acknowledge that there was a problem together with the reactions of English and Australian cricketers and politicians and the coverage of the crisis in the English press.

The ICC is made up of the various countries that play cricket at the international level. It is headquartered in England at a time when more than seventy percent of its budget is generated by cricket in the subcontinent. The internal politics of the body have, for some years, been enmeshed in person-ality clashes as well as racial conflict. The current president of the BCCI, Jagmohan Dalmiya, is the former president of the ICC. Dalmiya's election to his former job had been contested bitterly by the English and Australian cricket boards and race was never far from the center of that dispute. The current president of the ICC, the Australian Malcolm Gray, had lost to Dalmiya in that earlier election. As such there is no love lost between the ICC and Gray on the one hand, and the BCCI and Dalmiya on the other. When the ICC and Gray brushed aside Indian concerns about the Denness deci-sions that animosity almost certainly influenced the manner in which the issue was handled. To be fair to the ICC, the body was not procedurally equipped to deal with the crisis that developed in South Africa. There were no existing means by which a match referee's decision could be appealed or reviewed. There was a fear that if any of the Indian demands were conceded, the bureaucracy would have to stir itself and solutions would have to be developed. This partly explains the sheer clumsiness of the ICC's initial response which included a farcical press conference in which Denness refused to answer questions by claiming that the ICC did not allow it. But it also needs to be kept in mind that the ICC's position was firmly in line with the old cricketing tradition of the inviolability of umpiring decisions. What the ICC did not take into account however is that the tradition of umpiring and the signifi-cance of umpiring decisions had already changed. Cricket after Packer is a fully commercialized sport and there are no amateurs left at the international level. There are obvious ethical and political problems with telling a profes-sional player that he cannot appeal against a penalty. More importantly, in the era of instant replays, third-umpires and other recent technological and managerial innovations (innovations that include the office of the match referee) umpires no longer possess the infallibility of God, or even that of the elite white man. Indeed, the ICC did not take its own nature into account. The International Cricket Council retains its initials from the days when it used to be the Imperial Cricket Council but the body today is made up of post-colonial member-nations, the majority of which are largely non-white. Throughout the crisis the ICC insisted that only two men spoke for cricket's highest organization. These were the two Malcolms: President Gray and Chief Executive Officer Speed, who were both Australian and both white.

Since they had decided to support Denness, any challenge to Denness' authority was interpreted as a challenge to their authority, which was represented as defiance of the ICC. Ultimately, however, there was no escaping the realities of who plays, watches and pays for cricket in the world today. The eventual compromise reflected the fact that the ICC cannot afford, financially or politically, to force India out of world cricket. The Indian position had a great deal of support in the other Asian countries, including Pakistan (Dawn 27/11/01),[5] and forcing a vote on the issue would have made the racial divide of the sport a little too visible for comfort.

However, it was Dalmiya and the BCCI who were blamed for 'tearing cricket apart'. In column after column English and Australian cricket journalists made three points. One was that the conflict was rooted in Dalmiya's ego. The BCCI chief was demonized as both the cause and the instrument of impending calamity: 'the central force behind the entire crisis' (Guardian 27/11/01), a 'ludicrous' megalomaniac (Guardian 28/11/01), a man who 'has gone too far' (Sydney Morning Herald 24/11/01) and a 'strongman' given to 'bullishness' and brinksmanship (Independent 28/11/01). Another was that the Indians were threatening to destroy international cricket because they could not stomach the fact that Tendulkar had been caught cheating. The last was that the Indians were challenging the umpire's decision, which was simply not cricket. All three of these allegations have a familiar ring as they echo the colonial discourse of the childish, unmanly native who cannot control himself on the cricket field and who lacks the stoic character and sense of sportsmanship which might enable him to accept adversity without complaint. When the compromise was reached between the ICC and the BCCI, and Sehwag did not play in the first match of the India-England series, this was interpreted bizarrely as a climb-down on the part of Dalmiya (Guardian 30/11/01). It was forgotten that Sehwag's inclusion had never been the BCCI's primary demand and it was only when the ICC refused to review the Denness decisions that the BCCI had insisted that Sehwag would play.

In India, where Denness was quickly nicknamed 'Denness the Menace', a sense that the affair was the newest battle in an old colonial war suffused newspapers and television and spilled over into Parliament, into diplomatic channels and on to the streets. When the episode began, members of the government and the Opposition demanded that the Indian team be brought back from South Africa if Denness was not replaced as matchreferee. Prime Minister Vajpayee was evidently in touch with Dalmiya throughout the crisis and provided quiet support even as his Australian counterpart John Howard openly supported the ICC. Thabo Mbeki instructed his country's cricket board to side with India, which is South Africa's single biggest trading partner. There was also the fact that a premature termination of the Indian tour would have cost the South African board four million dollars in lost advertizing revenues and raised the spectre of lawsuits by angry television companies (Guardian 24/11/01). Meanwhile, on the streets of Calcutta, cricket became anti-colonial performance art in a very literal sense. Angry crowds burned Denness in effigy, paraded a donkey with a 'Denness' figure on its back, and organized a mock cricket match in which referee 'Denness' made a series of ridiculous decisions to the delight of onlookers (Times of India 21/11/01). Yet the outrage extended far beyond the figure of Denness, the message boards of Internet portals like Rediff.com and the online edition of the Times of India were awash with a perception that Denness was only one face of a much larger problem of institutionalized racism in cricket. Demonstrating how transnational capitalism actually reinforces nationalist self-assertion, ESPN India took to endlessly repeating a lengthy and provocative video clip. This showed that showed the Australian player Michael Slater challenging the Indian umpire Venkataraghavan and abusing the batsman (Rahul Dravid) while Australian captain Steve Waugh stood impassively by. The TV channel reminded the audience that Slater and Waugh were not harassed by the ICC or its referees.[6]

How are we to explain Denness' original decisions, the Indian reaction and the Anglo-Australian response? Until this episode began Denness had a relatively low profile in international cricket. A modestly talented batsman who had led England in the mid-1970s he was not one of the more flamboyant characters of the era as were his team-mates Tony Greig and Allan Knott. At the end of his playing career he had quietly joined the old-boys' network of English cricket and from there the 'paid holidays' of match refereeing came as a natural second career. Denness had served as the referee in nine matches involving India before the second Test of the South Africa series and all passed without incident. There is little reason to claim, as many Indians did in letters to the media, that Denness was a straightforward Indian-hater (Times of India 20/11/01). Nevertheless, the idea that Denness seems to be blessed with a particular vision of cricket and race is not totally absent from that picture.A particularly striking image of Denness can be found in Sunil Gavaskar's autobiography as it shows the England captain with one arm around Gavaskar's shoulders while his other arm is fending off Indian spectators who had invaded an English cricket field (Gavaskar 1991). When he became a match referee Denness remarked that he intended to 'clean up' cricket. What, at the beginning of the twenty-first century, does that phrase mean? It means doing away with corruption scandals like 'Cronjegate' for which the Asians, rather than the Cronjes, of the cricketing world are ultimately held respon-sible. It means, also, restoring a particular order to the cricket field, in which players and fans know their place.

However, this is not a self-evident concept. It is unlikely that Denness expects cricketers of colour to genuflect before their white adversaries. There is, however, a distinct understanding in England and Australia and in India as well that the same rules do not apply to all cricketers. During Mike Denness' own playing career in the 1970s Knott and Greig took the 'phony appeal', an elaborate war-dance designed to fool the umpire into declaring the batsman out, to a new level of perfection and confrontations with the umpire were not unheard of (Gavaskar 1991: 102–111). This was considered acceptable gamesmanship and the protagonists of those high-spirited times are now firmly in the ICC's camp. Greig, who once poured urine on a fan in Australia and who defended John Lever in the Vaseline scandal of 1976,[7] is now outraged by the Indian defiance of Mike Denness. Australian players' spokesperson Tim May recently explained that 'cricket is played in different cultures' and that these cultural differences must be taken into account in judging players' behavior on the field (Rediff.com 07/12/01). He was defending Australian fast bowler Brett Lee, not Sehwag. In other words umpires and referees are asked to accept that Australian and South African players will be aggressive on the field and that this is different from Indians and Pakistanis behaving in the same ways. When Shaun Pollock, Brett Lee or Michael Slater curse the batsmen or remonstrate with umpires, then that is Antipodean gamesmanship. When Sehwag or Ganguly do it that is misbehavior because it transgresses the allowances of culture.

The ICC's endorsement of Denness' mission to 'clean up' the game thus meant enforcing a code of conduct in which race is implicit and in which white athletes, especially those who conform to certain expectations based on class and geography, must be treated with indulgence when they ignore the elaborate ethos of self-control that C.L.R. James (1963: 39–46) called the public school code. There are deep historical foundations under this mindset. Australians, South Africans and working-class English fast bowlers like Larwood and Trueman were not the amateurs who were expected to embody the perfectly-controlled gentleman on the field. They served the gentlemen-amateur and the gentleman-fan as team-mates and opponents who supplied, from a comfortable social distance, the overt aggression that is sometimes necessary to win games. They also supplied the Other that is necessary in the construction of the Self.

Such separation was most visible a century ago but it has not vanished altogether. The amateur and the professional, the gentleman and the thug, now co-exist in the same individuals who represent England, Australia and South Africa. The separation is built into the essential schizophrenia of modern cricket which allows the public school code to remain relevant in an era when corporate sponsorship and nationalism have made failure and defeat increasingly unacceptable. As such, when Mike Denness cleans up cricket it is understood that some of the 'dirt' is a necessary part of the sport and must be allowed to remain. If all cricketers were public school athletes international cricket would become a very dull game and the concept of 'cricket', with all its moral baggage of acceptable behavior and appropriate leadership on and off the field, would become meaningless. The coloured cricketer is of course even more an Other than the Australian, the South African white or the working-class Englishman. As such his transgressions of the public school code are interpreted quite differently and this interpretation has evolved considerably over the last one hundred years or so. When nineteenth century Indian (and Caribbean) cricketers failed to control themselves on the field, English observers could react with amusement and a comfortable disdain. Lord Hawke (1924: 171, 274), on tour in 1892, was only slightly surprised to see that Parsis (and Antiguans) wept when umpires ruled against them and, during England's first Test series in India in 1933–34, it was noted that Dilawar Hussain failed to show the right stoicism when he was injured (Bose 1991: 87). But neither the Parsis nor Dilawar Hussain *confronted* the umpire who, like the ICC bosses of today, was white and who represented a power structure that was, and is, extremely reluctant to entertain a challenge. In a moment of hyperbole, in the middle of the Denness affair, the ICC president told a reporter that the Indian players had 'attacked the umpire' in South Africa (Rediff.com 26/11/01). Because contemporary South Asian cricketers like Javed Miandad, Sehwah and Ganguly can be directly confrontational they represent an overtly political challenge and a more serious threat than confrontational whites like Michael Slater and Jacques Kallis. Moreover, the aggression of the Indians and the Pakistanis does not contribute to English or even Australian victories; these men are quite literally the Other team. They confirm the enduring colonial fantasy of white moral superiority but in the era of decolonization the firm political grasp that allowed the white-imperial Self to play cricket with the brown-colonial Other, even when the Other misbehaved, has weakened considerably. The Malcolms must now contend with the Dalmiyas, the Gangulys and the Sehwags. It is now even more important to react forcefully against anychallenge to the public school code and its guardians. This is why Lord McLaurin, the head of the England Cricket Board, issued loud warnings of 'anarchy' when the Indian board defied Denness (Guardian 26/11/01; Independent 17/11/01).

It is not that the English press was altogether oblivious to the issues at stake in the Denness dispute. Writing in the Guardian, Mark Lawson noted that 'two long-standing problems in international cricket– colour and money' had resurfaced for the first time since the apartheid-era controversies over rebel tours of South Africa (Guardian 25/11/01). Lawson explained:

> Like association and rugby football, and then union and league rugby, the game may be headed for separate codes or leagues, decided in this case by race or historical hatreds. It's not, as they say, cricket. But the implication behind that old English phrase – of the right of the old, white world to decide the manners and rules of the game – is what's being challenged in this high-pitched row.

I shall not speculate as to what 'historical hatreds' Lawson had in mind. In any case Indian players, officials and fans did not come out in favor of aggressive appealing, weaker umpires or the right to tamper with the ball. In fact, the language that was deployed against Denness and the ICC in the Indian press was marked by a stubborn defence of the public school code. The Times of India expressed its outrage over the incident by declaring that Tendulkar was one of 'the game's gentlemen' (Times of India 25/11/01; Independent 26/11/2001) and irate fans told reporters that *unlike* Australian, South African and English players, Indian cricketers were gentlemanly to a fault (Times of India 20/11/01). As such the clash was not so much about the content of the moral baggage of cricket, as over ownership of the bags. Dalmiya was quite explicit about this: even as he rebelled against the ICC he declared that he had no intention of wrecking the governing body. The fight, he announced, was about 'who is in charge of it' (Guardian 28/11/2001). The issue of ownership is not simply about moral superiority or sentimental claims on culture. Obviously enough, it is also about dollars and cents, which are now in the hands of people of the wrong colour. As a money-spinner Tendulkar is to cricket what Jordan was to basketball; he is probably the only athlete in history to have a car named after him.[8] Teams and companies from the Indian subcontinent generate the lion's share of the ICC's revenues. The last World Cup was held in South Africa but the big sponsors were WOC Pepsi India and Hero Honda, which poured in ten million dollars through advertising sales alone (Guardian 24/11/01). Quite literally, India and Pakistan own world cricket today. This financial clout resulted not only in Dalmiya's forced entry into the top of the ICC but also in his unpopularity with English and Australian cricket administrators, who saw him as the archetypal wealthy but unwanted gatecrasher at the country club.

Money was very much at the forefront during the Denness crisis when the English press focused angrily on the financial considerations that led the South African cricket board to side with India. South African cricket is a white-dominated establishment still openly traumatized by the inclusion in the national side of black players like Makhaya Ntini and Justin Ontong,[9] but its peculiarities were barely noticed in the English press. When one journalist referred to South Africa as a 'tinpot country' the Indian scribe Prem Panicker retorted: 'Did the Republic of South Africa become 'tinpot' once the last vestiges of British colonialism were overthrown?' (Rediff.com 26/11/01). Mbeki's determination that his country's cricket board 'keep India happy' was seen in England as unacceptable fiscal-political interference in the purity of sport, much as opposition to playing cricket with South Africa in the era of apartheid was once seen as an unwarranted politicization of sport (Guardian 24/11/2001). It was also noted that the England board would lose up to eighteen million pounds in revenues if the crisis resulted in the cancellation of India's 2002 tour of England, and that, because of Asian solidarity with India on the Denness issue, England would be hard pressed to find an alternative opponent and source of income (Guardian 28/11/2001). Under the circumstances Dalmiya became the face of a potential South Asian secession from or takeover of world cricket, a second Packer crisis, all the more potent because this time money was the apparent vehicle in a transfer of power between cultures and across borders.

The Tensions of Transfer

This subversion of ownership is not limited to the politics of the ICC or even to a shift in the relationship between the 'east' and the 'west.' It is reflective also of tensions between the easts and the wests *within* the societies that play cricket in the modern world and that have been subject to dramatic movements of race and class. In England these tensions generated the 'Tebbit test', that is the perception articulated by Lord Norman Tebbit that proof of Britishness in immigrants and their children lies in whether or not they cheer for England when England plays India or Pakistan at cricket. Nobody expects Australians, Canadians or white South African migrants to England, let alone their England-born children, to submit to the Tebbit test, as it is understood that such investigations are necessary only for 'visible minorities'. It is also understood that the Tebbit test is not a mechanism for expanding the boundaries of British identity. It is an instrument of exclusion and of clarifying the political relationship between white Britons and the communities that Salman Rushdie has called 'the new empire within Britain' (Rushdie 1991: 129). As Raj Kaushal (2001) has pointed out, the British sporting arena in the throes of nationalist exultation is not a racially welcoming cultural space and it is hard for an Asian supporter of England to show his support for the home team when the crowd is chanting 'I'd rather be a Paki than a Turk' (Observer 26/11/01).

The tension between race and nationality on the cricket field only worsens when the England captain is himself, well, not a Turk. Not only was Nasser Hussain born in Madras (and greeted a little too warmly by the natives during the 2001 tour of India), his teammates include Mark Ramprakash, whose father's family migrated to England from India via the Caribbean and Pakistan-born Usman Afzaal. On the surface this is a wonderful advertise-ment for multicultural Britain. Nasser Hussain is popular with English fans and the press and a recipient of the OBE to boot. Below that surface one wonders if Hussain would have been quite so well received without his English mother and light skin. It is one thing to embrace a solitary interloper such as Ranjitsinhji and quite another to embrace a black captain when you feel besieged by black immigrants. It is not surprising then, to find Hussain endorsing the Tebbit test by declaring that he cannot understand why British-born Indians and Pakistanis continue to support India and Pakistan (Observer 26/11/01). He later backpedaled and claimed that he was talking about third and fourth-generation British Asians but it is difficult to avoid the sense that he is under a different scrutiny than Mike Brearley (to whom he is often compared) was when he led England against India in the 1980s or Douglas Jardine (born in India like Hussain but without the complication of a black father) was in 1932. Hussain's captaincy of England, like Dalmiya's ascen-dancy in the bureaucracy of international cricket, marks the transfer of power. Unlike Dalmiya, however, Hussain must represent England and it is no wonder that he feels the need to underline his identity by echoing Tebbit and also by directly criticizing the Indian board on the Denness issue (Guardian 28/11/2001).

Within India, the tensions of the transfer manifest themselves along the lines of class. This is not entirely new of course even in the earliest days of Indian cricket elite patrons of the sport needed marginal athletes like the untouchable Palwankar Baloo to win matches and some patrons, like Nagendraprasad Sarbadhikary, were far less central to the demographics of the sport than others (Majumdar 2001). This did not compromise the hegemony of the elite because the outsiders they allowed into their teams and clubhouses were relatively few and not especially vocal. They could be incor-porated into the circles of elite cricket and any residual dissonance could be ignored. At the beginning of the twenty-first century the situation is quite different because the nature of the crowd and the nature of patronage in Indian cricket has changed dramatically over the last twenty years. Indians who had substantially accepted the public school ethos must now contend with very large numbers of new fans who come from the margins of middle-class respectability but who watch satellite television, read the sports columns of vernacular newspapers and have money to spend on tickets and endorsed products. They compete with the elites over ownership of Indian cricket just as the elites compete with the white old-guard over ownership of the ICC. The cultural clout of the new Indian cricket fan was highlighted by the success in 2001 of the film *Lagaan*. On the one hand *Lagaan* is an intensely conservative text that, as Nissim Mannathukkaren (2001) has pointed out, is careful to nullify any challenge to the feudal patriarchy of the Indian village. It is also, however, an extraordinarily subversive text because it narrates a political, sexual and athletic challenge to British authority in colonial India and also because it presents a radically different picture of the moral universe of the cricket ground in which the 'old' middle class has no presence, let alone control. The 'first-generation' cricketers and fans in *Lagaan*, peasants who have formed a team/nation to play/fight the local British, have never heard of the public school code. They laugh, cry, jeer and applaud with abandon, they bat and bowl in shockingly unorthodox ways, their bodies are without any apparent discipline and their clothes are far removed from cricketing whites. Their nationalism binds them to middle-class audiences in India (and also in England where the film's success with British Asians indicates that the Tebbit test has not found many takers) but their true counterparts in the cinema hall are other newcomers to the cricket ground: the taxi drivers, the 'export-import' businessmen, diasporic South Asians in the Persian Gulf, the first-generation arrivals in the urban economy and the fans in smaller Indian cities that are new on the map of international cricket. They are too numerous and too lacking in diffidence to be easily co-opted into the 'gentle-manly' ethos of Indian cricket. Rather, they threaten to co-opt the gentlemen by altering the norms of behavior on the field and in the stands.

The relationship between the 'old' and the 'new' cricket fan in India is not uniformly or consistently hostile. Each is transformed by the other, and the numbers, the aggression, and the money that the new fan brings to the cricket ground is essential to the pleasure and the marketability of the modern sport. I would argue that, for the contemporary middle-class cricket fan in India, the new spectator serves as a kind of semi-acknowledged alter-ego that allows the 'gentleman' the vicarious excitement of being able to abandon decorum, curse opponents and throw bottles on to the field. Nevertheless, as much as the English and the Australians, the new crowds represent a challenge to the editors and sportswriters of English-language newspapers in India, pushing them to insist that Indian cricketers are gentlemen. Like the fictional heroes of *Lagaan*, Sehwag and Tendulkar must be claimed by the gentlemen because they are also claimed by the 'peasants' and Nasser Hussain must be claimed by England, lest he be claimed by the other side. For the 'old' cricket fan in India the arrival of the new spectator raises two simultaneous threats. On the one hand it erodes the ability of the 'old' cricket establishment in India, that is the post-princely, salaried, urban middle class that dominated the sport in India between the 1930s and the 1980s, to determine the moral meanings and behavioral norms of the game. On the other hand, it makes Indian cricket vulnerable to critics like Denness, who can raise the colonial spectre of the undisciplined native. This weakens the middle class' ability to control its 'own' house and expand its influence in international bodies like the ICC.

Conclusion

How is ownership asserted and contested in cricket today? During the 2001 series between India and Australia, Cammie Smith, the match referee from the West Indies, favoured the Australians in a series of controversial decisions. This led the Indian cricket writer Rajeev Pai (Rediff.com 03/03/01) to grumble:

> Why doesn't someone give Cammie Smith a good, hard scrub and wash? If we can just get that black paint off him, we are sure to find underneath, if not a white man, an Indian 'prince' in awe of white skin. A pity that such Uncle Toms continue to exist in the twenty-first century.

It would be difficult to find a more cutting articulation of the politics of race and anti-colonialism in cricket. The tensions of the late nineteenth century game have acquired a few additional layers of complexity in the early twenty-first century, as the actors and the stages have multiplied. It should be noted that Pai's attack on Anglophile princes was directed at cricket administrator Raj Singh Dungarpore who, along with Smith, had apparently tried to appease the Australians. Nevertheless, the broadside against Smith and Dungarpore echoes the nationalist critique of Ranjitsinhji in the 1920s and '30s when the Indian press saw him as a deracinated apologist for colonial rule (Wild 1934: 276–279). It also echoes Appadurai's choice of the term 'brown Englishman' to describe the first Indian to play cricket for England (1996: 23–48).

In the era of the circus-like cricket tournaments of Sharjah Appadurai wrote that all cricket is Trobriand cricket. I would like to amend his assertion, by pointing out that Trobriand cricket (Jerry Leach's term for cricket in which the codes have been co-opted by the natives) began when Ranjitsinhji first walked into the Fenner's ground in Cambridge. Undoubtedly, he understood the possibilities of racial transgression and took advantage of the anomalous cultural roles that cricket allowed him to play. At the same time he knew that he could enter the citadel of the imperial sport only as long as he did not jettison his skin and on the condition that he did not appear to be in the vanguard of an outright invasion. It is worth noting that when Ranjitsinhji first played for England one writer warned the editors of the *Daily Mail* that not only would seditious Indians ('especially the Bengalese') take heart from his success, but that the stage was now set for an invasion of English cricket by talented natives (Cricket 1896: 436). Hussain and Ramprakash had been prophesized. Today, this fear, which was probably expressed tongue-in-cheek a century ago, has come true, not only in the metropole which is in danger of being relegated to the periphery, but also in the erstwhile periphery which is staking its claim as the new metropole. Each is faced with a dual challenge. Those at the old white center of the game must contend, on the one hand, with the pressure of culturally and politically assertive immigrant populations, or with a post-apartheid black majority, that disrupts the order of the cricket ground and the wider society and that require uncomfortable readjustments in what it means to be British, South African or gentlemanly. On the other hand, they must face the reality that formerly subordinate opponent-subjects are now not only openly insubordinate, but in control of the sport's finances. As such they can infiltrate the ICC or secede and leave the ICC a pallid shell. Hence the strictness towards subcontinental 'misbehavior' alongside the leniency towards white players, the recriminations when Cronje is caught cheating, the anxiety when Denness is challenged and the outrage when Dalmiya emerges at the head of an outright rebellion. This is not the indulgent smugness with which the Empire faced an apparent anomaly, as it did when Ranjitsinhji eclipsed English batsmen between 1895 and 1905. It is a defensive response and an acknowledgment of a transformation that is already far advanced. Meanwhile, elite Indians feel pressured by the new cricket fans of the subcontinent even as they challenge McLaurin, Denness and the Malcolms. The pressure is made all the more compelling by the fact that middle-class Indians *need* the new fans, much as elite nationalists need the masses: without the numbers, the voices and the disorder of the latter, there can be no effective anti-colonial revolt. The trick is to manage the disorder much as the English managed Ranjitsinhji, by putting the 'peasants' in cricketing whites but carefully preserving the strategic aspects of their peasant nature.

6

THE SOCIAL HISTORY OF THE ROYAL CALCUTTA GOLF CLUB, 1829–2003

Paul Dimeo

Introduction

As this volume demonstrates, the cultures of recreation, sport and the body in South Asia have increasingly attracted the attention of academic researchers interested in exploring aspects of South Asian society. Understandably, the more obviously 'important' pastimes were the focus of early work. For instance, the histories of cricket (Cashman 1980; Bose 1990; Guha 2002) and football (Dimeo and Mills 2001; Dimeo 2002) have been well documented as have some of the more salient indigenous body cultures (Alter 1992; Zarrilli 1998). Other studies have focused on specific individuals or times and places, thus drawing out the micro-level motivations and strategies of key participants. Such studies were bold and innovative, bridging the gap between sports studies and South Asian studies, and leading to a wider awareness of sport among social historians.

Golf has been in South Asia for over a century, playing an important role in colonial relations but failing to keep up with global developments in the period after Independence. In this, the sport's fate mirrored that of football. Unlike football, however, golf has been almost entirely ignored by historians, perhaps because there are no moments of historical gravity to compel nationalist re-visioning or no radical oppression of indigenous traditions to fire up post-colonial critics. Yet golf is full of potential to the historian because of its value-laden institutional culture and the demands that it makes upon the individual's behaviour patterns and somatic styles. In Australia, for example, Phillips (1990) has shown that golf represented many of the values so cherished by British colonialists as 'civilized'. With its emphasis on etiquette and sportsmanship, golf consciously and openly promoted an identifiably 'Western' system of ethics that insisted upon control over one's emotions alongside mastery of one's clubs. In India, this culture of discipline and regulation had its own sociological character. Golf clubs were among the most class-biased and racially exclusive institutions in colonial India. There was no room for working-class Europeans or for Indians whatsoever. These facts alone may lead to an interpretation emphasizing Marxist elements or colonial criticism. It was, of course, from Marxist forms of historiography that the term 'subaltern studies' and various related studies first emerged. One can certainly view golf clubs as literal arenas of discrimination through which colonization of land and social exclusion were justified by recreation and social class.

However, as this chapter seeks to prove through a case study of the Royal Calcutta Golf Club (commonly referred to as the RCGC), such an interpretation risks over-simplification especially when the post-colonial era is taken into consideration. Indians wanted to join these clubs despite the clear colonial prejudices. When a small number were reluctantly accepted in 1946 there was no revolutionary impulse towards change. Moreover, Indians have since shown considerable respect for their club's heritage, glorying in the association with the Raj for decades after Independence (indeed using that association to stake claims of prestige in contemporary settings). In the post-colonial period the land which had been carved out by the British in Calcutta for their sporting amusement has become a focal point for class struggles at a localized, indigenous level. Thus, the legacy of colonialism is complex and far from benign. Conceptually, the simple dichotomies of colonizer-colonised or of working and middle-classes, have been disrupted. Some former subalterns longed for acceptance, achieved it and celebrate their new status. Others cast critical eyes on their treasure, accusing them of fawning to a former tyrant.

This chapter begins with a look at how the club was founded in the context of social class and colonial power. From there it will consider the post-colonial transformation of membership. Finally it will address the club as a contemporary legacy of the past, in which it has become a historical stage, playing host to the daily dramas of class conflict in urban India.

Early Days: 1829–1911

In the history of world golf the RCGC is renowned as the oldest golf club established outside Great Britain, apparently formed in 1829. While this is interesting in itself, the situation 'back home' was far from conducive towards such innovation in colonial outposts. The reasons for this faltering progress even in the sport's homeland lay with a number of factors: the impact of new industrial working hours, a rise in the cost of equipment, financial mismanagement and difficulties in securing exclusive use of enough suitable land. This was manifest in the fortunes of such clubs as The Honourable Company of Edinburgh Golfers, the Glasgow Golf Club and even the Royal and Ancient in St. Andrews, all of which faced bankruptcy and ruin in the 1820s and 1830s. The Honourable Company may well now be famed for being the first club in the world (established in 1744 in Leith) but by 1834 it had been, according to the golf historian David Hamilton, 'reduced to an inactive shell' as it was forced to sell off its clubhouse, fixtures and fittings and paintings. While the general background to the club's crisis was one of 'poor supervision, lack of interest and low morale at a time of general national unrest and uncertainty', the Company was not greatly assisted by one of their secretaries who 'fled the country, leaving behind personal debts, [while] money was missing from the club' (Hamilton 1998: 105). Similar problems were to be found in St. Andrews due to the sale of common land in the late 1700s and the declining status of the University, all of which produced a disgruntled and disaffected membership. By 1827 the Royal and Ancient was in 'temporary decline' as it lacked sufficient funds to rebuild its reputation (Hamilton 1998: 107). The situation was not much better south of the border as the sport was yet to flourish, so much so that by 1829 there was only one course in the country, that of the Blackheath Club in London (Stirk 1998). Further abroad, the early initiatives in the North American states of South Carolina and Georgia had petered out to the extent that the game had disappeared by 1815 (Hamilton 1998: 109). This all suggests that the fledgling sport was in decline wherever it had been played early in the nineteenth century, though of course its fluctuating fortunes were to recover in subsequent decades. As such, enthusiasm in India in this period seems at odds with the story elsewhere, and David Hamilton detects a certain stubbornness in the origins of golf in the Indian city: 'some Scottish soldiers doggedly founded golf clubs while on service in the Empire and in Bengal Major (later Sir) Hugh Lyon Playfair, a talented St. Andrews man, set up a club at Dum Dum' (109). In the early part of the 19th century Dum Dum was a small suburb to the north-east of the city. It was later to gain notoriety when in 1898 Captain Bertie Clay invented a bullet with a soft lead nose in its small arms factory (Moorhouse 1998: 82). During the 20th century the suburb was chosen as the location of the city's airport. However in 1829 it was home to the city's European settlers, mostly British people who were in India to work for the East India Company, the Indian Civil Service, in other commercial enterprizes or in related services such as teaching or missionary work.

Major Playfair was part of the military elite in the city, indeed he was commander of the 4th Battalion of Artillery at Dum Dum in the late 1820s (Playfair 1984: 57). He came from an influential golfing family that helped found the club in Prestwick on Scotland's west coast as well as to establish the Open Championship Belt in 1860. Born in Dundee in 1786, he took a degree at St Andrew's University where his father was Principal before joining the East India Company's Bengal Army in 1804. After returning from two brief visits to Scotland, he stayed in India until 1832 (Brehend and Lewis 1998: 104). Upon retiring from the East India Company he returned to St. Andrews to become both Captain of the Royal and Ancient and Provost of the town. He was responsible for renovating part of the course and for establishing the Clubhouse that still exists today (Ward-Thomas 1980: 23–4). In this way, and with continued involvement in the club, he became one of the most important figures in the early history of golf in St Andrews. At this time the sport drew its enthusiasts from a limited section of society, largely comprized of middle and upper class men with powerful connections in politics and business. In 1856 Playfair reflected on his youthful golfing days in a way that showed up the inherent class elitism of the game:

> The national and gentlemanly game of golf was, at that time, confined to the 'Upper Ten' and was looked upon by the common people, who could not afford to pay for clubs and the stout leather case stuffed with feathers, called a golf ball, as a pastime fitted only for those whom they considered to have 'mair siller [silver] than sense' (cited in Stirk 1998: 37).

Certainly, this notion of the 'upper ten' rang true for the founding fathers of the RCGC, described in the *Oriental Sporting Magazine* of December 23 1830 (cited in Pearson 1979: 7) as 'the list of subscribers to the Dum Dum Golfing Club' and players of 'that noble and gentlemanlike game'. They were: Brigadier Sir A. McLeod, C. N. Hon. C. R. Lindsay, Alex Ross, Esq., Dr Playfair, Lieut. Bennett, Lieut. Horsford, Lieut. Jarvies, Dr Wood, Capt. Ietric, A. McLeod Esq., Capt. Graham, Capt. Geddes, Lieut. Seppings, Lieut. Craig, Lieut. Austin, Lieut. Cooper, Lieut. Backhouse, Dr Montgomery, Dr Strom, the Right Hon. Lord Ramsay, Lieut. Kinliside, Capt. Cartwright, Capt. Tennant. Major H. L. Playfair, the Hon. Col. Ramsay, Capt. W. M. Ramsay, Capt. Morland, G. J. Gordon, Esq., J. Calder, Esq., and J. Storm, Esq.

As a point of historical accuracy it is not entirely clear why 1829 has been accepted by the RCGC as the year of its foundation. The above report is dated late 1830 and other evidence that comes from the Minutes of the Blackheath Club, to which the RCGC has retained a strong connection to this day, is in a note to the effect that a Golf Club has been formed in Calcutta on 12 June 1830 (Stirk 1998: 185).[1] However, the club's own records referred to 24th March 1829 as the day of inception with Lord Ramsay as captain, but this information in only available second-hand from a book published in 1906 by W. H. Carey called *The Good Old Days of the Honourable John Company*. Actually the year given by Carey was 1839 and the author of the club's only printed history, Surita Pearson (1979: 15) argues that '1839' is assumed to include a typing error and it should be '1829' because of other available evidence. Given this, however, it is unclear that any of Carey's testimony can be accepted and there is no supporting evidence for his claim that 'A Golf Club was established in Calcutta on the 24th March 1839 of which Lord Ramsay was captain' (1906: 115).

The historically important connection between the clubs in Blackheath and Calcutta clubs seems to have emerged from the fact that many of the senior executives and major shareholders in the East India Company were members of Blackheath. David Stirk (1998) argues that many of these men were both Freemasons and from Scotland. It is not clear how Stirk arrives at the conclusion on the latter point, though he cites Major Playfair to be an example. However, on the Freemasonry question he does tend to make dubious assumptions regarding the conspiracy that led to the club's minutes from 1830–1876 being destroyed. Perhaps a stronger case could be made with reference to Playfair's later clubhouse at St. Andrews for which the foundation stone was laid 'with full Masonic honours' (Brehend and Lewis 1998; Stirk 1998). While the conjecture regarding Freemasonry should not detain us here since the evidence is negligible, a more substantiated and important aspect of the club's history is its link with British clubs, not least the Blackheath Club. For instance, copies of the Annual Minutes were sent to Blackheath and in the 1870s the clubs exchanged trophies. The London club sent out the Blackheath Club Medal and in reciprocation received a Silver Cup. In 1882 the club presented the Cashmere Cup to the Royal and Ancient as a second prize for medal competitors. To this day, the RCGC clubhouse bar is adorned with the Royal Blackheath insignia that is set alongside that of the Royal and Ancient. In doing this the RCGC has continued a tradition of association that has quite fascinating implications for the way in which sport developed in the context of globalizing imperialism.

In the origins of modern sport in India, the British clearly played a predominant role, as they had in other societies. In the history of cricket, for instance, one of the key figures was Lord Harris who energetically promoted the sport in Bombay during his time as the city's Governor. His connections with English cricket were cemented upon his return when he was appointed President of the MCC. Bombay was also the site of India's second golf club, established in 1842, and like the RCGC was linked directly to Blackheath. The minutes at the latter record the members in London drinking to the health of the new Indian club (Stirk 1998: 185). In 1845 the Bombay Golf Club gifted a medal to the Royal and Ancient club (Brehend and Lewis 1998: 115).

Meanwhile, the establishment of British sports clubs in the capital, Calcutta, was also done in a manner that highlighted their essential Britishness. The Calcutta Football Club was first set up to play rugby, but when the enthusiasm for this sport gave way to that for soccer, the club's silver was refashioned into the Calcutta Cup. This was presented to the Rugby Football Union in 1894 and is still played for annually between the Scotland and England national rugby union teams.

This continuity with 'home' implies a particular attitude towards life in India, a type of diasporic attitude that held 'home' to be central and of ultimate importance and that privileged cultural forms from Britain. Life in India was assumed to be temporary and therefore it made sense to transplant Britishness into the colony for the benefits of this transient community who were, after all, intent upon returning 'home' at some point. Sports clubs then are best understood as British entities that just happened to have been on Indian soil. However, these clubs were about more than just sport, as they fitted in with a culture of socialising within carefully-controlled groups that enhanced the closeted, closed sense of British life in India. The social function of the club at this time, whether it was for sport or for more indolent forms of leisure, centred upon members' desire for physical and social distance from the locals and other perceived inferiors. W. O. Horne, a resident Anglo-Indian wrote the following just before the First World War:

> The life and work of the majority of the members required them daily, and in an increasing degree to mix with their Indian fellow-subjects, not only in work or business, but also socially from Government House downwards, and it was surely not asking too much that a man might have, after his day's work, a place where he could for an hour or two take his ease in the society of men of his own race, and those whose habits and customs were the same as his own.
>
> (Horne 1928, cited in Collingham, 2001: 192–3)

The social historian E. M. Collingham has reflected upon this culture by arguing that the club 'provided a venue where specific groups of Anglo-Indians could relax together, stretch out in a ... chair, cement social ties, play sports together, swap gossip or talk 'shop''. As such it was 'the most important site which daily reinforced collective identity' (162). Perhaps unsurprizingly then clubs such as the RCGC remained determinedly exclusive on racial lines: Indians were banned from membership until the time of Independence.

In the context of colonial sport, golf is therefore of a different social nature to games like football and cricket, which at times were used as pedagogical initiatives by missionaries and teachers who wished to use modern sports as means of moral training. The former was a site for constructing and emphasizing racial distinction, not an opportunity for 'cultural bonding' or for the diffusion of imperialist values throughout Indian society.[2] In this sense, the history of golf in India is radically different from that of cricket, hockey and football, which had been taught to Indians in educational settings, thus laying the foundations for the creation of Indian clubs. Therefore it is important to distinguish between forms of sporting culture in British India. The explicitly pedagogical sits at one end of the spectrum and is exemplified by the missionaries in rural India who promoted their 'muscular Christianity' through a range of sports but did not allow separate 'racial' teams. At the other end is the RCGC with its regulated and absolute exclusiveness. In the more ambivalent middle position are football, hockey and cricket clubs that were demarcated by community but which nevertheless competed with one other.

Turning specifically to the history of the RCGC, much of the background information has been laid out in Surita Pearson's history of the RCGC that was written to commemorate its 150th anniversary in 1979. Pearson was a member of the club at the time and has drawn from the committee's minutes to present a detailed and comprehensive but rather sanitized account of the club's development. There is much admirable information on the cost of membership and buying land, the shifting of the club from Dum Dum to the Maidan and back before the move to the southern suburb of Tollygunge, on the cost of equipment and the rise in membership. Perhaps more relevant for a study of the social aspects of this club are the indications of the 'clubby' and quite elitist atmosphere. For instance, the annual dinner in 1881 was held for 25 members at the prestigious Bengal Club, on which occasion the 'champagne was perfect and well iced' (Pearson 1979: 13). The following year a 'sumptuous dinner' was organised at the club for 40 members and another meal hosted by the Hotel de Paris in the city. With this conviviality came a higher level of organization and formalization. A new pavilion was erected on the Maidan in the late 1880s and women were permitted to play in the mornings. They were eventually granted the privilege of a club and a competition of their own in 1892. By this stage membership had risen to 420 and the annual dinner was being held at the Great Eastern Hotel. At this time it was proposed as host of the first Amateur Golf Championship of India (Pearson 1979: 20). The club had its first patron, the Viceroy Lord Lansdowne, whose immediate duty it was to present the Lansdowne Gold Medal, which is still one of the club's most coveted trophies. As the club's membership flourished even further, reaching 729 in 1893, it was evidently becoming one of the fashionable places to be and golf one of the fashionable sports to play. A rival emerged in the city, the Tollygunge Golf club, and it too has remained a part of the city's social fabric until the present day though it developed into a country club with a broader appeal. By the late nineteenth century the city therefore had two golf clubs with over 150 acres of land set aside for the exclusive use of just a few hundred people. In a city of almost one million inhabitants, the elitism of the land-sport relationship had become clear.

The RCGC was flourishing in all its racially elitist glory just as the politics of Bengal were reaching a crisis point. Opposition to the Vernacular Press Act of 1878 and the Ilbert Bill of 1883 had polarized the communities to the greatest extent since the 1857 Mutiny and had resulted in the formation of political bodies to represent Indian interests such as the Indian National Congress of 1885. Political tensions were heightened by economic problems in the 1890s and by the British measures to control plague in Bengal. Anglo-Indians became more introspective in their lifestyles and distanced from Indians who came to be viewed not only as a potential source of riot and revolt, but of degeneration and disease too. Moreover, the rise in educational opportunities for Indians had 'ideological and political implications and repercussions which were of almost immeasurable consequence in the making of modern India' (Brown 1994: 80). Many of the beneficiaries of this education used their talents to promote Indian culture in the face of the *Raj*, and included such Bengalis as Ram Mohun Roy, Swami Vivekananda and Rabindranath Tagore. The atmosphere in Calcutta was growing increasingly tense and divided and no doubt partly explains the attraction to the British there of the enclosed and cosseted world of such clubs as the RCGC. There was also the important consideration of prestige, as 'the British were convinced that a governing group could retain its *izzat* (prestige) only by maintaining a certain distance from the colonized' (Cook 1996: 131). Golf provided for this through its high costs of membership, the sacrosanct nature of its course and the essentially conservative symbolism of both its corporal practices and clubhouse politics. Embedded within the culture and the practice of the sport lay certain features that explain its popularity among the colonial elites of late 19th century Calcutta.

It would be misleading only to explain the club's rise with reference to the localized political conditions of Anglo-Indians in Bengal. The worldwide popularity of golf was having a definite impact upon Asia as a whole. For instance, the first club established in Ceylon was built in 1879 in Colombo, while in Singapore clubs were being developed from 1891 onwards and from 1889 there were clubs in Hong Kong. By 1912 there were 39 clubs in India and seven in the Straights Settlements (Stirk 1998: 186–8). The sport was growing across Africa as well with clubs being formed in Cape Town (1885), Johannesburg (1896), Durban (1892), Rhodesia (1898), Bulawayo (1893), Nairobi (1896) and by 1912 there were numerous clubs across West Africa.

Similar trends were to be found in Australia where British settlers established clubs in Melbourne (1847), Sydney (1893) and Adelaide (1892). The sport was also flourishing in Europe, the first club being established in France in 1856 by British players, which they christened the Pau Club. British players in France also formed a later club this time in Biarritz in 1888. Other ex-patriates formed a club in the same year at Antwerp in Belgium and in 1891 at Bad Homburg in Germany. Italy had to wait until the early twentieth century, as in 1903 a club was founded in Rome and this was quickly followed by another in 1907 on the shores of Lake Como. Further south their influence was to be found in the forming of clubs in Gibraltar, Malta and Egypt. In Canada the first club was formed in 1873, in Argentina it was 1900 and in Japan 1903. Finally, there is much evidence of golf being played in the USA so that by the end of the 19th century new clubs were 'springing up all over the States' (Stirk 1998: 181).

As has been well documented elsewhere this was a time when the British influence on world sport was predominant. The games that had been initially formalized at home were spread through trade and empire. By creating rules and governing bodies for international sport the British had facilitated competition between nations and thus set in motion the standardization of sport cultures. Therefore the progress of the clubs in India should be set in the context of the global popularity of golf and the process of developing an international standard of rules and conditions. The sport's major competitions such as the Open Championship (established in 1860) and the Amateur Championship (established in 1886) were fast becoming popular spectator events reported in the media, as were smaller tournaments and exhibition matches. Great players like Allan Robertson, Tom Morris Snr, William Park Snr, and Tom Morris Jr, were famed for their exploits in these events. Therefore the RCGC served the twin purposes of enhancing distinction in the context of local colonial politics but also of promoting a pastime that was quickly becoming one of the most popular sports in the world.

By the early 20th century the RCGC was fast becoming a respected feature of Calcutta life. In 1903 moves were first made to build a course in the southern suburb of Tollygunge, an area wealthy Europeans had begun to prefer for their residences, and that was already home to the Tollygunge Club (both clubs remain in the same place to this day.) It took four years to negotiate a deal with three landowners, Prince Bhuktyar Shah, Prince Gholam Mohammed and Baboo Hari Charan Bose. The total cost was Rs 75000 which included compensation for 'trees, huts, crops, etc'. With Rs 25000 in cash the Club funded this move through a debenture issue and rises in both the annual subscription and the entrance fees (Pearson 1979: 26–7). While the negotiations appear to have been viewed as irksome at the time by the Committee, the Club had been forced to move by the *Raj* government which had appropriated part of the Maidan course for the Victoria Memorial. However, by the time the new course opened in November 1910 there was a 'tremendous surge in interest' and a 'meteoric rise in the membership roll' to just over 700. For the first time, there was a waiting list and anxiety about overuse of the facilities (*Ibid*: 29). This led to a view that the Club required two full-length eighteen-hole courses despite the fact that the Tollygunge Club was offering another opportunity for play on an eighteen-hole course nearby.

Consolidation: 1912–1946

Not long after the main course in Tollygunge was opened the Maidan Course was temporarily closed altogether in preparation for the visit of King George V and Queen Mary. In commemoration of this visit, and after an application was made through the Viceroy and the Secretary of State, the Club was granted a Royal Charter in November 1912 and thus became the Royal Calcutta Golf Club. The political backdrop to this new status was the announcement in 1911 by the visiting King that the capital of British India was to be shifted away from Calcutta to Delhi. The decision to relocate the capital was a retreat from Bengal in the face of nationalist pressure and can be seen partly as a punishment and partly as an admission of defeat. It was a turning point for Calcutta as it lost its political and economic prominence to Delhi. It was also a turning point for nationalists who realised that pressure on the British could have results and they were soon demanding equality of political representation. Despite all this, however, the white colonial golfers were pleased with their new course, the sport was highly popular and the 'Royal' title was accepted with a minimum of fuss, something that Surita Pearson found 'difficult to reconcile' with the 'certain pride' felt to this day by the Club's members that it still has the Royal Charter (31).

For several years, the Club's reputation continued to be enhanced though such events as hosting the Amateur Championship for the first time in 1915 and again in 1919 after the competition had been suspended during the War. Surita Pearson's historical account includes a number of photographs from this period, one of the most striking images being that of a group of white players at the 10th hole bar. Eight of them are taking refreshments in the shade while their Indian caddies stand to the left side, without a drink and with hands on hips, awaiting their next instructions. Evidently this is a classical colonial relationship: that of the master and slave. In her review of how Ashis Nandy and Jean Paul Sartre draw from Hegel's notion of this relationship, Leela Gandhi writes 'the master and slave are, initially, locked in a compulsive struggle-unto-death. This goes on until the weak-willed slave, preferring life to liberty, accepts his subjection to the victorious master' (1999: 17). In this representation of golfers and caddies, the Indians are consigned to the role of slave. When it is also recalled that the land for this sport was bought from Indians using the economic power of the 'West' and was then cordoned off for the exclusive use of the 'Westerners' the dichotomous opposites of colonizer-colonized appear to have been exploited and reinforced through the sport of golf. While the representational nature of this example reminds us of Benedict Anderson's (1991) insistence on the textual underpinnings of nation-ness and imagined communities, there is an empirical reality to the RCGC's inequality that is spatial, physical, economic and social. It emerges from issues relating to how to play, where to play, whom to play with, how a social institution should be built around a sport and how the locals should be employed within the club. However, and perhaps inevitably, there are factors that complicate this picture of colonial golfing society. The first is the internal differentiation of the 'colonizer' social group. Working-class men of European origin were excluded and women had only partial inclusion. The second factor is that members were subjected to the disciplines imposed by the global culture of golf, namely the rules of play and the rules of etiquette. Thus the dichotomy of colonizer-colonized is challenged by realisation that not only is the coloniser group fragmented but that it is self-regulating as well as other-regulating.

A further challenge to this classical dichotomy relates to the varied ways in which local Indian people responded to the white-only RCGC. Two types of response shall be considered that not only disrupt the master-slave dichotomy of the colonial period but also reveal something fascinating about the postcolonial negotiations with the institutions of colonial power. The first is that of local working-class people who refused to be subjected and trespassed on the course, violating the land rights of the club and the sanctified nature of the course as 'sacred space'. They thus challenged Frantz Fanon and Mahatma Gandhi's recognition that 'the slave's hypnotised gaze upon the master condemned this figure to a derivate existence' (Gandhi 1999: 21). The second is of the middle class Indians who took over the RCGC after 1947 who left in place and indeed revered much of the tradition of the club in spite of its previous exclusionary policies. Their type of mimicry seems to resonate with Homi Bhabha's view of those 'almost the same, *but not quite*' (1994: 86), and yet it departs from his other notions of sly civility that use the language of colonialism to subvert colonial power through the 'logic of inappropriate appropriation' (Gandhi 1999: 150). They also challenge the anti-colonial assumptions of Indian nationalism being radicalized and in effect anti-British. Instead they typify an almost collaborative passivity towards colonialism and nationalism that Mahatma Gandhi criticised in his claims that 'we brought the English and we keep them. Why do you forget that our adoption of their civilization makes their presence in India at all possible?' (Gandhi 1938: 66), and 'we want English rule without the Englishman. You want the tiger's nature but not the tiger' (30). Yet, of course, what makes the RCGC curiously complex is that this appropriation occurred after the British had left and yet it was desired while the British were still in power. Clearly, these processes highlight the complexities around de-colonization and the range of competing views in Indian society on colonialism and it aftermath.

During the inter-war period when nationalist agitation demanded de-colonization, the club remained resolutely British. It played host to a number of archetypal athletic former public school boys like George Forrestor of Rugby School and Oxford University. Forrestor had captained university teams in cricket, rugby, golf and athletics while his wife was a distinguished tennis player. Upon arrival in Calcutta in 1919, he duly joined the RCGC and became captain between 1938 and 1942 after winning the Indian Amateur Championship in 1921, 1923, 1924 and 1925 (Pearson 1979: 47). However, the records from 1912 onwards testify to the beginnings of a class problem relating to so-called 'trespassers'. These were local working class people who had no respect for the snobberies of golf and the sanctity of the fairways and their appearance meant that notices were needed 'requesting intruders not to ride over the course' (Pearson 1979: 32). Further problems with saboteurs related to the theft of golf balls that were then being sold on at half price in the city's New Market. Such problems would continue throughout the century, and as will be discussed, created quite an intriguing post-colonial legacy for India's new golfing elite. Even though membership was flourishing at 1600 in the late 1920s and the club introduced a new social membership scheme, Indians were still explicitly excluded from membership and play. There is not even any evidence that high status Indian guests were invited on an ad hoc basis, as happened at other exclusive British clubs throughout India (Collingham 2001). On the occasion of the centenary in 1929 the Britishness was further reinforced. Congratulations were received from the Queen, the Viceroy Lord Irwin, the Governor of Bengal, Sir Stanley Jackson and various golf clubs including the Royal and Ancient, the Royal Blackheath and the Royal Bombay. A letter was also received from the American amateur and co-founder of the Augusta National (now home to the US Masters tournament) Bobby Jones, then the most successful golfer in the world who also passed on his congratulations (Pearson 1979: 56–7).

Curiously, Pearson argues that the years 'leading up to the Second World War were mainly uneventful' (1979: 64). Yet in the wider political context this was a turbulent period as Gandhi was agitating for independence,

Mohammed Ali Jinnah was leading the Muslim League's demands for Muslim self-governance and the British were struggling to make constitutional reforms work in the country. If the RCGC members considered all of this to be 'uneventful' then they clearly lived in a closeted world of fairways, greens, handicaps and medal competitions. The 1937 celebrations at the club that took place in honour of King George VI's coronation, and the greetings sent off to Buckingham Palace by its members, would certainly have acted as important rituals of self-reassurance for the British golfers. Later in 1937, the American professionals Joe Kirkwood and Walter Hagen played some exhibition games at the RCGC. This no doubt raised the profile of golf in India and it is interesting to speculate about the impact of these visits on Indians. It has often been claimed that colonised peoples took up sports like cricket and football to emulate their colonial masters and perhaps to beat them at their own game. However, the arrival of the American professionals provided a window on to a sporting culture beyond that created by the British in Calcutta, where there were exchanges on a global scale and where such entities as 'professionals' suggested alternatives to the British cult of the amateur.

Postcolonial Legacies

Pearson's sanitized history gives little impression of the attitude of India's aspiring golfers. However, he does amply convey the resistance to change on the part of RCGC's membership. It was after WWII and, oddly, precisely one year before independence was gained that the first Indian member of the RCGC was confirmed on 15 August 1946. By this time membership had fallen dramatically to under 1200 after British personnel had left for the War or because of the social crisis that had gripped India. While there is no evidence of how I. S. Malik came to apply for membership, Pearson does recount how several committee members 'black-balled' his application and so were over-ruled by the establishment of a new Balloting Committee. Soon there were several Indian members and Malik was joined by M. K. Powvala, C. Mukherjee, C. Sen, A. V. Mullick, K. K. Mitra and others. This was a quiet revolution and a very ambivalent one as it was in fact the start of a smooth transfer of ownership at the club. The transfer was smooth perhaps because it was so drawn out: it was not until 1963 that the first Indian captain was elected (contrast this with the Calcutta Rowing Club which did not admit Indian members until 1967).

The new establishment was to face fresh challenges that emerged from the politics of de-colonisation and independence. The 1947 partition of Bengal created refugee immigration from East Pakistan into Calcutta and these itinerant newcomers quickly populated the open lands of Tollygunge. As Pearson explains:

> Hitherto situated in a pleasant suburb of the city with the only the distant tinkle of a tramcar bell to remind members that the metropolis was extending ever outwards the Club, once you were within its boundaries, was a real haven of peace and quiet. Suddenly all this was shattered by the arrival of hundreds of refugees fleeing from the erstwhile districts of East Bengal consequent upon the partition of the country and the creation of Pakistan.

Evidently, this was the origins of an on-going problem for the RCGC:

> Large numbers settled down around the perimeter of the courses, particularly those areas bounding the southern and eastern extremities ... A weird assortment of shanties, mud huts and some brick bungalows sprang up as the weeks went by, and what more convenient place for recreation and exercise than the carefully manicured fairways of the Club. Eventually the problem began to assume serious proportions for these were, understandably, not only frustrated but somewhat angry people who had been displaced from their ancestral homes virtually overnight ... the Committee was finally compelled to surround the courses with a wall but, even then, breeches were knocked in this expensive structure and trespassing continued (1979: 71).

This issue was not helped by the fact that two rights of way traverse the course. The sporting space had come to symbolize post-partition conflict between communities in Calcutta. The indigenous West Bengalis looked down on these East Bengali refugees and, in turn, the latter considered the former to be snobbish and condescending. While it may have been diluted by generations of inter-mingling, this tension still persists in Calcutta, and is most saliently expressed through the passionate football rivalry between the Mohun Bagan and East Bengal clubs.

There is more to the history of this conflict than just one of immigration and belonging. The RCGC members remain to this day very proud of the club's association with the Raj, which they perceive as bestowing a higher form of prestige and status upon the club.[3] The clubhouse restaurant is still named the Mountbatten Room and the hallway is still adorned by large-scale portraits of Prince Philip and Queen Elizabeth. Throughout the 1950s and 1960s the committee took every opportunity to associate itself with the British Royal Family and thus to reinforce the status it had inherited from the British colonialists. Expressions of sympathy were sent to Buckingham Palace when King George V and then his son King George VI died and matches were suspended as a sign of mourning. The coronation of Elizabeth II was celebrated and a telegram is sent every year on the occasion of her birthday. However the status of the club in the eyes of the Royal Family had clearly declined: when the Queen and Prince Philip visited Calcutta in February 1961 they did not find the time to pay a visit (Pearson 1979: 86). The historical irony of the Royal Charter is that the British committee of 1912 do not appear to have celebrated it. Yet, in the post-colonial period the Indian members of the club are fiercely proud of its historical symbolism. Many members were surprized when the Royal Hong Kong Club dropped the Royal after the 1997 handover to China. For them the RCGC was the most prestigious golf club because of the term Royal (though other Indian clubs were also allowed this term) and its position as the first club outside Britain. Many members remain staunchly backward-looking and in the 1990s still readily related their opinion that the worse thing to happen to India was that the British left. One member explained that the British instilled a sense of discipline through many methods including golf and that this had now been lost in Indian culture. They continue to describe the RCGC as 'an English club' and have often argued about how to best preserve this sense of Englishness by, for instance, allowing dogs into the clubhouse.

Meanwhile, in 1955 a concrete wall 5000 yards long had to be built to exclude those people who did not aver to the *Raj*-inspired prestige and who continued to trample on the fairways, swim in the 'tanks' (ponds) and play cricket on the greens. These working-class people derogatorily referred to the RCGC members as '*desi sahibs*' or 'native white men'. Localised conflict continues and local residents continue to knock holes in the walls and 'trespass' right up to the present day.[4] The wall that symbolizes the class divisions in Tollygunge has been constantly enlarged, rebuilt in places and reinforced with barbed wire. The committee regularly complain to the police but the perception is that they do little to help. Indeed, the Government has reclaimed land for military use to the extent that there is only one course now.

While members speak fondly of making their once in a lifetime 'pilgrimage' to St Andrews, it is not clear that even this ritual will preserve their status in the world of Indian golf. The RCGC has new rivals such as the recently-built courses in Delhi whose exclusive members are attracted by highly modern facilities and courses designed by former professional players like Jack Nicklaus. These are now the preferred locations for national and international competitions. Golf is India's fastest growing sport and many young players are developing into world-class performers. In other words the RCGC is characterized by traditionalism and conservatism and beset by parochial conflicts which are underpinned by ideologies and positions relating to post-colonialism and class at a time when the game in India is attracting the country's young, entrepreneurial elites.

Conclusion

By way of final remarks the RCGC throws up a host of questions regarding colonial sports, post-colonial responses and the inheritance of cultural practices. It is significant that Indians so heartily accepted the role of the golf club in modern society as one of exclusion and chauvinism despite the fact that they had themselves been the victims of exclusion prior to 1946. It seems strange that the members have so much manifest respect for the agents of their exclusion. But perhaps again the point is to look beyond the local setting of colonial politics to the broader culture of golf. It is a sport that requires land and requires costly equipment and so has an element of exclusivity inherent in its very structure. If Indians emulated anything it is perhaps that structure as much as the specific idiosyncrasies of the British colonizers. If mimicry is about appearing to observe the 'political and semantic imperatives of colonial discourse' while 'systematically misrepresenting the foundational assumptions of this discourse' (Gandhi 1999: 50) then the RCGC case cannot be read as mimicry in any straightforward way. There is nothing in its history to suggest anti-colonialism, nothing to suggest any profound upheaval when Indians became members, just a set of questions about why the patterns of exclusion were so easily inherited and repeated by (some) Indians. Finally for those who, in Playfair's words, viewed golfers as having "mair siller than sense", the question of who is in charge of the RCGC, whether British or Indian, has been of little significance. And that shows once more that the diversions of class and taste complicate the history of colonialism, resistance, post-colonialism and globalization.

7

WARRIOR GODDESS VERSUS BIPEDAL COW: SPORT, SPACE, PERFORMANCE AND PLANNING IN AN INDIAN CITY

James Heitzman and Smriti Srinivas

Introduction: Of Cities and Spectacles

David Harvey (1985a; 1985b) describes a concentration of artifacts of consumption such as entertainment complexes, convention centers, gentrified neighborhoods or amusement parks as one type of development strategy available to cities under the conditions of late capitalism. Other authors, describing the city as a 'theme park' in the late twentieth century, have critiqued the end of public space and the increasing surveillance of citizens in American cities such as Los Angeles, New York, or Minneapolis (Sorkin 1992). More recently, by analyzing gentrification programs, beauty contests and sports events in Atlanta (Ruthesier 1996), Istanbul (Keyder 1999) and Beijing (Brownell 2001) scholars have theorized the relationship between cities and spectacles under conditions of globalization and liberalization. By contrast Orsi (1999) and Srinivas (2001) describe the continuing relevance of religious maps, architectural complexes and sacred processions for presenting alternative topographies and emotional geographies of the city in relation to suburbanization, capital accumulation and diasporic or regional labor movements. This article will attempt to contribute to this debate about cities and spectacles by tracing the embeddedness of specific body cultures,[1] wrestling and martial arts disciplines of considerable antiquity and 'sportized' athletics, within the larger space of 'urban performative genres'. The article suggests that we need to consider an entire range of performances, ranging from festivals and sacred processions to political rallies, sports events and beauty contests, in order to understand the relationship between urban planning, environmental history, and politico-symbolic contests over public space.

The concept of the 'sportization' of athletics, as developed by Bale (1994) and Eichberg (1998), refers to the transformation of activities of 'disport' or the discipline of physique into 'landscapes of achievement' through rule-based competition, the separation of players from spectators, regimentation, bureaucratization, professionalization and the proliferation of statistical knowledge alongside media involvement. They see sports as a colonizing complex that transforms landscapes into 'homotopian' sportscapes with manifold results for social and physical environments, ranging from the impact of stadiums on real estate prices to the alteration of forests by golf courses. From a political perspective Loy and others (1978: 287) noted that 'the relationship between sport and politics is one of the oldest and most pervading examples of institutional interaction', dating back at least to the ancient Greek Olympic Games. Much of the work in this field has focused on the more obvious interventions of the state within sporting events, ranging from the 'bread and circuses' phenomenon of the Roman amphitheater to the 1936 Olympics in Nazi Germany. In addition to studies of the state, recent commentary has focused on the political conflicts of sports organizations per se, intersecting with urban studies most spectacularly in the exposés of corruption within the International Olympic Committee engineered by city coalitions eager to host the games. The overarching framework for much of this scholarship has concentrated on rationalized sports as one of the 'archetypes of modernity', characterized by placelessness and technology.

In this article we will see the simultaneous projection of several different models of the city, expressed in the public sphere through distinct modes of ritual or spectacle. The older model, while obviously battered and increasingly disconnected from its original mode of production, actually stands as the largest civic ritual in the city, still gathering momentum and completely 'non-thematized.' The more recent model, while manifesting hegemonic tendencies, is constantly challenged by alternative visions of political mobilization and demonstrates limited ability to attract the allegiance of wide sections of the populace. The archaic Karaga festival expresses through its performance an implicit critique of developmental planning in the nation state which in turn confronts a variety of challenges from regional states, environmentalists and the poor. We would like to suggest that Bangalore, or the South Asian city more generally, contributes to this proliferation of genres because of the 'contemporaneity' (Augé 1999) of times past and times present, spaces near and far. What we intend is a serious exploration of such cities as theoretical objects; our lens is the relationship of body culture to public space.

We first focus on the historical development of a tripartite urban model in Bangalore from the sixteenth century onwards and the role played by the warrior/gardener caste of the Tigalas in this complex. We examine the Karaga, the annual civic festival of Bangalore, its relationship to the Tigalas and their body culture through the regimen of wrestling, and the changing parameters of public space in the late twentieth-century city. Contemporaneous with the Karaga performance and its body culture today is another type of performative and body culture, exemplified by the National Games held in Bangalore in 1997, which is discussed in subsequent sections. We follow the contests over public space that emerged in connection with the National Games and its consequences. The conclusion suggests that we need to analyze the National Games alongside the Karaga festival, juxtaposing their respective body cultures and implications for public space, rather than presenting them as disconnected worldviews and practices in the city.

In the study that follows, students of modernity or of body culture and public space, will find much that is familiar. We would caution at the outset, however, that this article is not a case-study of 'modernity' replacing 'tradition' or an example of underdevelopment, as if the phenomena described were but moments in a teleological progression toward a more perfected style of body culture and urban place. Rather, we want to articulate the two performance and city-views so as to insist on the joint processes at play as well as the representational fractures. Thus, for instance, while both the Karaga festival and the National Games are intimately linked to lakes as public spaces in Bangalore, the two 'mascots' of the events, a potent, martial goddess and an innocuous, androgynous cow, have different implications for the relationship between gender, sexuality and body cultures.

The Emergence of the Tripartite Urban Complex[2]

Bangalore originated in the activities of a local warlord, Kempe Gowda I (ca. 1510–1570), who established an oval-shaped mud-brick wall fronted by a thorn-filled moat to enclose and protect a series of bazaars and habitation areas associated later with different occupations (e.g. Balepete, the bangle bazaar or Akkipete, the rice bazaar). The choice of the location for the commercial centers (*pete*) and fort (*kote*) rested on the availability of water through an array of artificial lakes or tanks (*kere*) that Kempe Gowda constructed and augmented and which included the Sampangi and Dharmambudi tanks that bounded the city on two sides. The combination of forests and tanks provided an excellent defensive perimeter for the original fort as well as water resources for drinking and the cultivation of gardens, for which the city eventually became famous (see Figure 1).

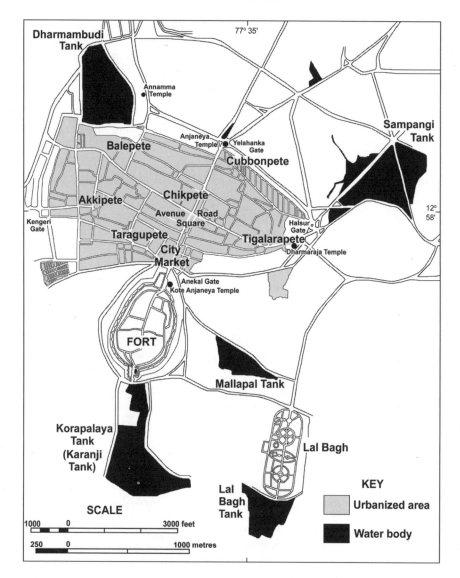

Figure 1. The archaic tripartite urban complex of Bangalore comprising of fort, commercial center and its fortification, and water bodies. (Credit: James Heitzman).

By the seventeenth century Bangalore was part of the expanding kingdom of the Odeyar (or Wodeyar) kings from Mysore and later came under the authority of their general Haider Ali, after he assumed formal control of the kingdom in 1766. He embellished the city by laying out the Persian-style Lal Bagh (the 'Red Garden') and its tank southeast of the fort and completely

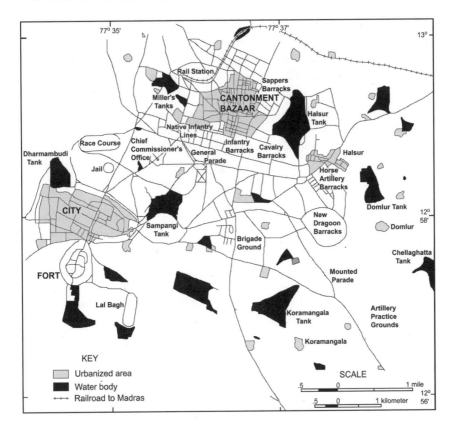

Figure 2. The dual urban pattern of the old City and the Cantonment in the late 19th century. (Credit: James Heitzman).

rebuilding in stone the fort south of the commercial centre. His military adventures, and those of his son Tippu Sultan, led to the formation of an opposing coalition by the expansive British East India Company based in Madras (Chennai). This overran Bangalore in 1792 and then again in 1799 when Tippu Sultan died fighting. Shortly after, the East India Company reinstalled the Odeyar kings and in 1807 the Mysore kingdom signed a treaty that allowed the British to maintain a military Cantonment northeast of the Old City beyond the Sampangi Tank. This established in the city the familiar dual pattern of urbanization under colonialism. The forested area between the Old City and the Cantonment became Cubbon Park, which was bordered by a variety of public buildings. A connecting road bisected the Sampangi Tank by 1870 (see Figure 2) and was a harbinger of the slow and steady transformation of the city's hydraulic system that has continued apace until today (Hasan 1970; Census of India 1981; Sundara Rao 1985; Kamath 1990: 41–94).

Among the military forces assembled by Haider Ali and Tippu Sultan during the eighteenth century were personnel from a number of martial communities established in the Bangalore region. These included soldiers from the community of Tigalas, who retain clear traces of their connections with martial communities in the northwestern parts of neighboring Tamil Nadu and whose ancestors may have been present in southeastern Karnataka even before the expansion of the Mysore state. The 250,000 Tigalas around Bangalore today, although members of a Backward Caste, view themselves as 'Vanhikula Kshatriyas' or warrior descendants of fiery ancestors and the goddess Draupadi. Their livelihood as military personnel did not decline dramatically with the installation of British colonial rule and their martial concerns remained entwined with gymnasiums or wrestling houses (*garadi mane*). These days they are locally famous for their skills in cultivating vegetables, fruits and flowers in garden plots. During the nineteenth century they controlled much of the land around the Sampangi Tank and other tanks in villages south and east of the Old City of Bangalore. For their horticultural activities they used water that came through canals leading from habitation areas to the tanks carrying organic waste for fertilizer. The discharge of waters from one tank overflowed into another, forming an interlocking system of reservoirs. The Tigalas' occupation as gardeners remained intimately connected with the fate of the tank-based systems that surrounded the Old City.

From the seventeenth-century onwards four female deities stood near water bodies on the boundaries of the Old City, and a quadrilateral network of festivals centred on them began to emerge. Today these goddesses still have a heterogeneous clientele drawn from different caste and religious groupings; all four are 'pox' goddesses in various forms concerned with skin diseases of several kinds. Each goddess commands her own temple and the Annamma shrine near the old Dharmambudi Tank is the closest example near the Old City. Each of these shrines continues to have a ritual jurisdiction over 'villages' in the vicinity, locales that are now part of the urban fabric of the metropolis. Every year, usually in the hot months between April and June, the goddesses have their own festivals with chariots being drawn through the city areas apportioned to them. In some cases telephone and electric cables and other constructions have made large chariots impossible but the goddesses' processional images, carried aloft by devotees, still visit 'villages' and households. These festivals are not exclusively religious configurations but reflect all kinds of transactions at household and public levels and a range of aesthetic and healing experiences. The Old City also had a quadrilateral pattern of shrines dedicated to the monkey god Anjaneya (Hanuman), who stood as the guardian of the 'gates' of the fort. This association of Anjaneya with fort gates was probably related to a pattern of organization inherited from the

Vijayanagar empire (fourteenth to sixteenth centuries) to which the founder of Bangalore owed his political allegiance. Anjaneya shrines remain in Bangalore today, several existing since the late eighteenth century and the others probably more recent replacements of older shrines. The two prominent shrines stand on the northern side of the Old City near the Yelahanka Gate and south of the Anekal Gate, northeast of the old fort. The patterns of goddess and Anjaneya shrines and associated ritual cycles are reminders of the centrality of water bodies, the structure of the Old City and fort and the complementarity between the goddess and the celibate-warrior.

The Goddess and her Wrestler-Sons

Bangalore's largest annual celebration is the Karaga festival organized by the Tigala community, and this continues to attract hundreds of thousands of people on its final days and to reflect the culture of the Old City. During festival time, city dwellers are to be found out on the streets making the rounds of temples (practically every street has a small shrine), listening to scriptural recitations, transacting business, eating at hotels or watching movies, the market areas remaining functional throughout the night. The official center of the festival is the Dharmaraja Temple, an unimposing structure dating to about 1800 in the southeastern corner of the Old City, a neighborhood known as Tigalarapete or Tigalarapet. The festival revolves around the manifestation of the cosmic female power (*shakti*) in the Sampangi Tank in Chaitra, the first month of the Hindu calendar (late March/early April). The *shakti* is Draupadi, the polyandrous wife of the five Pandava brothers, heroes of the pan-Indian epic the *Mahabharata*. In consequence of a promise made by Draupadi to this community of gardeners she manifests herself every year on the thirteenth day of the month in the form of an elaborately decorated red icon called the Karaga which must carried by a priest from the community at his waist (see Figure 3). On the fifteenth day of the month the priest carries the Karaga on his head wearing a woman's wedding clothes with bangles and flowers. At the end of the festival the priest as Draupadi weds Arjuna, the bowman-hero of the Pandava brothers. Protecting the priest is a ring of 'hero-sons' (*virakumara*) carrying sharp swords and wearing a distinct attire of white pants, white turbans with gold work on the fringes, and red and white checked neck-cloths (see Figure 4).[3]

Most families of the Tigala community send male members to the performance as hero-sons, who take vows to perform the service of guarding the deity. During the period of their vows they must remain celibate and are separated from their women-folk, especially their wives. They are required to eat only one meal a day which is usually uncooked food or food cooked in a special pot. They do not consume meat or alcohol during this period, although

Figure 3. The Tigala priest wearing a floral headdress of jasmine flowers carrying the Karaga in his left hand and holding a dagger in his right hand. (Credit: Smriti Srinivas).

ordinarily this caste does consume both. Purity is also maintained by not visiting a house where a marriage or a death has occurred or where there is a menstruating woman. A sword and a wrist-band symbolize their allegiance to the goddess and their participation in the festival. Every family that supplies a hero-son maintains a sword in their possession, while the wristband is regarded as a sacred thread of celibacy that binds the hero-son to the goddess and represents the strict demands made on his sexuality during the performance. The hero-sons train regularly in wrestling houses where the main deity is Anjaneya, who also serves as one of the guardian deities at the Dharmaraja Temple.

Figure 4. The hero-sons perform swordplay for the goddess Draupadi. (Credit: Smriti Srinivas).

Indian-style wrestling is a form of martial arts tradition that dates back at least to the period of the *Mahabharata* (probably about the beginning of first millennium BCE). In north India wrestling may have absorbed some elements introduced from the ancient Hellenistic world and from the form of wrestling brought to the sub-continent by Mughal armies in the sixteenth century. In south Indian versions of the *Mahabharata* there are also many descriptions of wrestling and in practice the Pandava brother Bhima, described as a great wrestler, remains perhaps the favorite personage revered at the Dharmaraja temple. The South Indian ruler Pallava Narasimhavarman I (630–668) had the title of 'Mahamalla' or 'the great wrestler' and there appears to be a continuous history of wrestling up to the time of the founding of Bangalore in the sixteenth century. There are descriptions, for instance, of wrestling at the court of the Vijayanagar emperor Krishnadevaraya (1509–1529) who ruled over much of South India. One historian has suggested that duels and contests were very common in the court of the emperor and lands were granted tax-free for running gymnasiums (Mahalingam 1975: 68–70). Northern and southern types of Indian wrestling resemble European free-style wrestling. However, there is a difference between the two systems in the theory of the body. Central to Indian wrestling is the belief that sexual energy and celibacy are linked and that strength is a function of structuring sexual energy. The variety of exercises that are part of the wrestler's daily regimen include jack-knifes and knee-bends which are linked to the production and control of semen. The latter is believed to be important for strength although it has to be kept in balance and should not be in excess (Alter 1992; 1995). Medical traditions like Ayurveda and Siddha, popular in South India, regard semen as a transmutation of blood and processes that increase the ingestion of food and the circulation of blood also lead to the production of semen. The pro-cesses for a wrestler include the correct diet (vegetables are important here, especially leafy ones), vigorous exercise through sparring and weight lifting and breathing during exercise. The wrestler becomes virile by channeling his sexuality and gains strength through his self-control (Alter 1992; 1995). The wrestlers revere Anjaneya because he was a great devotee; as he was unmar-ried and celibate he was able to contain all of his 'strength'.

The Karaga priest trains regularly in the wrestling house since the physical qualities built up there allow him to perform the strenuous activities that occur during the festival period when he must consume a meager diet of uncooked and vegetarian foods, observe strict celibacy, walk for eight to ten hours daily and carry the fifteen or twenty kilogram icon on his head without touching it once with his hands. The hero-sons must also train for they per-form equally strenuous activities during the rituals and both the priest and most of the hero-sons go without sleep for nine days. Strength and celibacy are interconnected during the performance and continue to exert a profound effect on the individual's everyday life. For the Tigala community the wrestling house is an important focus and boys and girls train there during childhood. Trained young girls perform acrobatics during the Karaga perfor-mance as part of a public display but after a girl child menstruates she is with-drawn from the wrestling house and adult women are prohibited from entering the premises. For the men and boys the wrestling-house continues to be a site for an everyday regime of the body as well as preparation for the Karaga performance. The wrestling house is a large room with traditional martial arts instruments (sticks, maces, stone weights and clubs) and a floor that is covered by red earth. There is usually a mirror leaning on one wall and a picture of Anjaneya. There are three wrestling-houses belonging to the community in the Old City and each is named after a famous wrestler or teacher. Each is visited during the Karaga performance by the priest and his troupe.[4] During the festival a ritual occurs at each wrestling house where the instruments are decorated and worshipped and a conical icon is made out of the red soil on which the wrestlers exercise, decorated with jasmine and ver-milion and surrounded by fruits to closely resemble the Karaga icon itself. The soft red soil, which is meant to balance 'heat' within the body of the wrestlers, covers the wrestler's body and maintains a required level of heat within it.

The circulation of fluids in the body, from food into blood and then semen, also appears in another form during the performance: as narratives concerning the female body of the goddess. The sanctum of the Dharmaraja Temple contains the central image of the Primal Goddess (*adi shakti*) surrounded by images of Draupadi and other heroes of the *Mahabharata*. The following narrative, recounted by Ramdas, who was a ritual player during the festival in 1996, illustrates the conflation of Draupadi with the Primal Goddess and other forms of the warrior goddess such as Durga:[5]

> There was a demon called Timmarasu. He was hiding behind a rock in the forest when Draupadi was passing by alone. He called out to her and made advances. The blood of the demon was such that if a drop fell on the ground a thousand prototypes were born from it. Draupadi, angered, shook the portion of her sari covering her breasts. From that … sprang the Virakumaras. They fought the battle against the demon but each drop that fell gave birth to a hundred thousand more. Finally the goddess felled him with one stroke and, before the demon's blood could reach the ground, she licked up the blood and also swallowed him whole (Srinivas 2001: 151).

The account here shows the transformation of Draupadi into a fierce warrior in the forest fighting the demon. During the course of the battle her hero-sons are born to join their primal mother in her contest. The narrative also reverses the relationship between blood and semen that is emphasized for wrestlers in the wrestling-house as Draupadi is reproductive from her own blood just as the demon reproduces from his own. Draupadi finally ingests the demon and his blood-offspring by eating him up like food.

The gardeners stress the roles of women as wives, mothers or unmarried and chaste daughters in everyday life, so that women have no roles to play in the street performance except as a supporting cast. Yet this control of women's bodies is linked to the power that is believed to inhere in their heat, blood and sexuality. The maintenance of celibacy for men during the performance is fragile, dependent on women's acquiescence, and in a way draws from their self-control. While this conceptual framework seems to circumscribe women during the performance, Draupadi's role is not constructed in a similar way. In fact, she has to go through several stages before she can be contained within it. From the beginning of the Karaga performance until the last day, Draupadi stands alone in her unmarried and singular state, bloodthirsty, martial and reproductive yet non-genital. The crowning symbols of her power are flowers of jasmine (white and considered to be 'hot like fire') that decorate the Karaga icon as well as the hair of the priest. Only the 'marriage' on the last day of the festivities returns the goddess to a state where this heat can be held in check, although paradoxically, this heat is channeled through the body of a man who has become the medium of the goddess. The heating of the goddess and her embodiment in the priest reveal most fully the ambiguities involved in the construction of sexuality in wrestling as everyday regimen and in the more intense situations of the festival.

The valorized celibacy and martial representations of the hero-sons are set in a contemporary context where the gardeners have experienced increasing powerlessness through loss of land in the city and through the extinction of the tanks that fed their gardens.[6] Soon after 1949, when a single Bangalore City Corporation came into existence through the amalgamation of the Old City and the Cantonment, the Sri Kanteerava stadium was constructed on the site of what had been the Sampangi Tank south of the main road that had originally bisected it. The bed of the old tank subsequently dried up except for a small, quadrilateral pool maintained in the old southwest corner for the use of the Tigalas during the festival. The current manifestation of the Karaga icon in a hall near this pool (See Figure 5) is but a distant memory of the large lake and the surrounding garden lands that characterized the environment of Bangalore two hundred years earlier.

The radical transformation of Sampangi Tank is only one example of a general tendency that occurred while the population of Bangalore city

Figure 5. The Karaga hall, key site of the performance, in front of the Sri Kanteerava stadium complex in the bed of Sampangi tank. (Credit: Smriti Srinivas).

increased from 228,000 persons in 1901 to 4.3 million in 2001and the metropolitan region increased to 5.6 million persons within 1279 square kilometers. An Expert Committee on Tanks released a report in 1987 that referred to 390 tanks within the metropolitan region. Of these 127 fell within the limits of the Bangalore conurbation with 46 dry and only 81 'live' tanks. The committee documented the reasons for the 'disuse' of water bodies and the agents responsible but, despite government orders designed to halt encroachments and preserve the remaining tanks, private studies indicate that the pace of destruction has continued unabated. By the mid-1990s water bodies covered only 1.89 percent of the territory within the metropolitan region and most were silted up.[7] Over 60 percent of the metropolitan residential sewage flowed into lakes together with industrial waste. During these processes the Tigala community changed from being gardeners to a petty bourgeoisie and an urban working class in the formal and informal sectors as tanks and gardens gave way to concrete after the 1950s. Fewer men attend the wrestling-house than fifty years ago and hardly any own land in the city.

During the Karaga festival the hydraulic environment of the old Bangalore based on artificial lakes achieves a weeklong 'virtual' reality through ritual action. The water bodies are recalled when the Karaga troupe travels to nine ritually marked points and performs rituals for sacred images unpacked at these locations by the priest who bathes and changes his clothes at each. Today these rituals occur within the interiors of various monasteries and temples but, before the 1950s, rites occurred at water bodies within or near the gardens belonging to the community. While one of these ritual sites was the Dharmaraja Temple itself, the troupe also visited three tanks, two large wells and a saltwater pond. Today, none of these water bodies exists as they have been filled by sewage, converted into a stadium or bus station, acquired by the city corporation or made extinct for other reasons. Because the fluids have dried up and no circulation occurs the Karaga priest has to metaphorically recreate the flow in the city in order to cool the 'hot' bodies of the hero-sons and his own. Potency through self-containment, though a dominant trope in the performance and in the ethic of the wrestlers who struggle to maintain heat from spilling over, is a deeply contested construct in this context.

The recollection of water-bodies in rituals, moreover, is not merely 'symbolic' and the festival itself is part of a process of political mobilization in the city between different Backward Caste communities. Several of these communities, also from working class or informal sector backgrounds like the Vahnikula Kshatriyas, have myths of origin that tie them in relationship of kinship to fiery ancestors like Draupadi and other martial heroes. Many of them sponsor separate festivals like the Karaga in different months in the city, have temples dedicated to Draupadi and other ancestors or participate in the

Karaga performance. Again, many erstwhile villages and towns in the periphery of Bangalore that have become part of the larger metropolitan region also celebrate Karaga festivals, which have become part of a growing network of public performances in Bangalore today. The political alliance between them has become more effective since the 1970s and has lead to their participation in the Bangalore City Corporation as a larger group calling themselves 'Tigalas' (including the sub-group that performs the Karaga festival in the month of Chaitra). While some of their claims relate to adequate representation in the legislature, as well as access to government-supported benefits, one of the most significant calls made by this alliance is for the protection of horticultural land within the city and the regime of water that supports it. For instance, one of the leaders of the Tigala community, S.M. Munivenkatappa, pointed out in the 1950s that 800 acres of land that could have been cultivated by the Tigalas of Bangalore for its growing population had been acquired for new urban extensions and planning efforts in the city. This included the Koramangala Tank, which he suggested be leased out or sold to the Tigalas for horticulture instead. He put forth a series of demands to state and central governments as well as the Planning Commission of India. More recently, rallies of Tigala groups in Bangalore and other sites focus on the displacement of these communities from older sections of the city, the loss of gardens and water-bodies due to planning and the creation of technology parks and even the suggestion that the founder of Bangalore was a Tigala. In other words, the Karaga festival and the political alliance that proceeds from it are part of contests over the direction of planning and the nature of public spaces in Bangalore today.

The National Games and the Re-definition of the Metropolis

The twentieth century witnessed the expansion of 'sportized' athletics in Bangalore in connection with national and transnational trends that stressed competition, segmentation, specialization and measurable precision. The most imposing venue for this type of body culture in Bangalore is the Cricket Stadium which is constructed on the northeastern edge of Cubbon Park and is the site of industry-supported or regional competitions and test matches featuring teams from the international circuit. One cannot over-estimate the attraction of cricket among wide sections of the population, especially the male working and middle classes, and the open spaces of the city are often full of young men playing pick-up matches. Football is the second most popular sport and has a long history in the city (Kapadia, 2001). In the Cantonment area one can engage in the ultimate expression of mechanized body culture at places like Steve's Gym, where middle-class men and women sweat on bicycle machines or lift weights. Annual award ceremonies for the most accomplished members might include appearances by champion body builders such as Mr. Karnataka. Alongside these standardized transnational activities are the originally village-based games such as *kabbadi* and *kho-kho* which have been undergoing standardization and reorganization in schools and professional bodies.

The standardization of local and transnational games is reflected in the manner in which bodies and their cultures are conceived. While many of the men and women who are players in 'sportized' activities may come from communities that still employ vocabularies of semen, blood and food, this is not reflected in the games themselves or the training procedures that lead up to them. Instead, the exercise regimens consist of sets of exercises, running, weights, etc. which are 'workouts' performed in numerical quantities, measured in terms of inputs and outputs, represented in conceptions of standardized body weights and heights for various games and skills and configured in professional relationships between trainers/coaches and athletes. While modern sport events are related to gender and some events tend to be 'male' domains rather than 'female' ones, this is a sociological rather than an ideological outcome. Unlike the body culture of the Karaga festival, where adult women are specifically excluded on cultural grounds from participating as players, sportized athletics are not explicitly tied to strictures about celibacy, menstruation or ritual practices associated with body fluids and calendrical festivals.

The Indian National Games originated in 1927 as a concept ostensibly designed to screen athletic talent in order to field teams for international events and especially for the Olympic Games. They first took place in 1970 and then in 1979 in Hyderabad. The success of the 1982 Asian Games in Delhi allowed a revival of the concept and in 1985 the National Games also took place there. By this time there were expectations that they could become a regular feature of the Indian sports scene, to be held every two years. But in 1987 when Kerala was hosting the Games there was so much political turmoil within the Indian Olympic Association that legal issues overshadowed events on the field. In 1989 Punjab was supposed to hold the Games but terrorist and police actions in that state forced cancellation. The next venue was Pune in 1993 but noncompletion of the stadiums and a major earthquake caused a delay until 1994 when they took place in Pune and Mumbai (Viswanathan 1997). As was the case with Olympic Games wherever they took place, the Indian National Games required extensive planning in order to provide housing for athletes and the construction or upgrading of infrastructure and venues to guarantee adequate facilities for events. Whenever they took place, the National Games linked the prestige of the nation state with the reorganization of space at the local level and thus exerted a perceptible effect on the local environment.

Karnataka Chief Minister Veerappa Moily of the Congress (I) lobbied during late 1993 and during early 1994 to bring the National Games to Bangalore. He paid Rs. 10 lakhs (US$32,000) to the Indian Olympic Association as a guarantee amount. Around April 1994 an announcement came down that the games would take place in Bangalore between 28 January and 7 February 1996. Preparations would include rebuilding Sri Kanteerava Stadium, the construction of an indoor stadium and the renovation of other arenas in Bangalore and Mysore together with a National Games Village to house an estimated 6000 athletes. The office of the state Sports and Youth Affairs Ministry moved into a building next to Sri Kanteerava Stadium in order to begin coordination for the events and in July 1994 there were several meetings of state government officials to decide what to do about construction issues. During these meetings there was an explicit linkage of the Games housing requirements with a proposed project for construction of multi-storied flats for Government employees at Koramangala on the southeast side of the city. The proposal was to allocate 47.6 acres of land owned by the Public Works Department (PWD) to the Karnataka Housing Board (KHB) for construction of about 5000 flats by November 1995. In return, after the Games ended in February 1996, the KHB would hand over to the PWD 968 flats for government employees and 232 for use by judicial officers. They would sell the remaining 3,800 flats to the general public. The money received from the public sales would cover construction expenses for all the flats which in effect gave the government 1200 free apartments for its personnel.

The site chosen for the National Games Village consisted of a shallow tank filled with plants that served as fodder for buffaloes that were visible all around the tank with white birds standing on their backs. The water in the tank was black with rotting vegetation and sewage that flowed into the site from a drainage canal in the north (see Figure 6). On the south side the campus of the National Dairy Development Board had already encroached on the tank on a one-acre quadrilateral campus. On the east side a series of gardens with tall, stately palm trees still remained. The Main Road between Koramangala and Viveknagar ran along the west side. Across the Main Road lay Ambedkarnagar (or Krishnanagar) one of the larger slums in the Bangalore area which consisted of a mixture of thatch huts and brick structures in various states of legality (Shiri (1999); Schenk-Sandbergen (2001: 199–203). A Christian church and a large concrete cross stood before the slum near the road. In local legend the water system in Koramangala was associated with the story of a woman whose suffering and death elevated her to the level of a goddess and she was worshipped during the twentieth century in a small shrine on the edge of a lake. The mythology of this water goddess was a

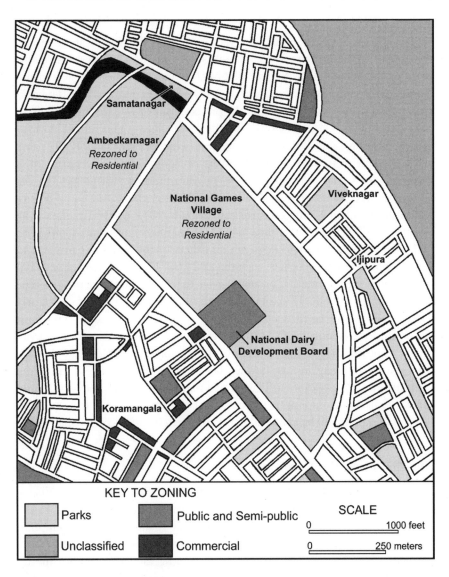

Figure 6. The National Games Village in the Comprehensive Development Plan. (Credit: James Heitzman).

feature of environmentalist arguments against further encroachments on the archaic hydraulic systems in the metropolitan region.[8]

By attempting to appropriate another water body for the largest apartment complex in the region, the state government began to run into problems connected with its own urban planning frameworks. The first issue was how to reconcile the construction of housing aimed entirely at middle and upper income groups with legislation that required the KHB to allocate a certain percentage of its housing to needy families. The solution was to devise a new label for the project as a 'Special National Games Scheme' that would not require construction of percentages of flats for low-income groups.[9] The government set up a committee to run the project, chaired by the Chief Minister, who was now H. D. Deve Gowda of the Janata Party. The central government's Housing and Urban Development Corporation (HUDCO) came under pressure from the state, the Ministry of Sports, and the Department of Housing and Urban Development to provide funding for the project. By November, HUDCO architects proposed a detailed plan for 4, 6 and 8 story buildings but planned the construction of only 2821 residential flats. The Government of Karnataka then issued a modified government order on 21 January 1995 with a revised plan that called for the KHB to hand over to the state government 600 flats, including 224 for judicial officers. The KHB would sell the remaining 2221 flats in order to pay for the entire project. The order authorized the KHB to obtain a loan from HUDCO for Rs. 270 crores (US$86 million) to construct buildings of four to seven stories. The most important legal action taken by the government during this period was an order[10] altering the zoning of the Koramangala site to 'Residential' from 'Parks and Recreation' as it was labeled in the draft of the 1995 Comprehensive Development Plan of the Bangalore Development Authority (BDA 1995). By accomplishing this change the committee could feel confident that it had satisfied all legal requirements connected with its own urban plans.

The 'Scam of the Century'

The first public reference to the project for a National Games Village occurred in October 1994. The non-government organization CIVIC-Bangalore, which lobbied regularly for increased democratic participation in planning and environmental protection,[11] heard about the September government order from a reporter who was covering the story and got the tip from a bureaucrat at KHB. By the end of December CIVIC and five non-governmental organizations had decided on an approach to the High Court to block the project and they filed a writ petition on 7 January 1995 to quash the government order authorizing the National Games Village. The writ petition, which attempted to block the activities of eight named government agencies,[12] presented three major points against the project. The equity argument stated that the project 'will benefit no one except a few well placed persons', that it was discriminatory because it 'amounts to conferring a benefit on those who are well placed and able to fend for themselves at the cost of those sections of society in respect of whom statutory authorities must take special care.' The environmental argument pointed out that the Asian Wetland Bureau was an international agency that had labeled the large Bellandur Tank to the southeast an important wetland as it was home for migratory birds and the most significant of the surviving tanks in the metropolitan area. The Koramangala site, which fed into the Bellandur Tank, should be preserved in order to protect the water body downstream. India, as signatory to the Ramsar Convention on preservation of the ecology, was legally obliged to conserve such places. Building on the Koramangala site would therefore constitute an abrogation of an international agreement and would destroy a precious ecological system while degrading the lives of people already living there.

The legal argument was potentially the strongest and claimed that the project was 'fraught with illegality and irregularity'. State law mandated that the BDA, as the state government's parastatal agency responsible for planning Bangalore, was required to publish drafts and elicit objections if there was a change in its Comprehensive Development Plan. This had not occurred. The writ petition was asking the court to decide if the decisions finalized in the BDA's planning document, and the procedures for developing such a document, were beyond the ability of other state agencies to alter at will without public participation. The petitioners could not be aware that the government would issue its second order two weeks later that officially altered the plan.

The press gave extensive coverage to the suit as it began and concentrated primarily on the ecological problems of destroying yet another tank in the Bangalore area.[13] The suit, however, became buried in court procedures and this cleared the way for the official inauguration of the National Games Village project by a group of luminaries including the Chief Minister, Deve Gowda, on 28 February 1995. As construction began a new challenge emerged when the Bharatiya Janata Party (BJP), in opposition in the state of Karnataka, used the National Games Village as a vehicle to accuse the ruling Janata Dal government of corruption. B. S. Yediyurappa, a member of the state legislative assembly and leader of the opposition, staged a protest in front of the state capital building along with some of his supporters on a Saturday in early March 1995. He alleged irregularities of Rs. 100 crores ($28 million) in construction projects for the National Games and demanded that the work be stopped immediately until the government provided information on its decision-making processes. During the protest a shouting match developed with police personnel and Yediyurappa was arrested. After his release he staged another protest the following day, this time in front of his house. Yediyurappa claimed that construction costs had been deliberately overesti-mated, that irregularities had already occurred in payments to contractors and that he had been blocked from access to relevant documents. The BJP backed up these allegations with an eight-page brochure describing in simple language the purpose of the Games Village and a list of reasons to oppose it which was interspersed with snide allusions to scandals in previous state governments. The brochure called the project the 'scam of the century' (*sata-manada hagarana*) and used simple arithmetic to show that housing 6,700 athletes and officials in three to five star hotels for 11 days would only cost about Rs. 11 crores ($3.1 million) and suggested therefore that the remainder of the Rs. 367 crores ($103 million) allocated to the project would line the pockets of government officials and contractors. After a brief period of mud slinging, however, the BJP protest disappeared and construction continued unabated at the National Games Village site.

Activists from CIVIC, its five allied non-governmental organizations and local slum populations, decided to hold a symbolic protest at the construction site on 19 March. By this time most of the tank had already disappeared under hundreds of loads of fill, leaving only a small section near the Milk Board for a few buffaloes. A barbed wire fence surrounded the site on all sides of with two entrances for vehicles on the north. The large numbers of construction vehicles and lorries coming in with loads of fill kept a steady supply of dirt airborne and the prevailing winds blew it in gusts across the road and into the slum. A parade of men, women and children led by a drummer and carrying placards and posters marched out from the slums to join a small group of environmental protestors. This swelled the crowd to about 300 people who milled around in the road and restricted the passable room for traffic to one lane. The line of demonstrators confronted lorry drivers trying to enter or leave and prevented them from using the road. The placards on display were mostly in Kannada and English but included a couple in Tamil and they expressed four main streams of opinion. Some signs drew on a strictly environmentalist perspective and demanded water or fresh air from the unspoiled tank or space for the migratory birds. Others demanded the establishment of a people's park instead of a concrete jungle although this contradicted the advocacy of an unchanged tank. The third stream attacked the government for functioning as a real estate operation. The fourth position wanted the government to work on affordable housing for the poor rather than elite housing for athletes over eleven days and then for sale to the rich.

The big media event occurred when the director of the Department of Housing and Urban Development showed up to hear the objections raised by the protestors. By this time the peak strength of about 500 people had been reached with maybe 200 gathered in a large circle around her and her security personnel. She stayed for a whole ten minutes of discussions and having done her duty on a Sunday morning the director departed. After an hour, in blistering sun and choking dust, the crowd began to thin out and the official demonstration broke up. Thus ended the most concerted effort to mobilize the public against the colonization of the tank-based environment by a coalition of sports and government officials. The organizers of the demonstration had been unable to reconcile the contemporary language of environmentalism with issues of poverty alleviation and had shown little awareness of the alternative vision of the urban fabric present in the Karaga performance.

The petitioners discovered that government ministers had given the Chief Justice of the state High Court a tour of the site in December 1994, one month before construction began, and no doubt in connection with projected allocations of flats for judicial officers. It is likely that judicial acceptance of the National Games Village concept underlay continuing delays in moving toward a judgement. Finally, in a judgement on the writ petition dated 6 March 1997, the High Court of Karnataka rejected the environmental arguments and the court declared that the state had followed due procedure: 'What is mandated with reference to a Planning Authority is not binding on the Government'. Ultimately, the court defended the state's sovereignty or, in effect, its ability to do whatever it wanted with its own institutions. The petitioners had argued to the end that there were still small areas of the tank that had not come under construction and were worth preserving, but at this point the Games were only three months away and the cause was lost.

A date for the Games in early 1996 had proven too ambitious. Plans to hold city council elections at that time introduced a high degree of political uncertainty and unseasonable rains from August to July delayed construction and lead to the postponement of the Games until October 1996. By then elections were in full sway and there were additional disruptions caused by a lorry strike. Another postponement pushed the Games to the middle of 1997. Behind all this lay funding difficulties. The original budget for stadium construction activities mooted by the Congress (I) government had been Rs. 38 crores ($10.6 million). But when the Janata Dal government took power in late 1994 more elaborate plans for additional infrastructure took shape as the leadership decided that the Games were an opportunity for Karnataka to challenge Delhi as the sports capital of the nation.[14] The total cost of the extravaganza excluding the National Games Village ballooned to Rs. 110 crores ($33 million) as elaborate plans were hatched that ranged from the complete reconstruction of Sri Kanteerava Stadium to give it a capacity for 40,000 spectators to new spectator pavilions at several neighborhood playgrounds.

Following the example of the Los Angeles and Atlanta Olympics, the National Games Organizing Committee decided to depart from past practice and to solicit funding assistance from private corporate sponsors. They hired a marketing agency from Pune, which had orchestrated advertising during the Games there, to direct marketing and attract sponsors. A special fold-out brochure described the advantages of sponsorship and the legal relationship entailed. While the Congress (I) government had been in power in Delhi Finance Minister Manmohan Singh had indicated that 100 percent tax deductibility would be available for donations to the National Games, but the new United Front government ruled this out. The result was a very lukewarm response from the corporate community.[15] The failure to raise funds from sponsors left the National Games Committee with a potential debt of almost Rs. 100 crores. Eventually the Government of Karnataka cobbled together a variety of contributions and loans amounting to about Rs. 85 crores ($23.8 million). The Committee was able to pursue construction activities and get the buildings into basic shape for the revised target date of June 1997 but even by that time they still lacked about Rs. 25 crores ($7 million) which remained an outstanding debt to contractors. Under these circumstances final touches and landscaping at the sports venues remained incomplete when the Games finally took place. Thus the first attempt to move the National Games away from a central planning model toward a more 'liberalized' agenda that drew on private funding yielded disappointing results.

The Ritualization of Spectacle

As the date for the inauguration of the National Games approached and negative voices were finally stilled (Heitzman 1999b), the language surrounding the upcoming events shifted from a bureaucratic discourse concentrating on funding and toward an explicitly ritual language invoking liminality. The National Games began in Bangalore on the afternoon of Saturday 31 May 1997 with a three-hour extravaganza at the renovated Sri Kanteerava Outdoor Stadium inaugurated by the President of India. Hot air balloons and sky diving began the festivities and were followed by salutations to the national flag. Yet even here, at the last moment, challenges appeared to the regimentation of the national citizenry as the host Karnataka contingent showed up without uniforms. While the teams were lining up for their dignified entry the Karnataka team milled around in warm-up suits and street clothes and showed every intention of entering the arena in that condition, to the embarrassment of the state. Although one story claimed that the company supplying the uniforms had backed out at the last minute there was also an element of protest in this situation. The secretary of the Karnataka Amateur Athletic Association was threatening to withdraw from the Games if changes were not made to the 'sub-standard track' at the stadium (Ikram Khan 1997; Ferraz 1997). While officials agonized over what to do, the police had to resort to a baton (*lathi*) charge against their own athletes. The Karnataka team marched onto the track as they were. After the state contingents were all present the Karnataka state flag and the flag of the Indian Olympic Association were hoisted, air force helicopters showered flowers from above, the masses sang patriotic songs, a torch arrived and the lighting of the ceremonial flame took place. An article in the Times of India captured the moment:

> The magnificence of the Kanteerava arena is breathtaking; straight out of a fairytale picture book or a science fiction Hollywood set. It produces surrealistic rumblings, memories of the main LA Olympic stadium mixed with montages of Muhammed Ali lighting the flame at Atlanta. There's this mystical feeling of magic in the air hitting all those standing around (Cherian 1997).

If the body culture of the Karaga rested on the invocation of fiery power from the water of the city in an explicitly localized ritual, the symbols of the National Games used fire to connect with the commercialized transnationalism of the Olympics.

After the flame was lit the theme song of the games was played and Nandu, the mascot of the games, arrived. This was a smiling, bipedal brown cow wearing a yellow T-shirt with the Olympic logo across it which held aloft an Olympic torch (see Figure 7). The brochure circulated to all present described this moment:

> Oh … Nandu is coming to plunder the hearts of each onlooker. Oh … what a scene … what an inviolable voice. Oh … the voice which can transform mundane things into metaphysical poetry… Nandu the sweet heart will be welcomed in a grand traditional dignity and decorum which befit the cultural ethos of the State with traditional musical instruments such as Kombu, Kahale, Maddale … Nandu detours and salutes VVIPs and greets spectators, then takes leave.

The President and other leaders then delivered short speeches. The big spectacle occurred afterwards, when the cultural program took place. This included a welcome chorus, demonstrations of 'traditional' dancing and drumming, aerobics by over 1000 school children, a pageant depicting the trauma of modern man in the industrial age by another 1000 children and the dance drama called Noopura Cauvery.

> The grand mythological story on the genesis of the mother river Cauvery, the life source of the State. According to the myth Cauvery was

Figure 7. Nandu, the smiling cow mascot of the Indian National Games.

born by a sheer chance of divine design when the sacred bowl or Kamandala of sage Agasthya was dropped at the instance of lord Ganapati. The ballet like Noopura Cauvery will be presented with the brilliant blend of traditional and Folklore musical idioms. Over 425 artistes present the events with Rashmi Hegde a well known dancer and choreographer.[16]

The spectacular characteristics of the opening rituals include invocations of modernity through synchronized aerobics and depictions of traumatic industrialism (the latter a standard Gandhian theme) but their most noticeable features include musical and dance envelopes that conjure the goddess. This time it is not the warrior goddess, but the river Kaveri, which provides irrigation water for much of southern Karnataka and most of the drinking water for Bangalore through the expensive, state-directed system that replaced the old tank-based water supply. Here again, as in the initiating Karaga rituals, we see male figures presiding over the birth of the goddess in the form of the sage Agastya and the elephant-headed Ganapati, together with the recurring image of falling to the earth. The simulated, archaic features of the performances produce, in a manner reminiscent of the Karaga rituals, a peculiarly androgynous, fiery figure. Whereas the Karaga foregrounds the man-become-goddess emanating an eternal heat, the National Games produce a cartoon-like figure that is decidedly non-muscular and meant for children, and who carries the inextinguishable flame of the international Olympics. And as the goddess in the Karaga visibly moves onlookers in the streets of Bangalore to expressions of heartfelt devotion and prayer, so Nandu, the sweetheart, plunders the hearts of viewers, although the quality of adult irony rather suffuses the latter construction.

Athletics, Audiences and Contests

As the scene of action shifted to the athletic competitions, the basketball tournament exemplified the informational complexities and agonistic processes of modern athletics. The first round of this tournament, held free of charge in the new Indoor Stadium in old Sampangi Tank, attracted a big crowd because one of the two games featured Karnataka against West Bengal. The electronic scoreboards were sitting in place on two corners of the hall's first floor but they were not installed and wired so the names of the teams and the scores appeared only on cardboard sheets mounted on easels in two corners on the ground floor. When a team scored young women changed the score manually by hanging numbers on these boards. Their locations in the corners made it impossible for at least half of the crowd to know the running score. For members of the crowd sitting at the other end of the arena, with seats too far up to read the tiny lettering on players' shirts, it was impossible to determine even the identity of the teams playing on the second court. The absence of knowledge concerning teams or the score effectively altered the process of viewing the game from a mathematical exercise to a play-by-play appreciation of athletic skills and tactics. The almost entirely male assembly watching the Karnataka/West Bengal match did cheer lustily for the home team whenever they scored and Karnataka finally won the game.

On Monday 3 June the Corporation Playground in Wilson Garden, on the south side of the city, was laid out with three fields for the first round of the *kho kho* competition and one field for ball badminton. The men's *kho kho* match between Karnataka and Tamil Nadu was a rout in favor of the home team, which was a treat for the almost entirely male crowd. The several electronic scoreboards on site were not working but fortunately the public address system was working and a good summary of scoring occurred in English and Kannada after each quarter. When the Karnataka/Tamil Nadu men finished several hundred male spectators on the other side of the field shifted down to watch the women's *kho kho* match between Kerala and West Bangal but as soon as the men's badminton match began they all shifted again toward the middle of the stands to watch the men play. On several occasions badminton shuttlecocks flew out of the men's court into the playing field of the women's *kho kho* match but no one seemed to worry about possible injuries or disruption to their competition; someone from the sidelines simply ran onto the playing surface and retrieved the objects while the ladies kept running.

On Wednesday 5 June there was no need for tickets to the basketball finals, and anybody could enter the Indoor Stadium. In the first game, the women's final, West Bengal defeated Maharashtra. The place was almost full for this game but became packed toward the end as the ninety-nine percent male crowd prepared for the men's match between Bihar and Punjab. This time there was an electronic thirty-second clock near the court that worked intermittently but it had no impact on the game because both teams were trained to put up shots as soon as possible. The two electronic scoreboards were working this time and showed the teams, the score and team fouls. Strangely, they operated independently and regularly displayed different numbers based on the speed with which the operator(s) entered data. The crowd and players had no way of knowing how much time was left in the half or the game. This was a stark contrast to a sportized fascination with blocks of time and the strategy of using time-outs at the end of the game to prepare specific plays and to disrupt the opposing team in American competitions. During the warm-ups for the men's game it was apparent that the Bihar team included a player of African descent who entertained the crowd by repeatedly dunking alley-oop passes from his teammates. He had been instrumental in the close victory of Bihar over Punjab earlier in the tournament. There was a long delay at the beginning of the game because a controversy developed over the eligibility of this player who carried a Kenya passport. The Punjab delegation demanded that he be excluded from the competition because he was a foreigner. Although he had been playing with the team for several years officials declared him ineligible just before the game and he had to watch from the bench. With most of the stadium cheering for Bihar, its team struggled valiantly but finally ran out of steam in the final quarter and lost. It was an emotional and physical contest that left the entire Bihar team in tears at the end.

The low point of the Games occurred on Sunday 9 June in three separate incidents. At the Football stadium a penalty awarded to Kerala in a match against Karnataka led fans to throw bottles and chairs onto the field and resulted in some brawls in the stands. Later, at Sri Kanteerava Stadium, the Karnataka 4×100 metre relay team was declared disqualified after its lead-off runner committed two false starts. This also resulted in the throwing of bottles and chairs, one of which hit a Punjabi athlete on her face and she required treatment at a hospital. A delay of one hour resulted until the crowd settled down (Khan and Ferraz 1997). Meanwhile, logistical negotiations among feuding parties within the Indian Triathlon Federation broke down, causing cancellation of the triathlon event.

The Fourth National Games ended on 11 June in another massive spectacle at Sri Kanteerava Stadium. Public sector employees received an official holiday during the afternoon so they could attend. This reduced the afternoon rush, complicated by the arrival of the master of ceremonies, Prime Minister I. K. Gujral, whose motorcade tied up traffic on the east side of the city. With Nandu present the ceremonies featured the typical congratulatory speeches by political leaders although the Prime Minister was almost drowned out by the shouting crowd who were doing the wave. The closing ceremonies also featured more performances, including the presentation to the Prime Minister of a 'Karaga icon', along with demonstrations of sword play by a troupe of 'hero sons' who performed completely out of context as an example of 'traditional' or 'indigenous' culture. The event culminated in a large display of fireworks. With this manifestation of fire, the enclosing envelope of tradition completed the traditional framing of the liminal space of modern sports, as conceptualized and enacted by the organizers of the National Games.

Fallout from the Games

The Games had been a big success for sportized athletics in the home state of Karnataka, which garnered the largest number of medals among the participating teams. Despite the various conflicts and administrative glitches the athletic competitions on the playing fields in general came off quite well as a whole with hundreds of medals awarded in 26 major sports categories. Reports in the newspapers on the following day gushed over the lavish spectacle and the accomplishments of the sport administrations but suggested that exploitation of the facilities now available would require careful organization by the athletic federations of the state. The Committee was still looking for private sponsors and was exploring the possibilities of long-term leases of the indoor stadiums to private firms that would manage them as money-making ventures. One of the first uses of the Sri Kanteerava Indoor Stadium, however, was a government-sponsored rally on the holiday of Id-Milad Unnabi

(18 July) which was attended by state political leaders and representatives of the Muslim religious leadership amid heavy security.

The site of the National Games Village had become an impressive visual spectacle. Two giant blocks of towers marched for half a kilometer down each side of a divided access road with a large open park in the center of the project (see Figure 8). Each tower of seven stories contained 200 individual apartments of two or three bedrooms, with space on the ground floor for parking and lifts giving access to the upper levels. Approaching the site from old Koramangala village, one could drive past the Dairy Board with its verdant landscaping and the new Indoor Stadium, and view the lines of towers as an impressive backdrop of massive construction. The apartments sold for up to 28 lakhs ($78,000) and offered for their middle-class clientele the possibility of insulation from the cares of the outside world and, for those with a car or motorcycle, easy road access to the center of Bangalore in 15 or 20 minutes.

Unfortunately KHB experienced difficulties in unloading the flats. By June 1997 the Government of Karnataka had arranged as planned for the purchase of 936 flats, including those allocated to defense personnel.[17] The marketing situation went downhill quickly thereafter. The collapse of Bangalore's housing boom after 1996, combined with the increased availability of quality housing from private developers in the late 1990s, made this

Figure 8. The multi-storied apartment complex of the Indian National Games Village. (Credit: James Heitzman).

government project unattractive to private buyers. Stories of shoddy construction, poor security and inadequate services scared away most private citizens. By 1999, after completion of a total of 2,534 flats in 14 buildings, the KHB had only been able to sell about 350 additional flats to Indian Oil Corporation and several banks. At the end of 2000 many flats still remained unsold. With HUDCO's payment due, the state government would have to pay for the National Games after all.[18]

As a footnote to the proceedings, a report in July 2001 released by the Indian government's Comptroller and Auditor General, detailed mismanagement that cost the state government money amounting to over Rs. 38 crores ($10.6 million) during the planning and operation of the National Games. For example, the state had to pay Rs. 18.59 crores ($5.2 million) in the form of interest on overdrafts accrued from banks because it did not release funds on time. Some of the causes of over-expenditure hinted strongly at corruption while others exemplified a lack of 'capacity' within state government administration that was pressed for time during the course of the project.

Conclusion: Performing the Urban, Constructing an Armature

The Karaga performance emanates neither from a radial map in which certain portions of the city occupy a central node in a hierarchy nor from the grid patterns that apparently democratize space for citizens. The entire Old City is the site of the spectacle and the priest moves through city streets enjoying a completely horizontal (and densely crowded) relationship with the spectators who are standing, praying and walking through the streets. The movement of the priest in the festival creates mobile maps of the urban space, a kind of labyrinth of possibilities that allows for playing with constructs of place. These refer to elements drawn from Bangalore's multiple cultural histories: one axis of the Karaga festival is the network of goddess worship within which it is embedded; the second is the urban mnemonic in which shrines and their festivals are located between the vanished nodes of the fort, the Old City and the tank. Its sites occupy a position within a scheme of complementary symbols: the monkey god and the goddess, the Old City and the fort, water bodies and gardens.

The National Games, deeply implicated in the valorization of the national project and the re-deployment of participants and audience, had a permanent visual impact. Standing in front of the Bangalore City Corporation offices one can see the painted dome of Kanteerava Indoor Stadium, with the light towers of the Outdoor Stadium standing as a frame behind it; the ensemble providing a modernist backdrop to the traffic jams and the air pollution. In fact, the stadium's light towers are the most prominent vertical extension of the central city and are clearly visible during the day from hills up to ten kilometers distant. Verticality is a feature that had been lacking in Bangalore for the shreds of the 'Garden City' paradigm restrained the construction of really tall high-rise buildings despite the large numbers of structures up to 15 stories coming up during the late 1980s and 1990s. In this context the stadium appears as a preliminary token, or the positioning of a major piece, within a larger, long-term game of urban construction that is expected to extend vertically in the near future. The stadium would, in fact, seem more at home if silhouetted against a skyline of tall buildings. This all seems natural because one becomes accustomed, or inured, to the look of Atlanta and its Olympic facilities or New York, Los Angeles, Tokyo, Sydney, London, Frankfurt, Bombay or Kuala Lumpur. In those environments skyscrapers full of private corporate offices fill the vertical plane and the stadium provides relief through a massive circularity or a quadrangular form firmly rooted in the earth. Thus, when Bangalore 'challenges Delhi' it stakes a claim to inclusion within the category of metropolis in the early twenty-first century with its definitive, transnational architectural manifestation. The stadium betokens what the city is becoming, and how it may appear, within an emerging development paradigm.

The life world of the archaic model is a system of connected flows best served by the practice of cultivation in which land is composted with civic waste and effort is spent in watering vegetables, fruits and flowers which in turn feed the city. Previously, the city consisted of settlements interwoven with gardens and tanks over an area that was much larger than the core area inside the Old City, the fort next to it or the Cantonment. Power tended to be dispersed among many community associations that functioned at the local level, such as merchants of bangles or rice, and the various settlements entered into a variety of transactions with each other. There were many publics, they functioned according to local rules of self-regulation within and between themselves, and the authority of the kings or the British was partial and incomplete. During the 1950s, with the creation of Bangalore as the capital of the state and its evolution as an industrial city, the urban armature became more elaborate and resulted in a concrete city that appeared and was conceptualized differently. In this city civic power, especially over land, was clearly in the hands of a few government authorities, property-dealers and corporate capitalists. Bangalore later arrived on the world stage and became a spectacle to be consumed by tourists as a science-industrial city and as a node in the flow of software rather than a controlled system of circulation of waste, waters and bodily fluids in civic space. The social manifestation of the Karaga performance's model, this hearkening to an alternative vision of the environment, became confined temporally to the nine-day period of the festival's celebration although paradoxically it has spread spatially to new towns and villages absorbed by the Bangalore Metropolitan Region in the form of smaller Karaga performances. Clearly, the ability of the performances to mobilize communities and suggest other visions of the urban has not been lost. In the case of the National Games Village, despite the technocratic attempts to alter planning procedures, documents and physical space, alternative discourses presented models of ecology and the city that claimed their own space in the courts, on the streets and in the media. At no time did the leaders of the opposition achieve theoretical unity or the power to mobilize mass action and they proved incapable of derailing a planning paradigm critiqued in its own terms. The Games provided, however, an opportunity for different models of the civic and the city to stand alongside the developmental paradigm on an equal basis, if only for a limited period.

Moving into the performative space of the Games, where one might expect the duality of 'a distinct, formalized and aesthetic staging' alongside 'the crowd's interpretive conception of city life' (Nielsen 1995: 21) one finds numerous instances when resistance to the 'panoptic' qualities of sport erupted. We can see these moments in the non-regimented dress of the home Karnataka team, the incompleteness of landscaping, the lack of concern with temporality and statistics during matches, the ability of the crowds to physically move in the stands and to intervene physically on the playing surfaces and the constant struggles over the interpretation of rules or even the qualification of athletes. As for the athletic competitions, tickets were not even required for most events and the pressure for seats even at final competitions was minimal, in marked contrast to the scalping of tickets characterizing National Games in China (Brownell 1995a: 105–07). The 'topophilia' connected to sporting events worldwide was muted although manifested periodically in patriotism toward the home state of Karnataka and preferences for (or against) other states. The most pronounced public preferences for the mostly male audiences attending events, in fact, were gender-based, as seen in the pointed discrimination against the women's *kho kho* match. Compounding a general lack of fan involvement was a lack of emphasis on the fans by the organizers of the Games, who were having enough trouble getting the event off the ground and dealing with their own managerial problems. As such, the community of spectators was a decidedly secondary consideration. The result of all this was that the image of the Games as national, and their function as rituals of community, remained divorced from the actual behavior of the audience and their conscious involvement in the sports scene.

The Karaga performance, and the wrestling-houses that produce the performance through everyday routines, structure the body in several ways.

While the separation and control of male and female spaces occurs in the wrestling houses and at other sites, the boundaries between male and female break down in the performance. This blurring of somatic regimes in the festival occurs because of the intersection of heroic warrior-figures with the martial goddess. The emergence of the goddess from water, the process of heating and her final embodiment in a male body choreograph a hydraulic sense of the body-in-the-urban that relies on a representation of the civic as place, defined and bounded by a living ecology. That this model is potent, virile, hot and then cold allows the exchange of fluids in life and death and conceptualizes the city as a human construct embedded within nature. The tripartite understanding of urban space within the archaic model, a network of tanks and their gardens, fort and settlement, provides a stage for the display of the body in its several forms. It appears even today as complete system of meaning that retains its power and relevance.

The program of the nation state juxtaposes a series of monolithic images emanating overwhelming power and responsibility with a series of regional variants embedded within cultural assemblages. From the national perspectives, the Games are a successful deployment of political figures and symbols of the state such as the President, the Prime Minister and the teams representing national unity and the next generation engaged in the synchronic manipulation of their bodies. From the regional perspective one views the bowdlerized representations of Karnataka culture, such as the Karaga festival and other 'folk' performances before the television audience and a disengaged crowd with mother Kaveri (the source of southern Karnataka's irrigation systems and Bangalore's drinking water) defining the outer rim of community. The centerpiece of this overloaded matrix of signs and the link to the transnational is the smiling, bovine, androgynous athlete, Nandu. This is a childlike figure standing at the center of a performative genre attracting a predominantly male, adult fan base.[19]

The configuration of body cultures and the range of performative genres in the city of Bangalore defy the kinds of heuristic dualities of traditional/modern/post-modern or sacred/secular. We see, instead, the qualities of a 'contemporaneous' world wherein the city becomes a site for several struggling histories and models. The Karaga, while standing as a historical construct arising from an older organization of society and space, remains vibrant not simply as a 'religious' festival or as a celebration of the model of the gardeners' city but as a means of political mobilization. The processes of sportization or the national project represented by the National Games, while demonstrating their dominance in the planning model of the city, cause no attrition in the 'fan' base of the Karaga which continues to expand politically and spatially. Both types of performances, with different modes of body culture, intersect in the politics of public spaces in the city. Athletics and ritualized body cultures and a range of performative genres such as festivals, rallies and the Games therefore become modalities or optics for analyzing the culture of contests over planning and urban environmental history in contemporary cities.

Acknowledgements

Smriti Srinivas received support for this research from the Institute for Social and Economic Change, Bangalore in 1995 and from the India Foundation for the Arts, Bangalore in 1996–97. James Heitzman received support from a Fulbright Senior Research Grant in 1994–1995 and funds for professional development from Georgia State University, Atlanta in 1997 and 2001. Earlier discussions of parts of this research appeared as Heitzman 1999b and Srinivas 1999b.

8

'NUPILAL': WOMEN'S WAR, FOOTBALL AND THE HISTORY OF MODERN MANIPUR

James H. Mills

Introduction

In June 2003 Manipur beat Bengal 2-0 in the 11th Women's National Football Championship to clinch the title. The newspapers reported it as a straightforward affair. Manithombi Devi and Sakhitombi Devi were the goalscorers in the 5th and the 50th minutes and while *The Hindu* newspaper noted that 'in Alpana Seal Bengal had a gifted midfielder who single-handedly tried to control the proceedings' (*The Hindu* 25/06/2003) overall it felt that this was 'to no avail against the nimble-footed Manipuris'. Indeed, a little research shows that Manipur had strolled the competition. Over the course of the four games in the competition they had scored nine goals and conceded only once. A longer perspective still on this game further reinforces the impression that Manipur were deserved champions. Since the competition began they had won nine of the eleven trophies and had beaten Bengal in the final in each of those nine victories. 2003 was their sixth Championship in a row and was perhaps their most remarkable. The date of the competition clashed with the Asian Football Confederation's Women's Championships and eleven Manipuri players had travelled to Thailand with the Indian international squad. Many of the Manipuri team were thereforerelative newcomers and A. Sakhitombi Devi, the hero of the final who set up the first goal and scored the second, was making her debut for the state team. Contemplating this game, and the history of the Championships in general, *The Hindu* concluded that Manipur's record reflected 'a dominance rare in Indian sports'.

This chapter will explore the origins and meanings of this football phenomenon as there is much, at first sight, that seems unusual or incongruous

about the story. The most striking feature of the tale is the gender of the
teams: this competition is for women footballers only, unusual in a country
where the emphasis is commonly placed on carefully controlling female
corporal behaviour, so that in many regions a 'girl soon learns to become
modest about her decorum, the clothes she wears, her body movements'
(Sharma and Vanjani 1993: 35).[1] Also to be considered is the reversal of
sporting traditions. Manipur's triumphs at first appear unlikely given the history
of football in India. Bengal is the powerhouse of Indian soccer as the country's
first trophies were competed for there, the earliest Indian teams emerged in
Calcutta and it was teams from this region that mounted the challenge to the
supremacy of British based clubs during the colonial period and which have
maintained a dominance of the sport ever since (Dimeo 2001a; Dimeo 2001b;
Majumdar 2002).[2] Finally there is the political shock of seeing Manipur
succeed at all on the national stage and receive positive coverage in the media.
It has been noted in the past that 'national newspapers make absolutely no
reference to Manipur except while reporting acts of killing or atrocities' (Dev
and Lahiri 1987: 16). The region is a peripheral legacy of British colonial
anxieties, tacked on to India as a buffer zone in 1891 and reluctantly ceded to
India in 1949. It retains the air of a frontier: ethnically heterogeneous, riven by
fractious political movements that pursue self-government, economically stag-
nant and under the shadow of the military presence of the national army. In
exploring this story the chapter will focus on political, economic and social
aspects of Manipuri history. It will be argued that the football success of the
women's team is actually built on the history of the region while at the same
time it reffects the more recent tensions and processes of Manipuri society.[3]

Women and Power in Manipur

Women have played a remarkable role in Manipuri history that reflects their
unusual position in Meitei society.[4] Visitors to the region have often commented
on the way in which Meitei women have been given greater responsibilities
and have assumed more active participation in their societies than women
elsewhere in India. For example, one of the first British women to visit the
region, Mrs Grimwood, the wife of the colonial Resident in the 1890s, was
careful to note that 'the Manipuris do not shut up their women, as is the
custom in most parts of India, and they are much more enlightened and intel-
ligent in consequence' (Grimwood 1975: 58). One particularly notable aspect
of this female activity is the presence of women in the economic sphere. The
Archaeological Survey of India observed that 'women have a major role in
agriculture, animal husbandry, collection of fuel, fetching potable water, managing business, weaving and so on' (Singh 1998: xvi) and that 'Meitei women
contribute about 50–80 per cent towards maintaining their respective families'

(Rizvi and Mukherjee 1998: 153). Perhaps the most visible manifestation of this is the 'women's market' in the capital:

> One of the most outstanding features of the Meitei community is the management of internal trade and exchange of the produce of villages, exclusively done by women. An outsider while travelling in the valley may come across innumerable bazaars located at convenient spots by the road-side, where women congregate and sell their produce. Imphal possesses the largest and the most important of these bazaars which is called sena kaithel meaning golden market. It is said to have been founded by Mongeanba during 1580AD. Now it consists of a number of embanked platforms allotted for different traders, such as cloth-weavers, dried fish vendors, roots and tuber vendors, vegetable vendors and others (ibid: 157).

This market was the scene of the famous 'Second Women's War' of 1939. At the time, the British Political Agent reported that over 6000 women traded at the market and it seems that the British had never succeeded in imposing order on the bazaar, the Governor of Assam noting that 'Manipuri women are notorious for their independence and their proneness to take direct action to get their own way'. In the winter of 1939 the colonial system of rice exporting and the environmental conditions of the harvests threatened a food shortage. By the end of November it was becoming clear that the Manipuri women were failing to get supplies for hand-husking and that as such the local market was being starved of its staple diet. The response of the women was to begin ambushing the cartloads of rice being transported to warehouses for export. As this proved an unsatisfactory tactic they banded together to put pressure on the British authorities. Four thousand of the women marched on the Assistant Political Officer's office and demanded that he track down the Maharajah and insist that a ban be imposed on all rice exports. His response was to telegraph the Maharajah who was out of the state at the time and the ruler was not to be found. Upon returning to inform them of this he was besieged in the telegraph office and was told that he would not be released until he had succeeded in eliciting a response from the Maharajah. Effectively taken hostage by the women, the Assistant Political Officer was only able to regain his freedom when one of his junior officers led a platoon of Assam Rifles to disperse the crowd. This was done violently and the sight of the women being manhandled by these troops caused the Meitei men to become involved. Over twenty of the crowd had to be treated for their injuries. Although the Assistant Political Officer was free, the women had not been defeated. A group of 10000 assembled the next day and marched on the office of the chief British Political Officer who had hurried back to the capital from a tour of duty. The women threatened to descend upon the rice mills themselves to destroy them. The chief Political Officer spent over two hours talking with their leaders and then promised to see that their demands were met. He was able to let them know that the Maharajah had agreed to place a ban on rice exports and he himself personally drove to the rice mill at Matripukhri to remove the electric switch and immobilize the mill. He then instructed the Hydro-Electric Board to suspend supplies of electricity to the other mills to ensure that they could not produce rice for export. In short, the female market traders of Imphal had won the Women's War (Parratt and Parratt 2001: 905–919).

While this was the most spectacular women's resistance to colonial rule it was not the only instance of successful protest at British government. The first 'Women's War' was staged in 1904 to oppose orders from the Political Agent that Meitei men should rebuild the bungalows of colonial officers destroyed in an arson attack. The women felt that this was an unfair imposition of *lalup kaba*, or forced labour.

> The women folk of Manipur were very much agitated against the oppressive rule of the British. They came out in large numbers and demonstrated against the order and entered the Residency to see the Political Agent. Law and order completely broke down. The Military was requisitioned to restore law and order. But the women closed the Bazaar and continued the agitation for several days ... women agitators were beaten up. But the movement continued. Ultimately the administration was compelled to abandon Lallup. The first Nupilan was successful (Venkata Rao et al. 1991: 189).

Indeed, the Nupilals are only the two best known examples of direct female Manipuri action against British policies. In the late 1920s an English administrator found himself dumped in a lake by angry local women and a couple of years later one of his successors was forced to reverse a decision on fishing rights in order to avoid a similar fate (Murthi 1984: 66). Such collective action on the part of Manipuri women has continued into the post-colonial era. Since the 1980s women have focused their activities through the women's groups known as the *Meira-Paibis*, or 'torch-bearing women':

> The Meira-paibi's predominant role has been, to see that the social order is maintained ... Any anormative behavior that goes against the social customs is discouraged and denounced ... today they roam in the locality to keep a watch on drunkenness and drug-abuse. They make a human wall in cases where innocent local youths are forcibly being taken away by the Armed Forces in the name of insurgence. They are the only ones

who can dare to warn and scold the people in under-ground movement for their excesses. Everybody is cautious of them. They dare to get lathi charged, to sit for hunger strikes and even go to jail for a right cause (Vijaylakshmi Brara 2001).

As recently as 2001 women confronted security forces operating in Manipur. On July 5th tens of thousands of women defied a curfew and battled security forces in the greater Imphal area in night-time demonstrations against a ceasefire extension. Eyewitnesses reported that women 'grappled with police commandos' and 'Meira paibis converging towards Lamlong bazar were stopped by security forces who fired several rounds in the air and teargassed the rallyists'. The night took a fatal turn as Laishram Ongbi Tamphasana Devi died of a stroke brought on by the effects of tear-gas (*The Imphal Free Press* 05/07/01).

These incidents were not spontaneous or extraordinary, they were based on traditional, and culturally sanctioned, patterns of behaviour. Before the arrival of the British, women had their own court in the Manipuri legal system which was known as the *Paja*. The *Paja* comprised eleven members headed by the king's mother and the female members of the royal family. This court dealt with matters such as adultery, divorce, wife-beating, assault and a range of other cases where women were involved and its function was to decide the form of punishment. Outside of this formal structure, there existed a custom whereby older women could collectively approach the king if they felt any injustice in the exercise of male authority over women. A strong collective protest by such a group against the death penalty of a criminal, for instance, was sometimes enough to force the king to change his verdict (Chaki-Sircar 1984: 29). Such female assertiveness had three sources. The first was cultural. In pre-Hindu religions the female priests were more important than the male priests, certainly in ritual performances, and it has been suggested that this was because the priestess appeared first in the development of that religion (Basanta 1998: 71). The second source was both practical and economic and has been mentioned already. Women's work as traders in central markets gave them an economic significance in Meitei society while also giving them the tangible experience of negotiation and the benefits of collective action. Indeed, their experience of collective action seems to extend beyond the economic and political and can be found underpinning many female activities, or as Chaki-Sircar concludes in a detailed study of women in the region:

Another noticeable aspect of Meitei culture is the collective spirit of women in different contexts, a bond which can be traced throughout their life cycle. I described various forms of bonding such as the *marup* credit associations, *khulongs*, the rice cultivation teams, *nupilalas*, associations for religious singing and dancing, and many others in economic and socio-religious spheres Chaki-Sircar 1984: 196).

Thirdly, and perhaps most importantly, this female assertiveness was contained within a patriarchal social system and was only unleashed in defence of that system. A number of commentators have been careful to emphasise this. In assessing the Women's Wars of 1904 and 1939 N. Jojkumar Singh concluded that 'the women's movement in Manipur never asked for the upliftment of their status in society. The basic objective of their movement was for the improvement of the economics condition of the state' (Jojkumar Singh 2002: 137). N. Basanta similarly concluded that

> There was an expression of feminism in Meetei patrilineal culture which encouraged women to be individually self-reliant and collectively powerful without necessarily involving sex war. Arising out of a collective spirit it acted as a moral backing to men. It was an integral part of the patrilineal social system and did not act against it (Basanta 1998: 59).

The picture of women and women's direct action in moments of economic and political crisis is vivid and complex in Manipur. Women have a history of such action at these moments and this history seems to be founded upon a number of aspects of Meitei society which include unusually high degrees of female economic participation and of female activity outside the immediate family and a patriarchal culture that prescribes such female initiative, albeit in carefully defined situations.

History and Sport in Manipur

Manipur has a distinctive history, born largely of its position between south and south-east Asia. Lying between Myanmar (Burma) and India the contemporary state is part of the modern day Indian Union. About 8500 square miles in size, the state is composed of a central valley about 36 miles by 18 miles across surrounded on all sides by hills. The central valley is dominated by the Meitei ethnic group which makes up about two-thirds of the 2 million population, the hills are inhabited by the Nagas and the Kukis (Parratt and Parratt 1997: xi).

The Meitei group has traditionally provided the elites of the region and the cultivators of the valley. Their language is classed as 'Tibeto-Burman' and anthropologically they are classed as 'Mongoloid'. In other words 'it is clear that the Meiteis came into Manipur from the east, not from the Indian sub-continent' and it seems that they arrived in the region about two thousand years ago (ibid.: xii–xiii). The impact of South Asian cultures became pronounced only in the eighteenth century when the ruling king converted to Vaishnavism and Hinduism was forcibly imposed on the population of the valley. The king, Garib Niwaz, had also succeeded in reversing Manipur's relations with its neighbour and had plundered northern Burma for much of his reign. Upon his death in 1751 the Burmese wrought their revenge and repeatedly attacked the small state. In their desperation Garib Niwaz's successors cast around for powerful allies and as early as 1762 the British in Bengal sent troops to their aid. By 1826 the British had established Manipur as an independent state in the Treaty of Yandabo that ended the first Anglo-Burmese war and in 1835 they set up a Political Agency there. It was not until 1891, and the Anglo-Manipuri conflict of that year, that the British took a more direct control of the region as the Viceroy of India assumed the right to select the successor to the throne who was now deemed simply a 'rajah', a demotion from his predecessors' status as Maharajahs. Manipur remained a *de facto*, but never a *de jure*, part of British India until the departure of the imperial power in 1947 (Parrattt and Parrratt 1992; Dena 1984). Finding independence with the sudden disappearance of the British, elections were organised in Manipur in June 1948 and the rule of the Rajah was replaced by a democratic government. However, India absorbed the state in 1949 and this government was swept away (Lokendra Singh 1998).

From such a history emerges two particularly relevant facts for understanding women's football in modern day Manipur. The first is the long tradition of recreational physical activities. Sport is so markedly a feature of Meitei society that it was identified as a distinguishing aspect of their culture by the Anthropological Survey of India. It noted that:

They are very devoted to sports and games as a result of which they are physically very fit. The principal games played, such as foot-hockey (khong kongjei), have had Manipuri boys who have represented Indian in hockey at various world and Olympic competitions [sic]. Polo was introduced during 1600 AS by Khagenba. This game was made popular because of patronage by the royal families. Their teams of polo players represented Manipur state in many competitive matches played as Calcutta and Delhi as far back as 1901. Besides these, some other sports popular among the rural folk are javelin throwing (rambai hunba), boat racing, long distance running (lumchel), wrestling and a game played with the seeds of a creeper (kang sanaba) which is peculiar to the Manipuri (Rizvi and Mukherjee 1998: 157).

Elsewhere in the book the Anthropological Survey of India compilers were careful to emphasize that it was the Meitei groups, rather than their Naga or Kuki neighbours, who had such sporting traditions; 'games such as *hiyang*, resembling a boat race, *mukha*, resembling wrestling, *khong khiangjei* and polo are exclusive to the Meitei' (Rizvi 1998: 4). Other writers have similarly reported the sports of the region. G.K and Shukla Ghosh noted *lanchel* or running races between villages and *rambai hunba* or javelin throwing. Team games included *khong kang je* or hockey, played between nine a side teams with sticks of bamboo and a ball fashioned from a root and *yubi lakpi* or rugby, played with an unhusked, oiled dry coconut (Ghosh and Ghosh 1997: 207–209). These activities are not simply past-times or ways of alleviating boredom. Physicality is central to the religious rituals of the region, both in pre-Hindu times and today. Dance is a key element in the most important festival of Meitei culture, for example the Lai Haraoba festival, through the *noiba*, 'a creative dance which releases the sacred fecund energy of the lais to bring about cosmic and human creation' (Parrat and Parratt 1997: 183; see also Arambam 2002; 132–159). Yet sport is also at the heart of this festival. At a key point in the rituals there is a reconstruction of the race to the shrine between three male and three female participants. At such moments as the arrival of a god and the selection of a wife in the performance a local hockey stick recurs as a prop. The *phibun*, a cloth ball, is a sacred object in a number of the rituals and is handled by the priests to the accompaniment of its own rhyme:

> Where the sovereign god throws it,
> The hill where the maiden goddess catches it
> Where the seven goddesses throw it
> The hill where the nine gods catch it

Indeed, the wider culture integrates sporting activities into its celebrations and understandings. The rituals of the Lai Haraoba festival are traditionally succeeded by days devoted to sports played between village teams. Meiteis believe that at the beginning of creation the gods played seven-a-side polo and that competition was a feature of their contests, 'the male and female gods have decided to race their boats' go the lyrics to the *Hijing Hirao* recital. Such is the significance of these sporting activities that anthropologists have concluded that within Meitei culture there exists 'the idea that the play is itself cosmically creative' (Parrat and Parratt 1997: 184). A further feature of such activity in Meitei culture is the participation of women in the sports. It is noticeable that this participation is sanctioned in ritual and belief. The race above to the shrine is between a male and a female group, the rhyme details male and female gods playing the cosmic game of catch and the boat race is a competition between the two genders of the heavens. The Meitei culture does not simply sanction the playing of games by women it allows the playing of games by women and men together. This is reproduced in practice. Among the games played in Manipur is *kang sa-na-ba*, first described in 1886:

> The in-door amusement in its season is kang-sanaba, a game as peculiar to Manipur as hockey on horseback was. It is played only in the spring, the players being generally young women and girls, with a sprinkling of men on each side. The game seems to cause great excitement, and there is great emulation between the sides. The kang is the seed of a creeper; it is nearly circular, about 1/1/2 inches in diameter, and about 3/4 of an inch in thickness. This is placed upon the ground upright, at one time with its broad side towards the party by whom it is to be struck, at another, edgewise. When the kang is placed with its broad side to the party, it is to be pitched at with an ivory disk; when it is placed edgewise, it is to be struck by the disk propelled on its flat side along the surface of the ground, by the force of the middle finger of the right hand acting off the forefinger of the left. A good player can propel the disk in this way with great force and precision. The side having most hits wins. The whole is closed by a feast at the expense of the losers (Dunn 1886: 396).

Khangjing sanaba is more interesting still. It pitted women against men, was performed on moonlit nights, and was essentially a game of tug-of-war using a strip of bamboo green (Ghosh and Ghosh 1997: 208–9). In short, Manipur is a region with an unusually active history of organised games and sports. These activities are celebrated in and integral to local rituals and belief systems. Women's participation in many of these games and sports is both common and culturally sanctioned.

Ethnicity and Identity

One further set of processes is important for understanding modern Manipur. Since the 1940s Manipur has become divided by the emergence of politicised ethnic identities, based on pre-existing communal groups. From the late 1930s onwards political agitation was focused on the expulsion of the British from the region through such political parties as the Manipur Mahasobha and under the leadership of politicians such as Irabot Singh. With the withdrawal of the colonisers from South Asia in 1947 Manipur was left under the leadership of its Maharajah and popular protest lead to the organization of an elected assembly in 1948. However, the Maharajah was pressured by the newly independent Government of India to merge his territory with the larger state.

Eventually, he was held hostage on a trip to Assam in September 1949 and forced to sign the merger agreement despite the fact that he argued that he was simply the constitutional head of Manipur and that the recent elections had demonstrated that sovereignty was now vested in the people (Joykumar Singh 1992: 104–110).

From 1949 onwards dissent has focused on the extent to which the various groups in Manipur were coerced into the membership of India by this forcible merger. Those intent on asserting Manipuri independence include the United National Liberation Front (UNLF) and its armed wing the Manipur People's Army (MPA). Founded in 1964, their objectives have been summarised as 'to restore the lost political sovereignty of Manipur and her neighbours, to establish and independent sovereign republic comprising of Manipur and her neighbours, and to regain the lost territories of Manipur from Myanmar (Burma)' (Tarapot 2003: 180). Opposed to such integrationist visions of an independent Manipur, however, are such groups as the National Socialist Council of Nagaland (NSCN), the Kuki National Army (KNA) and the Zomi Revolutionary Army (ZRA). Each group has a vision of uniting all of its ethnic members in nation states composed exclusively of those ethnic members. In each case this would involve pulling territories from the currently existing states in the region (variously including pieces of Manipur, Assam, and Tripura in India and districts in Bangladesh and Myanmar) (ibid.: 12–15).

The Meiteis have interacted with this politics in two ways. The first is as champions of an integrated Manipur. Meiteis have been among the most active participants in integrationist movements, key activists include Irabot Singh, the founding father of Manipuri nationalism, and the 'educated Meitei youths under the leadership of the late Arambam Samarendra' who founded the UNLF (ibid: 179). Part of the reason for this is that the Manipuri state has historically been a Meitei state. Its territorial boundaries were established by the succession of Meitei kings that ruled from the valley between 33 AD and 1955. Often 'Meitei' and 'Manipuri' are words that are used interchangeably, or as a recent study concluded 'the most popularly known and numerically the most dominant community inhabiting Manipur are referred to as the Manipuris. They are locally known as the Meiteis' (Zehol 1998: 116). Indeed, during the 2001 disputes about a ceasefire between Naga militants and the Indian Army a Naga politician explicitly argued that the Meiteis 'tried to sabotage the peace process as they want to suppress the Nagas of Manipur' and warned darkly that 'none could challenge the move to consolidate all the Naga inhabited areas in NE' (Matamgi Yakairol 11/06/01).

The second feature of Meitei interactions with contemporary politics has been their failure to represent their interests in relation to other ethnic groups in competition for resources. Groups such as the Nagas and the Kukis, through classification as 'tribals', gained access to a range of privileges drawn up by the Indian state to aid the development of people who were felt to have been historically disadvantaged and discriminated against. As early as 1947 there was a Manipur State Hill People's Act which classified these groups as separate and in need of special attention and subsequently a number of agencies such as the Tribal Development Schemes aimed to improve the lot of these target communities (Ansari 1991: 169–208). While resources have been directed to the tribal districts jobs have been reserved for representatives of these communities in government departments. The result of this has been that it is 'officers mostly from hill districts and outside the state who are holding key positions in the Manipur secretariat, the backbone of the state administration' and in fact 'the number of officers from the majority Meitei community holding key positions in the state secretariat or in the police department is far below the expectation' (Tarapot 2003: 52–3).

The response of the Meitei ethnic group to these interactions with post-colonial politics in Manipur has been to construct a distinctive identity and to emphasize its difference from other groups. One method of doing this has been to draw upon the past to come up with symbols and stories that emphasise the separate and unique nature of the Meitei community. An important feature of this process, which has been called the 'Meitei-ization of Manipuri society in modern times' (Chaki-Sircar 1984: ix) is the revival of *Lai Haroba*, the prime ritual of the Meitei religion mentioned above. This emphasis on the history of local religion and culture represents a deliberate 'de-Sanskritisation' of Meitei identity. Hinduism is associated with India and the gradual spread of Hindu religious practices from the early seventeenth century onwards is represented by Meiteis as a form of Indian cultural imperialism. Therefore, an emphasis on local religion and culture forms part of a challenge to India's hegemonic ambitions. As Chaki-Sircar has argued:

> Meitei society can be viewed as a field of conflict and compromise operated upon by two diametrically opposing forces, the process of 'Hinduisation' and resistance to it by Meitei cultural tradition. Recently, the latter has been spurred on by a burst of energy with a concominant rise in Meiteiisation (ibid.: 184).

In exploring this burst of energy Chaki-Sicar continues that 'data on Meiteiisation indicate that Lai Harouba also serves as a political symbol in the wake of regional awareness. A trace of secularisation of the sacred can be noticed in urban Lai Harouba' (ibid.: 225). In other words, the cultural and political imperialism of India are seen as one and the struggle for a sovereign and independent Manipur means that Meiteis have taken to celebrating

their difference from Indians and India. However, it has been argued that
this emphasis on the distinctiveness and difference of Meiteis may also feed
off of the second set of interactions of Meiteis with post-colonial politics
in the North-East of India. Meiteis are now seeking 'tribal' status in order to
access the privileges accorded to groups like the Nagas and the Kukis who
have long enjoyed the benefits of that label. Lucy Zehol's study of ethnicity in
Manipur has concluded that:

> There is the general understanding that the Meiteis are Hindus. This
> interpretation has now become a subject of controversy as the Meiteis,
> long known to be Hindus, would like to be identified as Sanamahis, the
> name of indigenous religious faith. According to some analysts, this rep-
> resents a process of religious revivalism. On a closer look we find that a
> complex set of political and cultural issues are involved, most of which
> have merged during the post-colonial period … the genesis here is from
> the increasing realisation of relative deprivation vis-à-vis the other ethnic
> groups in the state. Through experience the Meiteis have realised that
> they will need to enhance their capacity, and this is possible through a
> redefinition of their identity as a 'tribal community' as different from the
> current identity of a non-tribal community (1998: 116).

In short, the modern politics of Manipur has caused Meiteis to look for ways
of emphasizing the unique character of their community and their region.
The origins of these politics have been explained as in part a response to the
domination of India and the resulting search for a basis for measures of independence. They are also a response to the internal politics of Manipur where
'scheduled tribe' status brings with it privileges and rewards, prizes that have
been denied the Meiteis thus far, as they have appeared insufficiently 'ethnic'
or 'tribal' to qualify.

Conclusion

> In most studies that focus on the identities of dominated groups there is
> a failure to theorize sufficiently from the empirical data recovered. These
> data are rich in their revelation of subcultures and popular cultures,
> rituals and ceremonies, everyday life and habits that carve out and main-
> tain spaces within which these dominated groups can assert themselves
> with limited freedom and dignity. These are not practices and activities
> that originate simply as responses to powerful classes. Nor are they
> expressions of 'primordial', 'traditional' preferences and affiliations
> (Kumar 1994: 2).

The above account of Manipur is important in order to inform a reading of the story of the state women's football team. The achievements of the players are founded on the physical culture of the region, which is rich with a history of team sports and of female participation in such activities. This in turn is partly a reflection of the gender relations of the place. It is important not to over-estimate women's autonomy in Manipur and it is essential to recall the 'co-existence of Meitei women's power with a social ideology of male domination' (Chaki-Sircar: 11). Nevertheless, it remains the case that relative to conditions for members of their gender elsewhere in South Asia, Manipuri women enjoy greater power over their own lives:

> Women have the option and power to defy male authority within the family, the access to the use of the loom (a lucrative tool), and to their own earnings, the right to divorce a polygynous husband, the right to women's wealth (including land if it was given to her or purchased by her), the return of dowry on divorce, the normative power to keep the children after divorce, and above all, the option to choose their marital partners and their occupation (ibid.: 223).[5]

The sporting success of Manipur's women's football team can therefore be seen as resting on conditions of sporting participation and female power that have deep roots in the past. These roots are peculiar to, and deeply embedded in, the local history of the region.

However, the history and roots of the region do not entirely explain the phenomenon of women's football in Manipur. The photograph that accompanies this article (see Figure 1), taken of the winning team of 2003, suggests that the more recent processes of Manipuri history have contributed to the building of the sporting success. Clearly visible in the photo is the banner held by one of the players that declares that 'Manipur rules, We're no. 1'. At first this might simply be dismissed as an isolated moment of bravado on the part of winners aimed at their fellow competitors. However, in light of the high drama of recent politics in Manipur, such an explanation might fail to read this statement and its context more profoundly. After all, here is a group of Manipuri women using a national stage, and the attention of the Indian press granted to them because of their sporting prowess, to thumb their nose at the prevailing power relations that had only recently been forcibly reimposed upon their homeland. It should be recalled that the riots and demonstrations of 2001 that have been discussed above were about the perceived betrayal of the interests of all Manipur by the Government of India in granting cease-fires to armed groups who wanted to split up the region along ethnic lines. These events are now remembered as the 'June 18th Uprising' in Manipur, an

Figure 1. 'Manipur Women's Football Team won the 11th Senior Women's National Football Championship in Chennai', The Hindu 25/06/2003, photo K. Gajendran. The banner reads 'MANIPUR RULES WE'RE # 1'.

anniversary marked annually in honour of those killed by the Government's security forces on that day in 2001. That the football stage was being used to make a nationalist message is made all the more possible by the fact that Bengal was once again the beaten team. In some of the North-Eastern states of India it is Bengalis that are seen as a particular threat. This is in part because the British tended to use Bengalis as middle-men in their colonial rule and as such they came to be seen as agents of alien government and economic exploitation. It is also partly because of the experience of the North-East of mass Bengali immigration especially after the Bangladesh war of 1971–2 (Phukon 2003: 91). In Manipur in particular the Hinduism that is explicitly rejected as alien and Indian had its origins specifically in Bengal to the extent that one historian notes that 'Bengali became the medium of communication and communion' in the Sanskritisation process (Nilikanta Singh 1986: 80). As such, the Final can be seen not just as a football result but as a physical victory of Manipuris over representatives of a group perceived as a traditional foe.

Reading the football phenomenon as a political process also makes sense when viewed from the perspective outlined above: that Meiteis are currently engaged upon a process of creating a communal identity. All the players in the Manipur team are Meiteis and it is interesting to note the place of *Lai Haroba* rituals in the construction of a postcolonial Meitei identity. These rituals, portrayed as essentially Meitei and intimately connected with their origins as a community, emphasise the prominent role of women in the culture of the region and their physicality (Parratt and Parratt 1997). This female power thus becomes a symbol of the unique nature of the Meitei and a foundation stone of the difference between the Meitei from other groups and from India. Given the fact that Manipur is often used interchangeably with 'Meitei', there appears to be another layer still to the banner unveiled by the winning team of 2003 in front of the Press. Indeed, given the fact that Manipuri women have a long history of direct, political action, it is perhaps no surprise to find that the banner was a political message. Ultimately, the football success of the Manipuri women can be seen as rooted in a series of customs and practices that stretch back into the history of the region. However, it can also be seen as the outcome of more recent processes in the state, as the banner unveiled at the Final of 2003 hints at the idea that the players have been participating with, and were perhaps inspired by, a sense of the game having a wider significance.

The phenomena of Manipuri women's football is important for a number of academic discussions. Despite the ongoing success of female athletes[6] in India, no discussion of women in South Asia has yet to look at sport and sporting activities. It is all very well for studies of gender issues in India to complain that 'there is a failure to theorize sufficiently from the empirical data recovered' as does Nita Kumar quoted at the start of this section, but part of the problem may well be that the empirical data recovered is often circumscribed by the theoretical limitations placed unconsciously by researchers on where they go to gather that data. Kumar's collection seems typical in focusing itself on missionary activities, schools, kinship groups and the zenana when looking for 'spaces within which these dominated groups can assert themselves with limited freedom and dignity'. The assumption here is that women's experience in South Asia is typically one of dreary struggle for self-definition within social confinement. Yet the active participation of women in sports in India offers alternative visions, and this article has shown that female engagement in sport in South Asia can be a complex story that combines long-established patterns of female autonomy with the emergence of modern identities and agendas in which powerful women agents cooperate in a variety of acts of definition and resistance.

The account given here also has significance for those who have developed the field of sports studies. Many studies in this subject area that have concentrated specifically on women have seen the development of modern sports as a 'liberating' process (Hargreaves 1994: 5; see also Mangan 1987; Nelson 1998). Such studies present the practices and discourses of sporting activities in the nineteenth and twentieth centuries as opportunities to break free from and to challenge pre-existing norms imposed by patriarchal societies. A recent statement of this belief comes from Fan Hong, who introduced a recent collection of essays as follows:

> Without many remarkable women who devoted their lives to the cause of women's physical liberation, women's political and economic freedom would never have been achieved ... although different cultures have produced very different heroines, in this book they have one thing in common: the ambition to free women's bodies through sport (2001: 6).

The Manipuri example suggests that sport must not always be read as a liberating force for women. It shows that modern football is simply a new arena in which Meitei women can demonstrate a prowess based on a long-standing physical culture and experience of team games. In other words, the emergence of modern sport in Manipur reflects female physical autonomy rather than causes it.

The issue of team games is one made much of by other sports studies specialists who chart the introduction of modern sports into non-western societies. This process has typically been traced to colonialism and the intro-duction of western sporting activities as 'tools of empire'. The objective of employing these tools was not simply to refashion colonized bodies through physical exercise but to impose new ethics and modes of behaviour by enforcing group participation:

> The game carried within it a moral order based on the ethics of commitment and dedication, of team spirit and the subjection of the indi-vidual to the demands of the group and of valour and personal bravery. Colonized peoples were often portrayed as lacking just such attributes and thus football was seen as one method of introducing them to such desirable characteristics (Mangan 2001: 44).

The concept and dynamics of the 'team' as a social, and socialising, unit has therefore been constructed by sports studies such as J.A. Mangan, who wrote the above extract, as 'colonial' or 'western' imports into 'colonised' societies. A closer look at the Manipuri women's football story offers a clear example that challenges just such a construction. Manipuri women might be excelling in a modern team sport but this success is based on an indigenous tradition of team games and indeed on a wider base of social solidarity among women in the region. The concept and dynamics of teamwork were certainly not alien imports to this particular region of South Asia.

Finally, it is important to make sense of the Manipuri story in the context of the larger theme of this collection. Football in this story certainly features as a 'subaltern sport' as it is the site of resistance to groups or paradigms with dominating or hegemonic projects. Gender relations in Manipur are particularly complex as 'in spite of the socio-structural superiority of men, women can conceive of their lives as independent of men'. Women exercise a degree of control over their lives not available to women elsewhere in India and yet this scope for action remains circumscribed by male authority. Indeed, this seems to be increasingly challenged by men, as in recent years the Manipuri media has editorialized that 'we also need to remind ourselves of the rising crime graph and atrocities against women in our society. Rape and sexual molestation is no longer an alien subject today' (www.manipuronline.com 13/09/2003). It is argued that the high-profile successes of the women's football team on the national stage are an assertion and celebration of collective Manipuri female prowess, which is especially loaded with meaning given gender relations in the region. On the other hand the victories are intended to be statements of Manipuri identity and independence from India. India is seen as a source of unwelcome political and cultural imperialism, as the process of 'Sanskritisation' beginning in the eighteenth century threatened local religious systems and the forced merger of 1949 robbed the region of the political independence it had claimed in its 1948 elections. The football successes combine a number of messages of resistance and defiance, that Meitei society is different from that of India because of the prominence of its women, that Manipur can reverse traditional power relations and defeat Bengal, and that Manipur rejects the Indian sporting world and instead is a participant in global sports culture.

This last point is worth dwelling on, as it is notable that Manipuris refuse to play cricket and choose football as the medium of their successes. Cricket has come to be seen as an Indian game which was adopted and adapted as a vehicle for anti-colonial Indian nationalism before 1947 and for a more specifically Hindu Indian identity in the post-colonial period (Guha 1998; Nandy 1989; Appadurai 1995; McDonald 1999). Football on the other hand is a game which is a global idiom and it has been argued that in many Asian countries outside of India the sport 'symbolizes advanced modernity' (Giulanotti 1999: 169). The adoption of football in Manipur as the game at which to beat Bengal is itself significant then, as it at once rejects Indian sporting preferences and pledges allegiance to those of a larger and wider international community.

Writing in his recent account of cricket Ramachandra Guha stated that 'I do not myself support the placing of sports history (or indeed other emerging fields such as environmental history and women's history) in a ghetto of its own ... the attempt should rather be to use ignored or previously marginal spheres, such as sport or gender or environment to illuminate the historical centre' (2002: xiv). In adopting this approach in this article it is possible to see how the study of a women's football tournament sheds light on a historical centre that is Manipuri history. This is revealed to be a complex web of power relations in which gender, imperialism, nationalism, subalternity and modernity combine to make soccer a field fraught with meaning, ambivalence and defiance.

9

'PLAYING FOR THE TIBETAN PEOPLE': FOOTBALL AND HISTORY IN THE HIGH HIMALAYAS

Alex McKay

When not engaged on some work they play games, but not for money which is not their custom; he who loses sends for *ciang* and they all drink together. Their games are archery, or shooting at a target with a musket, at both they are exceedingly expert. At other times they play with heavy stones as we do in Europe with quoits. I do not know of any other game in Thibet, and these are only indulged in for exercise.

An Account of Tibet: the Travels of Ippolito Desideri of Pistolia S.J., 1712–1727, edited by Filippo de Filippi, Routledge and Sons, London, 1932, pp.188–89

Football, the State and the Stateless in the Modern High Himalayas

It was with those few words that the Jesuit missionary Ippolito Desideri filed the first sports report from Tibet early in the 18th century. Nearly three hundred years later a delighted striker for the exile Tibetan football team, Tenzin Dargyal, was quoted as saying that despite their 4-1 defeat by Greenland 'I have never been so happy in my life'. His team had actually gained an early lead when Lobsang Norbu had scored in the 11th minute of the game. But Tenzin emphasised that 'We're not playing for winning or losing. We're playing for the Tibetan people' (www.friends-of-tibet.org.nz/news/july_2001). The match was played in front of a crowd of 5000 people at Copenhagen's Vanløse stadium in 2001 but was not actually an official football international as neither Tibet nor Greenland is a member of FIFA and because neither state is recognised as an independent member of the world community. Indeed this 'Tibetan team' was composed entirely of exiles from the land that has been under Chinese control since the 1950s.[1] But the crowds waved the flags of the two states,[2] and the game did have international implications. China habitually opposes any manifestation of an independent Tibet and there were reports (downplayed by the embassy) that they had protested against the match being played at all (www.cphpost.dk/get/62172.htm). However, the match went ahead and as of 2 December 2003 the World Football Elo Ratings website rated Tibet in 223rd place out of 226 teams in the world, with a record of played two, lost two, two goals for and six goals against (www.eloratings.net/asian_qual.html). The Tibetan team now has a sponsor, the Danish sports clothing manufacturer Hummel, and has returned to Europe to play exhibition matches such as that against the Hummel All Stars in Arhus (Denmark).

The Danish connection with Tibetan football is a close one because Michael Nyorandt, a Danish supporter of the Tibetan exile cause, is the 'driving force' behind the Dharamsala-based Tibetan team. The Tibetans have also found supporters elsewhere in Europe. In 2002 a team selected from youths at the Tibetan Homes Foundation in India played in a junior tournament in Norway called the Norway Cup, which was attended by more than 25000 young players from all over the world. Among the other teams attending were four from China (www.friends-of-Tibet.org.nz/news/august_2002_update_19.htm). In 2003 a Tibetan under-13 team arrived in Marseille to play a series of matches against schools in Monaco, Marseille and Dijon. The visit was arranged by a Mr Thierry Marcade, a physical education teacher in Marseille (www.logic.at/Tibet/wtnn/wtnn-12.11.2003-II-9.html).[3] Although the Tibetans won 3-1 at a school in Auriol and 5-0 in Marseille they lost 1-0 to Monaco. Perhaps most importantly for them Prince Albert of Monaco was present at that match and expressed sympathy with their plight. They also had a mayoral reception in Auriol and went on to Dijon, with cultural events, talks, films and lectures on Tibet planned to coincide with their visit in order to 'create a general awareness [of Tibet] among the French people' (www.TimesofTibet.com/artman/publish/article_566.shtml).

The domestic game is also being strengthened. The Tibetan National Football Association is a member of the Tibetan National Sports Association, which was founded in India in 2001. In June 2003 it organised a competition in which the exile community in India was divided into eight regions. These played for the Gyalyum Chenmo Memorial Gold Cup, named after the late mother of the Tibetan leader, His Holiness the 14th Dalai Lama of Tibet. Later that year a Tibetan team also took part in a student competition at the Panjab University between six teams representing United Africa, Bhutan, Tibet, Manipur, Ladakh and Thailand.[4] At the GCMGC Cup the guest of honour was Ugyen Thinley Dorje, the 16th Karmapa, a youthful and important incarnation who had escaped from Chinese Tibet some years earlier. Before the match, played at the Tibetan Children's Village school ground, the 16th Karmapa gave a speech in which he emphasised that 'One must ... play a game with a spirit of true sportsmanship. One must be able to accept winning and losing as a part of any game' (www.Tibet.net.flash/2003/0603/020608.html). Perhaps he should have directed his remarks to the crowd, for after the home team lost 2-0 to a team based in Pokhara (Nepal), it was reported that 'for the first time TCV football ground saw hooliganism in form of throwing of empty water bottles on the field. But whether it was in support of the second goal or in dismay is not clear' (www.tibetanyouthcongress.org/tycnews.htm 07/06/2003).

The stated aim of the Tibetan National Football Association is:

To promote games and sports among Tibetan community in exile [and] to help achieve harmony and healthy physical growth and sportsmanship among Tibetans. Although the association has nothing in political nature [*sic*] but through games and sports it does help create better understanding and awareness of the Tibetan issue in the international scenario (ibid.).

The website of the team sponsors, Hummel, presents it somewhat differently. The site features a picture of a shaven-headed Tibetan with a football on his lap. He is apparently meditating and there is a Tibetan flag behind him. 'Both seriously and wilfully' reads the accompanying message:

The Tibetan national team players do their best to create great experiences, unity and hope. And they follow their own ways to create a characteristic cultural identity in finding a balance between the spiritual and secular worlds ... so that Tibet can create a football history of its own (www.hummel.dk/sw/273.asp).

While the marketing man who came up with this text enjoyed taking liberties with politics and cultural cliché, he was simply wrong in his final statement. Tibet already has a football history of its own, which is wound up in the broader politics and cultural dynamics of its past. Tibet has not been the only Himalayan state to make its mark, however humble, on world football. According to the Elo Ratings Bhutan, a mountainous Buddhist nation of 750000 people sandwiched between India and what is now the Tibetan Autonomous Republic of China, ranks 220th in the world. That places it behind Anguilla and just ahead of the Vatican, with a record of played 26, won two, lost twenty-three, with one game drawn and with fifteen goals for and one hundred and twelve against. While the Bhutan Football Federation has been in existence for some decades[5], the country was only affiliated to FIFA in August 2000. It first entered international competition at the South Asian games in Nepal in 1999 losing 7-0 to the home team. A series of defeats followed, including a 20-0 loss to Kuwait in the Asia cup in February 2000 (www.zenads/2599.zen.co.uk/bhutan/bhutan.html).[6] So poor was their record that by the summer of 2002 Bhutan ranked 202nd in the world with just one team, that from the Caribbean island of Montserrat, below them. However on the 30th of June 2002, while hundreds of millions of football fans the world over prepared to watch the World Cup final played in Tokyo between Brazil and Germany, 15,000 fans gathered at the Changlimithang stadium in the Bhutanese capital of Thimphu to watch another match: The Other Cup. This 'Other Cup' was sponsored by KesselsKramer, a Dutch media firm, and Robot, a Tokyo production company, and was played for by the two lowest-ranking teams in world football. To the delight of the home crowd Bhutan achieved its first ever win, a 4-0 triumph over Montserrat, with Bhutan skipper Wangyel Dorji scoring a hat-trick.[7] After the game the two teams sat down together to watch the Brazil-Germany match on satellite television. The Montserrat players must have been glad to relax, as their journey to Bhutan had taken five days and they had been troubled by the 7,600 foot altitude of Thimphu. Sportingly, they avoided using either factor as an excuse for their defeat. Bhutan meanwhile, could celebrate their FIFA recognised victory, which temporarily took them up to 199th place in world football (www.mypage.bluewin.ch/raoonline/pages/story/bt/btfootball01.html).

The fact that the players in the Other Cup could watch the World Cup on television was itself remarkable. The authorities of the devoutly Buddhist kingdom had long resisted the introduction of television but the rise of satellite television effectively made such a ban impossible to police. Bhutan's king, who is himself said to enjoy watching football, temporarily rescinded the ban for the occasion of the 1998 World Cup. That competition was at the centre of another Bhutanese football story, albeit one that was fictional. The Bhutanese film *The Cup* tells the story of three young monks at a Tibetan Buddhist monastery in India who are obsessed with football and determined to watch their Brazilian heroes progress in the 1998 World Cup. This brings the monks into a gentle conflict with the monastic traditions and authorities as they struggle to be allowed to watch the contest for world football's championship. *The Cup* was devised and directed by Khyentse Norbu, a Bhutanese Buddhist monk and football fan, who had formerly been an advisor during the making of Bernardo Bertolucci's 1993 film *The Little Buddha*. In contrast to *The Little Buddha* and so many other portrayals of the Himalayan Buddhist lands on film, *The Cup* did not mythologize its setting as a Shangri-la of meditating monks, wise old men and magic and mystery. Instead it offered a charmingly realistic picture of youth caught between tradition and modernity. Amidst the prayers and monastic rituals, the film's young heroes dreamed of football while the custodians of tradition wrestled with the question of whether this strange foreign game could be a permitted diversion within Buddhist monastic culture.

That football has increasingly found a place in Himalayan culture is clear from the report in June 2002 that Bhutan's Foreign Minister, Lyonpo Jigme Thinley, had expressed concern that football and basketball could replace archery as the national sport. D.K. Chetri, Secretary-General of Bhutan's Olympic committee, was quoted in support as saying that 'In Bhutan archery is more than a sport, its part of our cultural heritage, a festive activity deeply ingrained in our national character ... It is an expression of being Bhutanese as well as a social event' (www.news.bbc.co.uk/I/hi/wrld/south_asia/ 2036815.stn). But with the Bhutanese Football Federation benefiting from grants from FIFA to improve the national stadium and training facilities, football has quickly established firm roots in Bhutan. There are now nine teams in the Bhutan A League club competition with a further nine teams in the B league and a C league soon to start. The 2003 competition was won by the DrukPol team with a 6-2-0 record.[8] At international level too Bhutan has made progress since the days of the 'Other Cup'. Victories such as the 6-0 thrashing of Guam have been celebrated and have enabled Bhutan to progress to the recent Asia Cup in Saudi Arabia, where their performances against far-higher ranking sides have been reasonable.[9] The Royal Netherlands Football Association has provided a Dutch coach, Arie Schans, who now presides over the team and he rates several of his players as capable of earning a living as professionals in Europe.[10] The Word Cup finals may be a long way off, but the era of 20-0 defeats to the likes of Kuwait seems a thing of the past.

Football and History in Tibet

In a special edition of the *Newsletter of the International Association for Asian Studies* devoted to sports in Asia, James Mills noted the lack of academic research into sport in Asia. 'One suspects', he writes, 'that sport has been neglected as it often fails to fit easily within the tried and trusted categories preferred by Asian scholars, caste, economics, politics, agriculture, land tenure, marriage, kinship, ritual and religion'. He goes on to discuss two approaches that have developed in this field:

The first has been to examine discourses about sports, Asia and Asians, and to explore the ways in which games and physical activities have been used by all manner of groups to construct different identities and to assert or to challenge stereotypes. The second has been to focus on sports and power, and to show how sporting moments and activities have been implicated in the formation of, and important in the challenges to, the region's political and social systems [to demonstrate that] sports have often been central to the construction of the identities and structures that shape Asia today [and] sporting activities have just as crucially offered opportunities to challenge and transcend those identities and structures' (IIAS Newsletter 28/07/2002: 7).

In light of these remarks it is important to look again at the stories above. In two previous articles (McKay 1994; 2001) I have examined the history of sport in Tibet and focussed on the question of sports and power in the context of the British colonial project in the Himalayas. The expansion of the British Indian empire during the 19th century brought the British in India into direct contact with both Bhutan and Tibet. British military forces subsequently invaded both territories and imposed diplomatic agreements with the Himalayan states. A British Political Officer stationed in the Sikkimese capital of Gangtok was given responsibility for relationships with Sikkim, Bhutan and Tibet and the British subsequently endeavoured to befriend the local elites and guide them on a path of modernisation on the European nation-state model. The primary British concern in this project was the security of their northern imperial frontier and their presence in the Himalayas had an essentially military character. However, its chief impact on the Himalayan Buddhist states came as a result of its encouragement of the structures and processes of modernity and sport was part of the British imperial model of development. Apart from providing the imperial personnel with healthy leisure time activities, sport also served as a means to develop friendly ties with local people and was seen as a device through which the Himalayan states could develop a national identity on the modern model. This process was far more developed in Tibet than in Bhutan because Bhutan was largely secure from any threat from China or Russia to the north and consequently no British personnel were permanently stationed there.

In Tibet, the British maintained a permanent presence at Gyantse (120 miles south-west of Lhasa) from 1904–1947 and in the Tibetan capital itself from 1936–47. British diplomatic representatives, medical officers, soldiers, radio officers, technicians and clerks all served there throughout this period. During the early years of the British presence, football and other sports such as hockey were a means of keeping fit and passing the time. Tibetan employees of the British posts presumably began to join in these activities despite the fact that they were very different from the indigenous ideas of sport. The Tibetans had no history of ball games and their recreational activities centred on board and dice games (Finkel 1995) or sports deriving from martial pursuits. These latter activities consisted of wrestling, archery, horse-racing, long-jumping etc. but with military skills of low social standing in Tibetan society, competitions were apparently impromptu and at a local level. There were no written records kept and no associated infrastructure. Only among those monks responsible for monastic discipline, the *ldab-ldobs*, does there appear to have been a physical culture (McKay 2001: 93). Fights among these monks were common and they engaged in various trials of strength and exhibitions of martial skills.[11] They did not, however, develop any form of 'national' sport or establish a sporting culture in wider society. The Tibetans had to learn the written and unwritten rules of sports as understood by the British.

Sport first became an aspect of British policy in Tibet in the 1920s when a school was established in Gyantse under an English headmaster, Frank Ludlow (1885–1972). His pupils quickly learned to enjoy the game of football which Ludlow saw as a potential vehicle for modernity, not least in the development of a modern national consciousness on the Western nation-state model. At that time, while possessing a distinct identity and traditions, Tibetans did not have a sense of nationalism in the Western understanding of an identity based around a nation-state so the British sought to develop this in order to strengthen Tibet as a 'buffer state' against threats to their Indian empire. Ludlow therefore invented 'Tibetan colours' of yellow and maroon for the players' kit and while using the game to promote British sporting values, he also used it to enshrine Tibetan traditions. When a Political Officer awarded a cash prize to a school team, for example, Ludlow suggested they use the money to buy a picture of the Dalai Lama. In the mid-1920s, however, the Tibetan state turned away from modernity and rejected many innovations while attempting to preserve their traditional society and isolation. The Gyantse school was closed and football was deprived of an indigenous base. A new effort, however, was made in the mid-1930s when the Political Officer in Sikkim, Basil Gould (1883–1956), established a British mission in the Tibetan capital of Lhasa. Drawing on Ludlow's earlier attempts to stimulate the development of a national consciousness, he organized a football competition in Lhasa. The teams competing included a British mission team and two Tibetan sides, one composed of soldiers from the Dalai Lama's own personal bodyguard and the other a team called Lhasa United formed by Lhasa residents. The latter included Tibetans, Ladakhis, Sikkimese, Nepalese and even a Chinese tailor. In addition there was a team made up of players from the Nepalese community and another from the Lhasa Muslim community (mainly composed of Ladakhis). As the game became more popular in Lhasa in the late 1930s the competition grew to include 14 teams and until 1944 it remained the most popular foreign sport in Tibet. In that year the Tibetan government banned football. The decree stated that kicking a football was 'as bad as kicking the head of the Lord Buddha'.[12] While the overt cause of the ban was a hailstorm during a game, a most inauspicious event in Tibetan understanding, the real reason for the decree was opposition to the sport from the powerful monastic community. The guardians of Buddhist Tibet saw time and money being devoted to a non-religious activity, not least by monks, and saw passions and loyalties arising that were outside of the traditional structures of Tibetan society.[13]

The conservatism of the monastic elites is now recognised as fatal to any chance Tibet might have had to survive as an independent entity in the modern world (Dhondup 1986; Goldstein 1989) and I have previously concluded that had a Tibetan football team been created it would have made a small contribution towards the recognition of Tibet as a nation-state (McKay 2001: 102). But in the wider sense, the Tibetans defined themselves in religious rather than secular terms, and manifestations of popular secular culture were of little interest to the ruling elites, who failed to see in them the aspects of modernity that would enhance Tibet's prospects for future independence.

It is clear that in the Tibetan exile community today football is no longer seen by the authorities as being 'as bad as kicking the Buddha's head'. Sports have been recognised by the exile government as a valuable tool, both for the general health and welfare of the community and as an instrument for fostering Tibetan identity.[14] There is a wider context to this development. With the post-1959 establishment of a Tibetan exile community, based around the Dalai Lama and his government in Dharamsala (north India), Tibetan efforts to isolate themselves from the modern world have been abandoned. The policy of rejecting modernity that was formerly characteristic of the Tibetan state is recognized as having proved disastrous to its long term interests and the exile community today is increasingly engaged with the modern world. With the passing of time the majority of people in that community are now Indian-born. While refugees from the Tibetan Autonomous Republic of China continue to make the hazardous journey into exile across the Himalayas and elder authorities such as the Dalai Lama still recall a childhood in their native land, most of the exile community have been schooled in India and are more familiar with motorcycles than yaks, and are more likely to be found reading the racy novels of Harold Robbins than the Buddhist philosophy of Tsong Khapa.

As the Tibetan community has become increasingly embedded in Indian society new formulations of identity have arisen and the structures of Tibetan society have been altered to accommodate these changes. While such negotiations are the norm for long-term exile communities, the developments in

Dharamsala are complicated by the existence of an imaginary construction of Tibet as Shangri-La (Bishop 1989; Dodin and Räther 2001). In the popular imagination Tibet is a land of magic and mystery which is home to a race of enlightened beings, other-worldly monks who pass their existence in meditation. This image was constructed on the basis of a number of factors such as the earliest accounts by Marco Polo of a land of 'necromancers' up to James Hilton's 1933 novel 'Lost Horizon'.[15] In exile, the Tibetan community has found advantages and disadvantages in this imaginative association. On the one hand, their exotic appeal has enabled them to attract considerable patronage; their Indian hosts have been generous in the provision of land and Western sponsors have patronised both Tibetan institutions and individuals. However on the other hand, the image of Tibetans as somehow other-worldly has hindered their efforts to obtain political recognition in the real world and to locate themselves in that real world. Efforts to achieve the latter include the development of modern institutions such as biomedical facilities, democratic elections and sponsored social processes such as literary prizes and sporting infrastructure.

The main aim of the exile authorities has been to preserve and promote Tibetan culture and identity, which they regard as threatened with extinction in their homeland. This has involved defining certain cultural elements (such as dance and medicine) as distinctive of Tibetan culture and preserving and promoting those elements in an attempt to demonstrate that a distinctly Tibetan Buddhist culture can exist in, and contribute to, a modern world. Despite lingering conservatism they have also recognised the overwhelming impact of modernity and sought to maintain the unity of the exile community by tolerating the tastes of a new generation. Thus a modern Tibetan identity is emerging. Tibetans may wear jeans, eat hamburgers, listen to rock and roll and play football. But they will remain Tibetan, identify themselves as Tibetan and are manifestations of a modern Tibetan culture (Diehl 2002). Such new and negotiated identities are, of course, problematic. Tenzin Dargyal's happiness at 'playing for the Tibetan people' implies both a particular expression of a modern identity and a particular definition of the Tibetan people, one that includes Tibetans in China as well as in exile. The political cause of an independent Tibet is served, in this understanding, by a Tibetan football team and its flag-waving supporters. They demonstrate that Tibet is a nation and the sport offers the opportunity to promote the Tibetan national cause in Europe, where football supporters are invited to attend cultural events associated with the team's visit, and are thus drawn to the Tibetan exile cause. Similarly, the stated aims of the Tibetan National Football Association evoke the language of sporting modernity in terms of the promotion of health and desired or ideal behaviour patterns, while explicitly

claiming a role in the creation of international awareness of the Tibetan
political cause. They are thus identifying themselves as patriotic Tibetans. To
attack football would thus be to attack an instrument, and implicitly the ideal,
of the national freedom struggle.

The construction of a modern Tibetan identity embracing football is negotiated with tradition as their domestic football competition is played for a cup
that enshrines the memory of their leader's mother, a much-loved figure in
the exile community. Thus football acknowledges the authority of the traditional leaders through its honouring of one whose position is unchallenged,
locating itself within the community despite the many aspects of the game
that are foreign to those traditions. The 16th Karmapa's role at the football
tournament was also highly symbolic. In inviting the leader of the one of the
main sects of Tibetan Buddhism, football acknowledged traditional authority.
His presence also symbolised a new era. The leadership of the exile community has remained in the hands of those who escaped Tibet since 1959, most
notably in the grip of the charismatic figure of the Nobel prize-winning Dalai
Lama. But as that generation ages, the community is faced with a need for a
new generation of leaders. The Karmapa was born in Tibet and escaped to
India in the late 1990s and is clearly an outstanding individual with an important role to play in the future of the exile community. He is young, possesses
something of the Dalai Lama's charisma and is now busily learning the
English language skills he will need in his future dealings with the outside
world. Thus, he is seen by young Tibetans as both a traditional figure of
authority and also one of their own generation. The feeling is that he may yet
turn out to be a John F. Kennedy, if not a Che Guevara.

In calling for 'a game with a spirit of true sportsmanship' the Karmapa
filled multiple roles. He was an appropriate cultural figurehead for a 'Tibetan'
event. However, he also took on the traditional role of a world sporting
supremo by standing above the immediate event and espousing the idealised
values of modern sport in which the spirit of the occasion is valorized and
privileged above the actual outcome of the competition. However, the
spectators (many of whom were monks) were actors in another manifestation
of football identity; the supporter as 'hooligan'. The throwing of plastic water
bottles was, in this context, a rejection of idealised values and a manifestation
of the tribal passions that are equally well associated with sport, not only in
the modern world, but historically. It was precisely this tribal identity and this
passion that had been feared by the traditional monastic elites who had
banned football in 1944. Nor was the throwing of water bottles compatible
with the desired image articulated by the team's sponsor, that of Tibetan
participants 'finding a balance between the spiritual and secular worlds'. In
pre-1950 Tibet, regional and local identities were the primary identification

of individuals. In exile, and vis-à-vis a Chinese 'Other', a unified Tibetan identity can now be said to exist but clearly more localised identities may be reverted to, under certain circumstances, and that reversion perhaps encouraged by localised sporting identities.

The football history of Tibet is apparently forgotten in these negotiations of identity. Nowhere in the literature associated with the modern Tibetan team is it mentioned that the game was played in pre-communist Tibet, albeit under colonial auspices. The rejection of modernity in pre-1950s Tibet cost both local football and the Tibetan state dearly, with the fate of the game symbolic of the fate of the state.[16] Reminders of that failure are not, it seems, a desirable association in the modern construction of a sporting Tibet.

Football and Modernity in Bhutan

The recent development of football in Bhutan has much in common with that in the Tibetan exile community. During the colonial period Bhutan and Tibet both functioned as independent states and neither was under the direct authority of the British imperial Government of India. But unlike Tibet, which was recognised by the British government as part of China, Bhutan had entered into a treaty relationship with the Government of India that gave control of its defence and foreign relations to the British. After Indian independence in 1947 the new Indian government took over that guiding role. Bhutan remained an independent kingdom and is represented in the United Nations, unlike Tibet which became a part of China. Like Tibet, Bhutan is a Buddhist state and is essentially conservative in its tendency to see isolationism as a means of protecting its independent culture and identity. In recent years however Bhutan has, with considerable caution, increased its engagement with modernity and also sought to emphasise its independent identity. The Bhutanese have seen the effects of modernity on their Himalayan neighbours and have no desire to turn Thimphu into a city on the Kathmandu-Dharamsala-Lhasa-Gangtok model of cheap concrete high-rise, polluted air, lost youth, drugs, crime and exploitation by outsiders. They are tentatively seeking a new model which is more in line with Buddhist modernist principles and traditional culture. Thus new buildings must be in traditional forms, national dress is compulsory and the air in Thimphu remains pure and fresh.

Yet modernity has come to Bhutan and football is both an example of its encroaching nature and a factor that has further fuelled it. Whereas Bhutan's Indian and Tibetan neighbours were introduced to football by the British empire, the absence of a permanent imperial presence in Bhutan meant that foreign sports and games were not played there during the colonial period.

It was only in the 1950s when schools were opened in Ha and Paro that football began to be played. Foreign teachers, principally Indians but including some European Jesuits, were recruited to these schools and introduced the pupils to football as Ludlow had done in Tibet in the 1920s. In 1968 a Bhutanese team competed in the Indian Independence cup in Calcutta, but the team was composed almost entirely of non-nationals. This tendency continued, with 'Bhutanese' teams playing in the All Nepal Football Association Cup against China, Hongkong, India, Korea, Bangladesh and Sri Lanka. But financial restrictions saw the end of the recruitment of foreign players and the game stagnated until recently, when the heavy loss to Kuwait brought a fresh impetus to the development of the game. Some local players are now paid and many receive free accommodation, enabling them to devote more time to training and practice (www.mypage.bluewin.ch/raoonline/pages/story/bt/btfootball01.html).

The increasing popularity of football has brought with it the unanticipated desire to watch football on television and the introduction of television into Bhutan, with a Bhutanese channel inaugurated in 1999 to compete with the satellite channels available. Long resisted for fear of its impact on Buddhist society, TV is something that is still not universally regarded with favour and is blamed for any increase in crime or delinquency. While the benefits of access to television are still debated, the success of the movie 'The Cup' is a source of some pride to the Bhutanese and Khyentse Norbu has recently made a new film which explicitly confronts the difficulties of the Bhutanese encounter with modernity. In this film *Magicians and Travellers* the hero is a modern Bhutanese youth who wears a leather jacket and listens to rock and roll. Appointed to a minor government post in a remote village, he dreams of migrating to America. The opportunity presents itself for him to realise his fantasy and he readily sets off for Thimphu and his ticket to America only to be confronted on his journey by a variety of reminders of the essential goodness of his indigenous culture. Significantly, in *Magicians and Travellers*, there is a clip of an archery competition. Archery serves here as a metaphor for traditional village pastimes. The only sport with which Bhutan has been associated in the past has been archery and its only representatives at the Olympics have been archers. It is now feared that the supremacy of that sport is now challenged by football, and as we have seen, it has been constructed as a threat to Bhutanese identity and a rejection of the traditional 'cultural heritage'. In harnessing football as an aspect of modernity to the expression of the independent nation, other, more traditional sporting forms may be sacrificed in the construction of the new identity.[17] Football may serve several functions in Bhutanese society, but as well as providing an outlet for the energies and passions of under-employed youth, a Bhutanese national football team does serve to demonstrate independent existence as a nation to the outside world. While that independence is not immediately threatened, Bhutan's position between the two most populous nations on earth requires careful management and, as in India and China, the harnessing of national-ism is considered a tool of governance. Indeed, one factor that may have eased the introduction of football into Bhutan is that the articulation of sport-ing values is not inconsistent with Buddhism. Concepts of 'fair play' and 'the importance of taking part' are compatible with Buddhist ideals of compas-sion and humility. Football is thus seen by the Bhutanese as an aspect of modernity that may be harnessed for the national good without radically challenging the traditional forces and understandings within the nation.[18]

Conclusion

The official encouragement of football in the Bhutanese and Tibetan exile communities in the Himalayas is a recent phenomenon. Sporting cultures on the Western model have never existed there, although recreational activities and physical competition deriving from military pursuits were known, as in the case of archery in Bhutan. Although no attempts were made to introduce football into Bhutan during the colonial period the British did try to introduce the game into Tibet as a means of developing relations with individual Tibetans and to stimulate the development of a Tibetan national identity. But these efforts were resisted by the indigenous authorities who were hostile to the introduction of virtually all aspects of modernity into traditional Buddhist culture. This resistance led to the banning of football in Tibet. More recently, however, both the Bhutanese state and the Tibetan exile government have encouraged football as they have recognised in it a means of promoting national identity on the world stage. In the Tibetan case this marks a complete reversal of the policies of the pre-1950 period and a belated acceptance of the British understanding of sport as a political weapon. In addition, the pro-motion of a Tibetan sporting identity challenges the image of 'Mythos Tibet' with its imagined 'other-worldly' population. While the team sponsors may attempt to draw on that image the message of football-playing Tibet is of a nation capable of participating in the real, not the imagined, world. That there is an explicit political purpose behind this promotion is something acknowledged by the Tibetan National Football Association which, while on the one hand denying any political intent, openly states on the other that their sport assists 'awareness of the Tibetan issue in the international scenario'. In playing its initial 'international' against Greenland, another community seeking recognition of its separate political identity, the Tibetans gave a signal of their membership of a world community of 'would-be' nations, implicitly allying themselves with the Greenland cause. In the Bhutanese case, a game against fellow strugglers Montserrat also served a political cause, but one less urgent and dramatic than the Tibetan struggle to save their identity. The Bhutanese endeavour was more about what Mills describes as the urge to 'construct different identities and ... challenge stereotypes' than to challenge 'the region's political and social systems'.

In adopting and promoting football, the one true 'world game', the Himalayan kingdoms claim a place in the modern world. Indigenous traditions such as archery may suffer in comparison but in the constant process of identity formation the Himalayan elites judge that football may be used to consolidate 'Tibetan' or 'Bhutanese' national identities without threatening the core elements that constitute these. The earlier fears that football would lead to passions and rivalries harmful to the wider society have not entirely vanished, but by associating the game with traditional structures, authorities and objectives, it is hoped that these issues may be overcome. Football is, however, one of innumerable elements of 'modernity'. It brings with it other aspects, such as television and a non-traditional code of dress. While Bhutan enforce national dress in public places and resisted the introduction of television, both foreign elements have now been rapidly accepted into Bhutanese society, with as-yet unknown consequences.

One additional factor that may be considered here is the extent to which football in Bhutan, and to a lesser extent in the Tibetan exile community, contributes to state centralization around a capital (an essential element of the Western nation state model). The mountainous regions contain few areas of flat ground suitable for football pitches and the demands of subsistence agriculture inevitably take priority there. The result is that football tends to be concentrated in urban centres where land is not required for farming and level surfaces can be spared for recreation. At the grass-roots, spare flat land is something of a rarity in many other countries and an uneven playing surface of course does little to hinder the enthusiasm of the game's amateur players. But at a more advanced level, a Bhutanese or a Tibetan exile footballer who wishes to progress must move to Thimphu or to Dharamsala or one of the other exile centres in India or Nepal. Similarly, a supporter must journey to the capital to see his national team play. Thus sporting resources, along with so many other elements, are drawn to, and help to constitute, the physical centres of the Himalayas' modern nations.

10

COMMUNITY, IDENTITY AND SPORT: ANGLO-INDIANS IN COLONIAL AND POSTCOLONIAL INDIA

Megan S. Mills

Introduction

The Anglo-Indian community is a tiny remnant of a class that represents some of the uncomfortable paradoxes of colonial legacies (Carton 2000). Once granted privileges as a social group because of the blood relations with the colonial masters at the same time they were rejected and kept at a distance both by the colonizers and the colonized as somehow tainted by the 'Other'. Now that those colonial masters have departed they nevertheless remain in India as an uneasy reminder of the presence of the former. In the postcolonial nation they find themselves stranded with community institutions and practices that had been developed to emphasize separateness from all things Indian and at one with all things British. Their identity as 'almost-British' sits at odds with the urge, in postcolonial India, to privilege all things Indian.[1] This essay considers the place of sport in the development of an Anglo-Indian identity and the search for a role in postcolonial India by members of the community. In 1947 there were around 500,000 Anglo-Indians in South Asia and current assessments suggest an ongoing presence of 250,000 to 300,000 in a total Indian population of 1 billion. Another 300,000 Anglo-Indians have resettled in the West since India obtained Independence. In spite of the community's microscopic size, it has produced numerous Olympians as well as coaches, organizers and technical delegates at every level. Moreover, sport continues to play an important role in the socialization of Anglo-Indians as it remains central to the curriculum of the 300 or so English-medium schools that are run by or cater for the community. It is in these schools in particular, and in the community as a whole, that Anglo-Indian culture

continues in the postcolonial period to follow patterns of cultural transfer
from the West to Asia that are familiar from the colonial era (Mangan 1992).

A Hampered Population

The Anglo-Indians' 500-year history is one that Caplan (2003) has recently
written of as essentially a story of blurred boundaries, multiple identities and
creolized cultures and it might be useful to see the community as shaped by a
struggle for survival, as Smith has noted of many ethnic minorities (1992).
At first the British in South Asia followed the approaches of other European
powers in India by encouraging Eurasian enclaves as they appeared to lend
an impression of permanence in India. No distinction was made between
East India Company servants of European or Eurasian origin and, into the
early 19th century, a great many Britons continued to marry Indian women
of varied Asian, Portuguese, Dutch, French or British descent. However, in
the 1780s and 1790s persons of combined ancestry were excluded from the
Company's military and higher civil posts because the 'Indo-Britons' or 'East
Indians', as they were then known, were seen as a security risk (Hawes 1996).
It was observed that educated mulattos had aided the Santo Domingo rebellion
and the loss of the American colonies had sensitised opinion to threats of
insurgency everywhere. In short order colonial law and policy came to distinguish Anglo-Indians from 'pure' Europeans. As Eurasians came to out-number
Europeans in colonial India from the late 18th century it is possible to discern
an official aim of keeping the population down to prevent its political influence. Until the 1830s Anglo-Indians were forbidden to own land, to migrate
beyond East India Company stations or to send their sons to Britain for
education as had been customary. These sons could not inherit automatically.
Until 1947 and the firm assignment of Indian citizenship, Anglo-Indian
status 'approximated' that of the British in India for the purposes of education
and defense, while in all other respects they were designated as Indians. In
general, the obligations of British citizenship were required of them, but they
were denied most of its benefits.

The aftermath of the 1857 rebellion, and the expansion of India's lower
colonial service, brought reserved service roles for Anglo-Indians as a useful,
English-speaking population that had demonstrated its loyalty through the
course of the uprising. This preferment was a mixed blessing as in the long
term it discouraged economic diversification by the community. Furthermore,
Anglo-Indians earned a fraction of what was accorded Europeans in the same
services and they remained ineligible for responsible military service until the
20th century although they were conscripted for assorted conflicts, which was
never done with other Indian communities. Indeed, in the twentieth century

Anglo-Indians were obliged to serve in the Auxiliary Force India (AFI) as a condition of their service employment. The AFI was a militia organisation which was widely deployed to contain nationalist agitation. Unsuprisingly, it was disbanded in 1947.

It is an irony then that, at the same time as the community was being relied upon to provide soldiers in times of crisis, they were being constructed within the discourses of scientific racism as examples of the degeneration that came from miscegenation. An American social scientific offering of 1918, for example, stated that 'the Eurasians (Anglo-Indians) are slight and weak ... they are naturally indolent and will enter into no employment requiring exertion or labor. This lack of energy is correlated with an incapacity for organization. They will not assume burdensome responsibilities but they make passable clerks where only routine labour is required (Reuters 1918: 29–31)'. On the one hand the community was rewarded and privileged for being 'almost-British' and it was trusted to provide soldiers and administrators loyal to the Empire. On the other hand, however, the community was carefully constructed as 'not-quite-British', and its Asian ancestry was represented as the source of both mental and physical deficiencies. The privileges granted to the Eurasians served to secure their distance from local Indian society (for exceptions to this see Arnold 1979). From the perspective of the Indian communities the Anglo-Indians were representatives of the colonial order. Meanwhile, Anglo-Indians had been rewarded for their distance from local groups during the events of 1857 and therefore learned that their privileges relied upon the continued maintenance of an 'arms-length' relationship with Indians. While Anglo-Indians were therefore isolated by the British from the British elites, a mutually exclusive relationship with Indians imposed an isolation from local communities (Moore 1986).

Sport and Community

The lines were drawn then, so that the Anglo-Indian community was isolated from other groups in India and drew on British models of culture to define itself. As such, sports became important to the community, partly as a means of visibly displaying 'British-like' behaviour, partly because their community was divided into groups that lent themselves to the organization of teams, and partly because the experience of isolation meant that the community devoted great energy to developing its own institutions and cultural practices. The community's English-medium schools were founded by Christian religious orders arriving from the West after the 1830s on the English public school model. Families engaged in service work of regular rotations or remote postings frequently dispatched their children to boarding schools which typically demonstrated an ideal of competitive sports as a natural adjunct of education. Athleticism became a strong element of Anglo-Indian childhood. The colony-born, when writing of their youth, often mention railway colonies or other service enclaves in which there were always sufficient participants to allow for what could be a rather incessant round of hockey, cricket, soccer and other sports as leisure activities. Moreover, adult life was shaped by work in which the men spent their entire careers within one of the colonial service departments. The first of these was the massive South Asian railway infrastructure in which Anglo-Indians served into the 1960s and sometimes beyond. Anglo-Indians were also visible in the subcontinent's other service networks such as the police, forests administrations and public works departments. These various networks were organized in distinctive ways that emphasized corporate separateness and identity, to the extent that employees lived together in cantonments or 'colonies' where the housing was reserved to those in the relevant field. A perusal of issues of the Bengal-Nagpur Railway Magazine from the 1930s attests to the everyday prominence of sport in railways life. A July issue refers in its opening pages to football enjoyed by the young and an upcoming football tournament, to two women's bowling teams, and to the arrival of a tennis expert, Mr. S.A.Yusoof, at Khurda Road in what is now Orissa.[2]

Individual stories back up this view of a social life dominated by sports. Kenneth Wyllarde Blythe-Perrett, an electrical engineer for Bengal Railways, was a dedicated athlete in his youth who won national championships in discus, javelin and shot-put. He was also a successful sprinter and his boxing career ended only at his young wife's objection to bloody noses and he nevertheless maintained an interest in the sport as a boxing referee. He held several posts around Bengal and at each one served as the Railway's sports officer.[3] Mr. Jim Bannister of Chakradharpur Junction recently wrote of his life and career on the railways and referred to the local community of his youth as one, 'alive with sporting activities' (1998: 69–71). Chakradharpur was known for its boxers and December 26th was Boxing Day as, 'all of us would wait with bated breath, in our places, on the makeshift galleries around the boxing ring' (70). Mr. Bannister became a national boxing organiser in his home area. Overall, attachment to service, school, church and communal social life was central to Anglo-Indian society and culture and each association generated its own sporting teams and clubs. Membership of these teams and clubs was exclusively Anglo-Indian, as no British member would want to join, and no Indian would be admitted. Thus sports clubs became an important aspect of a separate Anglo-Indian way of life and at the same time they perpetuated and consolidated that separate way of life.

Hockey, India and the Global Sports Stage

Bengal Hockey Club was founded in 1908 and was followed by Karachi's Sind Hockey Association, which was established in 1920 and which went on to play an active role in systematising Indian hockey. The game's modest needs in terms of equipment and facilities rendered it a sport suited to corners of South Asia and, as was the case elsewhere in the British empire, hockey was regarded as a healthy passtime for both sexes. Eric Stracey's memoir of Bangalore in the 1920s and 1930s refers to the sports in which he and most other Anglo-Indians were involved, recalling that cricket was played in the summer, soccer belonged to the monsoon but that hockey had year-round appeal. Indeed, in this period cricket was the site of sporting confrontation between British and Indian elites, while football was increasingly monopolised by Indians (Dimeo 2001: 67–70). As such, as Stracey writes, it was hockey that the Anglo-Indian community made especially its own (2000: 12). This was contested by Indians though, and Stracey notes that in the 1930s the best of the community's teams, the Sappers & Miners, was rivalled by the Bangalore Indians (ibid).

The Golden Era of Indian hockey is considered to be the period 1928–1956 when India won six consecutive gold medals in Olympic competition. In fact, India won all 24 Olympic matches in this period and proceeded to take the gold again at Tokyo in 1964 and Moscow in 1980. These successes were founded on a number of factors, including the solid organizational structures of the Indian Hockey Association which was founded in 1925 and the introduction of the sport into the Indian Army in the 1920s. Anglo-Indian talent, however, was another factor. In Bengal the Calcutta Hockey League's annual tournament was won by Anglo-Indian teams seventeen times between 1905 and 1924 (Anthony 1968: 227). For many years Calcutta Customs was considered unbeatable, with other outstanding players belonging to the Calcutta Port Commission or the Bengal-Nagpur Railway. In Bombay the story was similar in this period and the city's Aga Khan Tournament was dominated by Anglo-Indian elevens such as Bombay Customs or Christ Church School's Old Boys of Jabalpur. The All-India Scindia Gold Cup was won repeatedly by a team chosen from fewer than fifty of the Ajmer railway workshop's apprentices. In 1926 an Indian Army team toured New Zealand and on the eve of their departure were beaten soundly by an Anglo-Indian team of the North-Western military. It is little surprise then that the team sent to the 1928 Olympics was largely composed of Anglo-Indian players. Eight of the eleven male players representing India in the Final were from the community, as was the manager (Antony 1968: 229).[4] The Anglo-Indian lawyer and parliamentarian, Frank Anthony, claimed that his community might easily have summoned at least six more teams of equally high standard at the time. The

1932 Olympic team contained seven Anglo-Indians, including R. J. Allen, who had played with the 1928 team and who was regarded as the world's best goal-keeper. While the 1936 Olympics is remembered as the event at which Jesse Owens confounded the Nazi regime's theories of Aryan supremacy by winning the 100 metres sprint, India's hockey team made a no less compelling point on the issue. There were six Anglo-Indians on the gold-winning Indian team and once again R. J. Allen returned to the Olympics. A team dominated by the products of racial miscegenation thrashed the 'racially pure' German team 8-1 in the Final to claim gold in Berlin.

Most of the 1928 and 1932 players hailed from northern and central India and well-organised inter-regional competitions meant that the international players of the 1930s often knew one another well. Hammond, Penniger, the Carr brothers and Allen were students of Oak Grove and Cullen and Emmett attended St. George's College. Both schools were in Mussoorie, Uddar Pradesh. While their roots were localized, their renown became international. Broome Penniger, for example, was known outside of India as the world's best centre and Leslie Hammond and Laurie Carr were famous arrivals in Australia when they later emigrated.[5]

Despite the disruptions of the War and the departure of the British, Anglo-Indian hockey continued to thrive and in 1948 India's hockey team proceeded to become the world champions at London. The star was an Indian, Dhyan Singh, but he was supported by a host of Anglo-Indian players such as Patrick Jansen, Leslie Claudius, Lawrie Fernandes, Gerry Glacken, Leo Pinto, Reginald Rodrigues and Maxie Vaz. This victory was the basis for a period of post-War domination of the sport by teams from India, as successes followed in 1952, 1956 and at Rome in 1960. Moreover, post-Independence Anglo-Indian emigration produced interesting developments abroad. At the 1960 Games in Rome India defeated Australia in the quarter-final by a single goal. Leslie Claudius acted as the Indian team's captain while his opposite number, the Australian captain, was a fellow Anglo-Indian Kevin Carton. Hockey in Western Australia was founded on Anglo-Indian immigrants who went on to dominate the game there. Fred Browne was Australia's first Olympic hockey coach in the 1950s and Eric Pearce represented Australia at the 1968 games in the company of his brothers, Gordon and Julian. In total five Pearce brothers played for Australia and Eric Pearce's daughter, Colleen, played on the Australian women's hockey team at the 1984 Los Angeles games.[6]

Indeed, Anglo-Indians also formed the backbone of Pakistani hockey as, in 1947, P.P. Fernandes and several other hockey players found themselves divided from former team-mates by the new border. Indeed, the defeat sustained by India at the 1960 Olympics was to Pakistan. The sport there is still concentrated in Karachi, Lahore, Rawalpindi and Peshawar, towns of once large

Anglo-Indian populations.[7] It remains organised along the familiar lines of school, occupation or armed forces teams.[8] In more recent times Anglo-Indians have played key roles in the game in South Asia. Cedric D'Souza, a former goalkeeper and Air India employee, was India's national coach at the 1996 Atlanta Olympics following on from a good performance at the 1994 World Cup in Sydney, victory in the 1995 Championship Trophy and gold at the 1998 Bangkok Asian Games. Since 1998 D'Souza has headed the hockey academy at Jullundur and staged hockey camps about the country (Chandigarh Tribune 06/05/2000). Equally significant in terms of the modern game is the Indian Hockey Federation's executive director, Robert 'Panther' Lawrence, a former cricketer and a public relations employee of Tata International.[9]

While Anglo-Indians have an active role in contemporary hockey, they have been co-opted as symbols of the game too. In 2000 Leslie Claudius was honoured by the Ballygunge Institute and the West Bengal sports minister as the Best Bengali Athlete of the Century. It is worth noting that in their determination to claim him, the Bengalis overlooked the facts, namely that Claudius is a native of Bilaspur in Madhya Pradesh and that he attended the Bishop Cotton School in Bangalore with his brothers. Claudius has 3 Olympic gold medals and a silver to his credit and for years his name appeared in the Guiness Book of World Records as the only Olympian to have won in this way for his country. In 1956 and 1960 Claudius was the half-back star of the Indian Olympic team. It seems to have been enough for the Bengali authorities that he has simply lived for a number of years in Calcutta to justify their claiming him as their own. Claudius's first love had actually been football but he was discovered by Dickie Carr of the 1936 Olympic team in 1946, when the latter happened to attend a match between the Bengal-Nagpur Railway's A and B teams at Kharagpur, then the main centre for railway sports.[10] Carr asked Claudius to substitute for a missing player and within a fortnight he was a member of the first-string eleven. He played for Port Commissioners and in 1949 joined Calcutta Customs, carrying on until 1965 when he retired from first-string hockey. Mr. Claudius's son, Bobby Claudius, showed similar ability and had been selected for the national team at the time of his tragically premature death. While Indians have set about claiming Anglo-Indian sporting heroes as their own then, the latter do much to maintain the flow of players from their own communities. This is most obvious in the activities of the All-India Anglo-Indian Association which has organised an annual hockey festival in Bangalore since the early 1980s. However, the flow of players is likewise secured by the commitment of former players to coaching, both in India and in the Anglo-Indian diaspora.[11]

An important part of the hockey story is that played by women. Anglo-Indian women were often pioneers in many of the occupations and pursuits now taken for granted by other educated Indian women. While women's work beyond the home was not considered respectable in other communities Anglo-Indian females went forwards into education, nursing, office roles and the military support services. This level of participation was similarly reflected in sporting activities and, until the 1960s, most of India's national and international women hockey players were Anglo-Indians and it was usual for most provincial women's athletic championships to be won by Anglo-Indians (Anthony 1968: 240). Among the most famous of the Anglo-Indian female players are Ann Lumsden and Eliza Nelson. In 1962 Ann Lumsden was the first woman to receive India's national sporting honour, the Arjuna Award, for her contributions to Indian hockey at the national and international levels. In 1982, Eliza Nelson of Bombay captained the Indian women's hockey team to gold at the Asian Games in New Delhi and was later awarded the Padma Shri and Arjuna Award (Rizvi 1999). Others such as Ida Stokes achieved more as administrators than as players and she was a famous, long-term director of the All India Women's Field Hockey Association who encouraged Indian women athletes to set their competitive sights higher as part of a mobilizing effort that has been many times manifested in a microscopic Anglo-Indian community. Indeed, female Anglo-Indian athletes were responsible for these mobilizing efforts in more mundane ways. Middle-class Indian families have long favoured English-medium education, and at the older schools there remains an element of physical education at the heart of the curriculum. Female instructors were routinely drawn from the Anglo-Indian community and my research frequently turned up stories of stern sports mistresses from their community overcoming all objections to ensure that all their girls received physical instruction. Many girls coming from orthodox communities, including an informant raised in strict purdah, have spoken of their girlhood exposure to netball, hockey or long distance running. For such girls this would have been a startling and unique experience with their own bodies and the transgression of multiple taboos about body and dress. While women like Ida Stokes used their positions to loudly advocate sport for women, her colleagues in the schools and colleges saw to it that the Indian girls that were their pupils experienced first hand the possibilities and the challenges of modern sports.

From Boxing to Billiards in the Colonial and Postcolonial World

The patterns familiar from hockey, of an Anglo-Indian society geared to the practice and ritual of modern sports which generated successive generations of sportsmen and women who went on to carve out many of India's postcolonial sporting accomplishments, is repeated in other sports too. Boxing was an activity encouraged in the British army and adopted by the Anglo-Indian schools. Stracey's memoir mentions his brother Patrick who was once insulted by a British Tommy, possibly on account of his darker complexion, and how their father had promptly sent him off to learn to box (2000: 27). Through the interval in which Anglo-Indians were obliged served in the Auxiliary Force India (AFI) as a condition of their service employment there was much friendly yet heated competition with British regiments' best boxers. As a result Anglo-Indian pugilists were significant members of India's boxing community on either side of WWII. India's middleweight champion of 1934–1937 was Duncan Chatterton of Jhansi, later an undefeated All-India Inter-Railway light-heavyweight champion. Bombay's Edgar Brighte was the Indian lightweight champion for many years. Another legend of the 1930s and 1940s was Arthur Suares who in his youth defeated western India's Jack de Souza and Harry Bell of Australia. As an all-India champion, Mr. Suares made several tours of Ceylon, Burma, Malaya and Singapore and later turned down an American boxing contract. Instead he enlisted in the RAMC in World War II and continued boxing, donating his prizes to the War Fund.

During the War Dusty Miller emerged as the Indian Navy's best middleweight boxer. In the 1951 revival of North India's boxing scene Miller defeated Charles Campagnac of the 3rd Gurkha Rifles, another well known Anglo-Indian who would later lead his regiment in the 1965 war against Pakistan. Miller held India's middleweight title between 1941–5 and also the India and Ceylon heavyweight titles of 1951–1952. In 1963 he joined the Anglo-Indian diaspora by emigrating to Australia where he resides in Perth. Peter Prince, many times a champion, also became an Australian as did Gene Raymond after boxing in India and in Britain. In 1948 and again in 1952 most of India's Olympic boxers were Anglo-Indians; Nuttall captained the 1948 boxing team and later emigrated to England where he emerged as a 1950s middleweight champion. The sporting Norrises made their mark too as Ron Norris became All-India lightweight champion before heading for the Helsinki Olympics with Oscar Ward, a fellow Anglo-Indian, and defeating Canada's Battila.

Cricket also followed suit and Bangalore's Roger Binny is perhaps the best-known example of an Anglo-Indian whose sporting prowess elevated him to an international stage. An ace bowler and all rounder able to bat at any position he contributed to assorted international victories, was the darling of India's 1983 World Cup triumph and was a member of the Indian team to tour Australia in 1981, 1984–1985 and 1985–1986. As with so many of his hockey playing colleagues, upon retiring from life as a player he has retained an interest in coaching. Indeed, he eventually turned his back on a career in banking to take the Level III coaching course in Australia and he went on to produce the Indian winners of the 2000 Under-19 World Cup.[12] His currency as a cricketer has allowed him to enter politics, and he represents his state's 12,000 or so Anglo-Indians as a member of the Karnataka legislature (Bala 2000: 36–37).

One of the most remarkable stories comes from athletics. Norman Gilbert Pritchard was born an accountant's son in Calcutta in 1875, where he attended St. Xavier's College. He taught in Lucknow for some years en route to becoming India's first Olympian. At the 1900 Paris Games, Pritchard finished second in the 200 metres to J.W.B. Tewksbury of the United States and became India's first Olympic medalist; he finished second again in the 200 metre hurdles. Pritchard received a hero's welcome upon returning to India, where he was later appointed an honorary secretary of the Indian Football Association, as the Anglo-Indian insisted on representing India at the Olympics rather than Britain, as had been suggested by the authorities. Like many others from his community, although somewhat earlier than most, he emigrated. He went off to California to embark on a career in silent film. Pritchard was succeeded at the Olympics by a number of Anglo-Indian athletes. The 1932 Los Angeles games saw an Anglo-Indian hurdler, Mervyn Sutton, reach the semi-finals in the 110 metre hurdles and sprinter Eric Philips and hurdler John Vickers represented India in 1948. Henry Rebello was born in Lucknow in 1928 and was favourite for the triple jump gold at the 1948 Olympics but was injured before he could compete. Derek Boosey of Karnataka's Kolar Gold Fields beat Rebello's Indian record in the event and in 1960 became India's national champion. He subsequently emigrated and reappeared on the British team at the 1968 Mexico games.

More recent developments point to the contribution of Anglo-Indian coaches to track and field. The Dronacharya Award honours the work of out-standing Indian coaches. In 2000 one of the three recipients was Mr Kenneth Owen Bosen, a graduate of the Doveton Corrie Boys School, Chennai and Staines School in Coimbatore. Mr. Bosen was a fine track and field athlete in his youth and also a promising cricketer. He represented India in javelin at the second Asian Games before a round of meningitis interrupted his competitive career. Mr. Bosen was engaged by the Southern Railways and was the Indian Railways Athletics Coach before joining the National Institute for Sports teaching staff at Patiala, from which he had been a first of class graduate. He has contributed to coaching as well as administration and planning and had two terms as national coach of the Indian athletics team, during which time he was appointed to the International Amateur Athletic Association. He is now to train India's female hammer-throwers, contributing his competitive experience to this newly introduced sport (Anglos in the Wind 2000: 3).[13] At the 2000 Sydney Games an Anglo-Indian became the first Indian to participate in the torch relay. Mr. Ivan Jacobs represented India at the Helsinki Games after breaking the Indian 400 metres record. He joined the Tamil Nadu police and continued as a sprinter in All-India police and national competition. He later emigrated to England in the mid-1960s and thence to Australia although like various other Anglo-Indians, Jacobs has returned to live in Chennai several times since emigrating to the UK in the mid-1960s (Anglos in the Wind 2000: 6).

The record is equally impressive in other sports. Wilson Jones became the first Indian to assume an individual world title when he triumphed at billiards in 1950 and he added to his fame by going on to win the world snooker champion in 1958. More recently, Leander Paes has become the darling of Calcuttan tennis followers and is best known for his individual bronze won at the 1996 Atlanta Olympic games and the mixed doubles title he secured at Wimbledon with Martina Navratilova in 2003. His mother was a fine basketball player and his father, Vece Paes, was a mid-fielder of the bronze-winning India Hockey team at the 1972 Munich games. In 1999 Leander Paes and Mahesh Bhupati won in doubles at both the French Open and at Wimbledon. Miss Nisha Millet is a current Anglo-Indian swimming sensation who represented India at the 2000 Sydney Olympics after a period of training in Australia. Ms. Millet is a psychology student in Mount Carmel College, Bangalore and from the age of 10 has been a frequent winner in national level competition. She was the first Indian woman to swim the 100m freestyle in under a minute, she was awarded the Arjuna Award and at the time of writing holds 10 junior and 7 senior records. The diversity of the contribution made by Anglo-Indians to India's sporting culture is best demonstrated by Leslie F. Wilson. He competed in snooker, billiards and played or knew 'everything' else before or during his years at the The Deccan Herald under Mr. Ron Hendricks whom he succeeded as sports editor. Mr. Wilson was an All India Radio commentator on cricket, tennis, soccer, hockey, boxing, swimming, netball and athletics, cycling and horse-racing.

Conclusion

The Anglo-Indian community's relationship with sport has endured across Independence although in many ways its meanings and impacts have changed. Partly founded on the community's sociological peculiarities through which it was organized into ready-made teams through educational and occupational experience, participation in sports clubs and activities were actively embraced because these consolidated the community's position in the colonial period. The sports engaged in were self-consciously British, as the community desired identification with the colonial masters and cultural distance from Indian neighbours. Moreover, the clubs that were founded acted as centres for self-identification and for reassuring community building in a colonial society where both British and Indian societies rejected them. In postcolonial India the endurance of such activities as the All-India Anglo-Indian Association annual hockey tournament suggests that sport continues at times to function as a means of perpetuating and consolidating the community. As its numbers dwindle and the population around it grows, such exercises in self-identification increase in importance. However, the community's sporting excellence has allowed it to engage in the processes of nation building in postcolonial India. Sports have at times been very important to the emergence of India's nationhood and the active participation of Anglo-Indians, in even those most important of moments in the nation's list of sporting triumphs, such as the 1983 World Cup cricket win, have allowed the community to demonstrate its allegiance to the postcolonial nation and to symbolically suggest its potential as a contributor to India's future. It must be remembered, however, that the Anglo-Indian community's contribution to India's physical culture has not simply come through the high-profile achievements of its most significant competitors. Many lakhs of Indians would have experienced startling new body cultures and the possibilities of modern physiological regimes through the organized games and drill of an Anglo-Indian games mistress or coach.

While sport is about power it is also about discourse. In pre-Independence culture the scientific racists constructed Anglo-Indians as fatally weakened by the presence of Asian blood in their veins. In the postcolonial world the Anglo-Indian has been constructed as deracinated and an incomplete citizen of the new nation through novels such as *Bhowani Junction* and films such as *Cotton Mary*.[14] As with other communities in India, which have used sport to challenge received notions about their physical and moral character, (Dimeo 2004) Anglo-Indian achievements stand as a refutation of the negative representations of the community's members.

Overall then Anglo-Indian sport presents a series of paradoxes. Founded on the experiences, agendas and structures of the colonial period, it has allowed the community to claim a place in the very different world of postcolonial India and to engage in the processes of building the independent state. At the same time, however, sporting prowess has allowed certain Anglo-Indians to interact with and to manage the challenges of global migration (Blunt 2003) and has helped them to make familiar life in Britain, Australia or Canada. Sport has been at the heart of a small community's strategies of survival in a period of transition from colonialism to globalization.

Acknowledgements

Special Thanks to Mr. Mark Suares and family of Bangalore and Australia and all other contributors and particularly those of 'The India-List'.

NOTES

Introduction

1 Mike Marqusee summarises this in concluding that 'on sport's level playing field, it is possible to challenge and overturn the dominant hierarchies of nation, race and class. The reversal may be limited and transient but it is nonetheless real. It is, therefore, wrong to see black sporting achievement merely as an index of oppression; it is equally an index of creativity and resistance, collective and individual' (1995: 29).

2 Sudhir Chatterjee tells the story of meeting an old man at the Ganges after the famous football victory over the British in 1911. The old man responded to the result by pointing to the British flag on Fort William and asking him when they were going to achieve their next victory by removing it (Armstrong and Bates 2001: 191).

3 That demonstrations of 'order-destroying power' by an individual can have political implications for the 'crowd' in colonial contexts where mature political institutions are lacking is discussed in Singham (1968).

4 Giulianotti explores the physical sensations of sports spectatorship and argues that 'the hope of experiencing these ecstatic moments is what keeps people going to matches, to participate on the pitch or in the stands' (1999: 173).

5 It might be instructive to think about Hobsbawm's (2003) model of the social bandit here. The social bandit is sponsored by a community that does not have the resources, or the desire, for head on conflict with the elites that dominate it. The community provides resources to the social bandit while he attacks the elites and their representatives, and he comes to represent their will to resist, while at the same time demonstrating the limited means with which they are able to do it.

6 To this extent sports events seem to fit analyses of carnivals and fairs in which power relations are ritually mocked or reversed but only within circumstances carefully controlled and specifically sanctioned by elites. Bakhtin (1968: 109) was sure that 'carnival celebrates temporary liberation from the prevailing truth of the established order'. Others have been careful to emphasise that 'carnival, after all, is a licensed affair' (Eagleton 1981: 148) where 'the release of emotions or grievances made them easier to police in the long term' (Sales 1983: 169). Burton's (1997: 263–267) take on carnival and sport in the Caribbean is especially interesting as he argues that such events as festivals or sports matches can present an opportunity for subaltern groups to celebrate opposition and resistance but in contexts where their (albeit small) stakes in the social order ensure that they do not want to be perceived as truly threatening to deliver upheaval and change.

7 The work of George Rudé comes to mind here, even though he preferred not to include crowds at sporting events in his analyses (1964: 4). For historical perspectives on spectators and sports events see the chapter on the crowd in Collins and Vamplew (2002).

8 For another consideration of the RSS and sport see McDonald (1979).

9 Other important studies of indigenous sports in South Asia include Parkes (1996); Zarrilli (1998); Azoy (1982) and Sreedhar (2000). Rather less helpful is Levine (2000) as it is a tourist travelogue in which she sets out on 'Asian adventures' searching for 'bizarre traditional Asian sports' for her own amusement.

10 For a recent celebration of this game and its result see Basu (2003).

11 It is important to read Bandyopadhyay's article after reading Dimeo (2001), which preceded it in print by two years.

12 This reads as a film review of 'Bend it Like Beckham' padded out with recent newspaper reports trawled from the internet. Majumdar continues to publish on sport in South Asia. His recent work appeared too late to be considered here.

13 See Bains and Johal (1998).

14 Mario Rodrigues argues that cricket in India is not popular at the local level where matches are poorly supported. Cricket's power in Indian culture is derived from its meaning when played at the international level. Football on the other hand is consumed at the local level and matches between the two Calcutta rivals have generated crowds in excess of 100000 people (2001: 122). Sen argues that Indian cricket fulfils the same functions as British football in terms of nationalist sentiment (2002: 27–37).

15 Other studies that have taken the issue of sport and the South Asian diaspora more seriously than Majumdar are Fleming (1995) and Werbner (1996).

1. '*Kalarippayattu* is Eighty Percent Mental and Only the Remainder is Physical': Power, Agency and Self in a South Asian Martial Art

1 Gurukkal, the plural of Guru (Master), is a title representing all past masters in the lineage of teaching.

2 By no means do all practitioners or theorists of 'new age' somatic disciplines fit this simple stereotype. A number of practitioners and theorists of somatic disciplines are perfectly aware of these problems of the reification and romanticization of the 'east' and therefore choose to resist such oversimplification in their own practice and thought. For example see Don Hanlon Johnson's important work on the body (1992; 1994).

3 In part our reading of India as the romantic, feminized, nonviolent (i.e. Gandhian) 'Other' has too long precluded reading the Bhagavad Gita in its appropriate larger Mahabharata context, that is, as part of a text in which the arts of war are practiced for the larger good.

4 P.C. Chakravarti, drawing on the Mahabharata, the Sarabhanga Jataka, Alexander's chronicles and the records of succeeding centuries points out that 'the popular notion that the military profession was the exclusive monopoly of the Ksatriya caste is wholly without foundation' (1972: 78–79).

5 Narayanan has clearly established continuity between the Kerala *cattar* of the *salad* and the *cattar* mentioned in this work (1973: 29).

6 Within living memory of *yatra* brahmins today are performances of the brahmin entertainment, *yatrakali*, one part of which included the demonstration of martial skills. *Yatrakali* texts record verbal commands (*vayttari*) which are identical to the commands still used in *kalarippayattu* practice.

7 Other passages in Agni Purana are concerned with topics related to warfare and martial practice, but they do not focus on fighting skills per se. Examples include (1) rituals

to be performed by brahman priests designed to give protection and/or success in battle (M.N. Dutt Shastri 1967: 840, 539) (2) construction of forts (Gangadharan 1985: 576–578) (3) instructions for military expeditions (Gangadharan 1985: 594) and (4) battle formations and deployments of constituent parts of an army (Gangadharan 1985: 612–615; 629–635). For a comprehensive discussion of the art of warfare in ancient India see Chakravati (1972).

8 Translated by Gautam Dasgupta.

9 See The Mahabharata, vol. 2, translated and edited by J.A.B. van Buitenen, "The Book of the Forest," 38.1–42.1 (1975: 296–303). All quotations from the story below are from the van Buitenen translation.

10 A similar pattern of development of powers is also found in *teyyam*. See Freeman (1991).

11 I am following David Edward Shaner's attempt to provide a more appropriate non-dualistic account of the relationship between body and mind. 'Although there may be mind aspects and body aspects within all lived experience the presence of either one includes experientially the presence of the other' (1985: 42–43). 'Bodymind' refers to this 'polar' and symbiotic, rather than dualistic, relationship.

12 It is impossible for me to either confirm or deny the existence of such subtle, esoteric powers. What is most important in terms of my argument here is that traditionally such powers were assumed to be actual and, therefore, remain part of the entire domain of powers with which a martial master might have to contend.

13 For further discussion of *gunam* and the Indian concept of the person see Carter (1982), Daniel (1984) and Davis (1976).

14 *Gunam* type determined at birth is still considered important by most Malayalis today, especially when considering a suitable marriage partner with whom bodily fluids will be exchanged. Even for many educated Malayalis, who view caste as a social and political evil, to consider marriage to a partner outside one's birth-group and, therefore, to one born with a different *gunam* complex is unthinkable.

15 In contrast to the unbridled impulses of the *rajasic* type Kakar characterizes the *tamasic* type as 'always appear[ing] sullen and dull to the ruling elites' (1982: 249). Master Govindankutty Nayar's use of *tamasa* to describe students prone to quick anger and impetuous, rash behavior is equivalent to Kakar's *rajasic* type.

3. Indigenous Polo in Northern Pakistan: Game and Power on the Periphery

1 A Tibetan etymology of the widespread term *bulá* 'ball'-hence Anglo-Indian *polo*–suggests possible Himalayan origins (Mahdisan 1981). On Persian *chaughan* (Old Persian *chosagan*), attested in Achaemenid Iran, see H. Bailey *Bulletin of the School of Oriental and African Studies* 23, 1960: 39.

2 This received history of the game (Watson 1989: 52–53) was characteristically disputed by G.W. Leitner, a somewhat cranky explorer of the northwestern enclave of what he called Dardistan (see Keay 1979: 14–22). I reproduce here his apparently unnoticed claim to precedence in introducing polo from Ladakh, which might be investigated: 'Although our first practical knowldge of "Polo" was derived from the Manipuri game as played at Calcutta, it is not Manipur, but Hunza and Nagyr, that maintain the original rules of the ancient "Chaughán, bazi" so famous in Persian history. The account given by J. Moray Brown for the "Badminton Library" of the introduction of Polo into England (Longmans, Green & Co. 1891), seems to be at variance with the facts within

my knowledge, for it was introduced into England in 1867, not 1869, by one who had played the Tibetan game as brought to Lahore by me in 1866, after a tour in Middle and Little Tibet. Since then it has become acclimatised not only in England, but also in Europe. The Tibetan game, however, does not reach the perfection of the Nagyr game, although it seems to be superior to that of Manipur' (Leitner 1889: Appendix IV.1 'Polo in Hunza, Nagyr'; cf. Frembgen 1988: 198 n.5).

3 The significance of the vizier thus serving as an auspice of human fertility is elsewhere illuminated by a conjugal analogy: 'The *tham* [king] is husband, the *wazir* is his wife. The prosperity of the house depends upon the wife, the prosperity of the country depends on the *wazir*' (Lorimer 1979: 126). On court rituals of polo, see Müller-Stellrecht (1973: 78–79; 260–64) on Hunza, Frembgen (1988: 205) on Nager, and generally, Jettmar (1975: 267–69).

4 Cf. Drew (1857: 386–87), who had foreseen several of these modifications as desirable for English players, if not indigenes.

5 The federally administered Northern Areas formerly comprised Political Agencies in Gilgit and Baltistan. After the dissolution of states and rajaships in this region (1972–74), Political Agents were redesignated Deputy Commissioners. Chitral State also had a Political Agent advising its Mehtar, prior to its dissolution in 1969, when the former principality was incorporated as a subdistrict of Malakand Agency (NWFP) under a Deputy Commissioner.

6 These costs are based on informants' estimates in September 1995 which I have not updated. A Punjabi polo pony then cost Rs. 25–30,000, and a trained groom (*sais*) expected a monthly payment of Rs. 1000 with similar additional monthly costs for his subsistence together with fodder.

7 Personal communication from S. Kassam on the issue of polo sponsorship in 1991.

8 On this peculiar 'independence struggle' of Gilgit in 1947–48, then claimed by India as a dependency of Kashmir, see Dani (1989: 326–401) and Staley (1982: 265–69).

9 Foreign tourism in northern Pakistan has suffered a devastating decline since its peak in the late 1970s (cf. Kreutzmann 1996), entailing widespread defaults on loans for hotel building throughout this region, whose social effects have yet to be properly documented and appraised.

10 See Staley (1982: 259–65, 270–71) for an account of such ruptures already evident in the 1960s; also Haserodt (1989) on more recent social and economic developments in Chitral.

4. 'The Moral that can be Safely Drawn from the Hindus' Magnificent Victory': Cricket, Caste and the Palwankar Brothers

1 This essay is extracted from a larger work on the social history of Indian cricket, *A Corner of a Foreign Field* (London: Picador, 2002). Copyright: Ramachandra Guha

2 The versions, respectively, of Baloo's nephew K. V. Palwankar (1996) and of an obituary in the *Times of India*.

3 This was a reference to the patriotic hysteria which overtook Britain during the Boer war.

4 There was actually a fifth brother, Krishna, who died very young. In deference to his memory P. Vithal titled a chapter of his memoirs 'Panch Palwalkar'. This is a reference to the greatest of all Hindu brotherhoods, the five Pandavas, or 'Panch Pandeshwar'.

5 Palwankar Ganpat died of consumption at the age of twenty-seven in October of that year.

6 The statement was probably drafted by L. R. Tairsee, the reform-minded Congressman and industrialist who was to later become the President of the P. J. Hindu Gymkhana.

7 Govindji Vassanji used to regularly advertise in Gandhi's own journal, *Young India*.

8 As recalled by J. C. Maitra.

5. The Peasants are Revolting: Race, Culture and Ownership in Cricket

1 'Bodyline' refers to the tactics used by the England captain, Douglas Jardine, to defeat Australia in 1933. Jardine's deliberate use of physical intimidation was widely seen as contrary to the 'gentlemanly' spirit of the game and nearly caused a diplomatic rift between England and Australia.

2 In the 1970s Australian media magnate Kerry Packer lured the world's top cricketers away from their national sides and paid them comparatively large salaries to play professionally. 'World Series Cricket', as Packer's scheme was called, severely disrupted the structure of international cricket, almost destroyed the system of national teams and led to a new commercialization of the game. It was seen by many as the triumph of money over patriotic duty.

3 The BCCI and the ICC became deadlocked over the composition of the review panel. The ICC rejected all of the BCCI's recommendations for the 3-member panel, and a new confrontation appeared imminent (The Times of India, 08/01/2002; The Telegraph (Calcutta) 12/01/2002).

4 Using fingernails to remove grass and dirt from the seam of the ball is ubiquitous in cricket and players generally ignore the rule that requires that they ask the umpire for permission before they proceed. In that sense Tendulkar's punishment was unprecedented.

5 *Dawn*, in particular, was critical both of Denness and of the ICC.

6 Steve Waugh was quick to announce his support for the ICC and the referee's authority when the Denness controversy broke. Some weeks later, when he was penalized by a Sri Lankan referee for 'showing dissent', Waugh came around to advocating a process of appeal.

7 During England's 1976-77 tour of India fast bowler John Lever was caught with a strip of gauze smeared with Vaseline. Grease is helpful in preserving the polish of the cricket ball which assists in fast bowling. It is quite illegal; in today's parlance, it amounts to 'ball tampering'. Greig was the England captain at the time.

8 The car is Fiat India's special-edition Palio S-10, where S for Sachin and 10 for Tendulkar (Rediff.com 11/01/02).

9 Both men were criticized by senior board members as undeserving and as affirmative-action inductees (The Times of India 03/01/02).

6. The Social History of the Royal Calcutta Golf Club, 1829–2003

1 Later minutes from 1833 record a visit from Major H. L. Playfair, who is described as the founder of golf in the 'East Indies'.

2 Without wishing to labour this point, there has been an over-emphasis on the 'muscular Christianity' approach to colonial sports history, to the neglect of the more complex reality in which various agendas informed the development of sport in India, South Africa, Canada, Australia etc.

3 The information in this section is drawn from observations and interviews made by the author in July 2001.

4 The author reviewed the Committee Minutes for the past 20 years and discovered that the problem of trespassers remains. Local people knock holes in the walls which the Committee constantly repairing, much to their annoyance and expense. Around the course lie blocks of flats that are densely populated with the residents having no obvious space for recreation. The golf course represents a good opportunity for relaxation, sport and social congregation.

7. Warrior Goddess Versus Bipedal Cow: Sport, Space, Performance and Planning in an Indian City

1 The idea of 'body culture' used here suggests Marcel Mauss's 'techniques of the body' as well as the institutional regimes that mark and mold habits of body and its performances in everyday and non-everyday life. See also Brownell (1995b: 10–13) for a similar definition and the relationship of this to the work of Pierre Bourdieu.

2 The tripartite model of old Bangalore is discussed in Srinivas 2001.

3 For detailed discussions of the Karaga festival, the roles of the Tigala community and Bangalore city see Srinivas (1999a and 2001). The paragraphs that follow summarize Srinivas 2001: 141–151.

4 The Tigalas are not the only community that maintains wrestling houses. Most old communities in the city, Hindu and Muslim, have their own gymnasiums where men and boys train daily. Many are known by the names of famous teachers and at least one street in the Old City bears the name of a famous wrestler from the community of gardeners. Until 1947, while the king of Mysore still ruled, grand contests would be held in the large grounds near his palace west of the British Cantonment. Competitions still occur between local wrestling houses in Bangalore in open spaces attended by large crowds and local politicians.

5 This explanation is more or less similar to that given in the oral epic recited on the final day of the performance, which explains the origins of the community of gardeners from Draupadi.

6 Taylor and Jamieson (1997) also point to the persistence of images of virility in advertisements and local practice and a reworking of hegemonic masculinity under conditions of political and economic marginalization for steel-workers in de-industrialized Sheffield, the city of steel, after the 1980s.

7 The work of the official committee in 1987 led to the unpublished 'Report of the Expert Committee constituted by the Government for Submitting Proposals for Preservation, Restoration or Otherwise of the Existing Tanks in the Bangalore Metropolitan Area.' Among environmental activists, K. V. Narendra (1993, 1995) founded a center, supported studies, and released publications that focused attention to the plight of water bodies. Figures on the percentage of land covered by tanks come from INRIMT (1995: 22).

8 L. V. Sharada Rao's *Kere Haadu* [Tank Song] (Bangalore, 1996), shown on the Indian Doordarshan TV channel and at a number of venues in Bangalore, used the story of this goddess as an introduction to the importance of artificial lakes within the urban ecology, and their neglect, encroachment and eventual destruction by developers.

9 'Construction of flats for the National Games 1996.' Proceedings of the Government of Karnataka. Order No. HUD 161 KHB 94, 2 September 1994. Proceedings of meetings of 7 July 1994 and 30 July 1994.

10 No. HUD 139 MNJ 1994, 5 January 1995.

11 The Citizens' Voluntary Initiative for the City (CIVIC) was a collective of citizens concerned with issues of democratic participation in the planning of Bangalore. During the previous three years the group had engaged in lobbying and convened a number of public meetings and seminars on a variety of issues ranging from transit systems to India's 74th Amendment (Nagarapalika Act). In 1995 CIVIC established a funding relationship with the United Nations Economic and Social Commission for Asia and the Pacific (ESCAP) and by 2000 was receiving funding from the Ford Foundation.

12 Writ Petition No. 758 of 1995. The organizations that filed the writ petition with CIVIC included the Bangalore Environmental Trust, Educator-Manufacturer Association, Indian Society for Environmental Studies, Karnataka Kolageri Nivasigala Samyuktha Sanghatane [United Front of Karnataka Slum Dwellers], and Ornithological Society of India. The government organizations named in the Writ Petition, in addition to the State of Karnataka, were the Housing and Urban Development Department, Government of Karnataka; Public Works Department, Government of Karnataka; Forest, Ecology and Environment Department, Government of Karnataka; Forest Department, Government of Karnataka; the Karnataka Housing Board; Bangalore Development Authority; Karnataka State Pollution Control Board; and the Housing and Urban Development Corporation.

13 Newspaper reports on the initiation of the Writ Petition include: 'Move to build Games Complex challenged' (*Indian Express*, 11 January 1995); 'NGOs allege violation of law in National Games village project' (*Sunday Times*, 29 January 1995); 'Kridagrama nirmana yojana kaydege viruddha' [Opposition to Rule on Sports Village Construction Plan] (*Praja Vani*, 29 January 1995); 'Kridagrama nirmana viruddha rit' [Writ Opposing Sports Village Construction] (*Samyukta Karnataka*, 29 January 1995); 'National Games township opposed' (*Economic Times*, 30 January 1995); 'Plea against 'illegal allotment' of land' (*Deccan Herald*, 31 January 1995); Ravi R. Prasad, 'Siberian birds may not visit Bangalore again' (*The Statesman*, 13 February 1995); Saritha Rai, 'Real Estate Rules' (*India Today*, 15 June 1995: 161).

14 Dr. C. M. Muthiah, Advisor to the Government of Karnataka for the National Games, said that the political leadership of Karnataka (formerly Mysore) under Chief Minister Hanumanthaiah had constructed in the state capital building (Vidhana Soudha) a building large enough to hold Parliament, making Bangalore potentially the nation's capital. In the same way, under Deve Gowda and his successor Patel the unofficial motto was 'We are challenging Delhi.' The details on the organization of the Games come from an interview with Muthiah on 16 July 1997.

15 Finally ACC Cements came through with Rs. 2 crores for the general construction fund, Canara Bank provided Rs. 75 lakhs as the official bankers of the Games, and at the end Videocon (best known as a maker of consumer electrical appliances) threw in Rs. 4 crores for transportation and food expenses, which were still eligible for 100 percent deductibility.

16 The River Cauvery (or Kaveri) was the major source of water flowing through the southern part of Karnataka state but describing it as the 'life source' ignores the equally important Tungabhadra River and others flowing in the northern part of the state. This presentation was thus a statement of a peculiarly 'Mysorian' vision of the state in distinction to a northern variant. It was also a clear reference to the ongoing legal conflict with Tamil Nadu over shares of Cauvery water, which in 1991 had burst into large-scale violence and massacre of Tamil speakers in southern Karnataka.

17 Defense personnel received flats through a deal whereby the Ministry of Defence conveyed 17 acres of land to BDA for the completion of the intermediate ring road (Bangalore Development Authority 1997: 31-32).

18 'KHB wants to sell brass at gold rate—but no takers except govt agencies' (*Bangalore Times*, 24 June 1999); CIVIC Bangalore (1999).

20 The tendency to create androgynous mascots for national sporting events seems to have started with the 1982 Asian Games in Delhi with a dancing elephant named *Appu*. The 2002 National Games in Hyderabad featured another smiling, bipedal cow standing with legs spread, its left 'hand' on its hip and its right holding aloft a flaming torch called *Veera*. The Press Information Bureau of the Government of India (http://pib.nic.in/feature/feyr2002/fnov2002/fl41120021.html accessed March 2003) stated that *Veera* 'means bravery. The mascot defines the character of the game. The characteristics of the bull have been strongly associated with the facets of an achiever – power, strength, passion, confidence and endurance'.

8. 'Nupilal': Women's War, Football and the History of Modern Manipur

1 For a broader discussion of the body in South Asian see Mills and Sen (2004: 1–15).

2 For more on football in Bengal see Dimeo (2001a); Dimeo 2001b; Majumdar (2002).

3 For those unfamiliar with the wider context of the history of football in South Asia see Dimeo and Mills (2001). A recent attempt to look at women's football in India reads largely as a film review of 'Bend it Like Beckham' but it does contain some useful information; see Majumdar (2003).

4 This article deals largely with women from the Meitei ethnic group as it is this group that supplies the footballers of Manipur. For some aspects of the women of tribal groups from the mountains see Chatterji (1996).

5 Contrast this with discussions of women elsewhere in India in, for example, Clark (1993) and Kumar (1994).

6 A selection of female Arjuna Award (India's national honour bestowed on its sporting elite) winners includes Anjali Ved Bhagwat, a World Air Rifle Champion, Sita Gusain, a former national hockey captain, P.T. Usha, the 400 metres Olympian and Malathi Holla, the para-athlete.

9. 'Playing for the Tibetan People': Football and History in the High Himalayas

1 The Tibetan state functioned as a de facto independent state during the period from 1913 until 1950, when the new Communist Chinese regime sent troops to conquer Tibet. In 1959, the Tibetan leader, the Dalai Lama, went into exile in India with around 100,000 of his people. China claims Tibet as historically part of its territory; a claim disputed by the Dalai Lama's exile government.

2 These flags had been distributed by a local newspaper.

3 Support has also been extended to teams in the Tibetan exile community. For example the Daily Record 21/09/2001 noted that Scottish film-maker Jack Milroy had helped a Tibetan team in Nepal with assistance from the Football Association and Glasgow Football Development and also arranged for Kilmarnock, Partick Thistle and Celtic football teams to provide team kit.

4 On Manipur see James Mills in this volume.
5 Internet sources give various dates for the founding of the Federation, including 1960, 1974 and 1983.
6 According to www.geocities.com/Colosseumm/Park/3802/AFC/bhutan.html their first seven games were all lost; with three goals for and 54 against; their best effort being a 2-1 defeat by Pakistan.
7 A film was made of the match entitled 'The Other Cup'.
8 Malik Riaz Hai Naveed and Hans Schöggl for the Recreational Sport Soccer Statistic Foundation, 31/07/2003.
9 The Bhutanese results in the Asia Cup held in October 2003 were; lost 2-0 to Indonesia; lost 6-0 to Saudi; lost 8-0 to the Yemen; lost 2-0 to Indonesia; lost 4-0 to Saudi and lost 4-0 to Yemen, giving Bhutan a final record of played six, lost six, goals for 0, goals against 26. Given the conditions in Saudi Arabia and the strength of the opposition the results were acceptable (www.asiancup2004.com/en/tournament/index.asp?cid-525).
10 Personal information from Bhutan coach Arie Schans, August 2003.
11 Even the *ldab-ldobs* did not, however, apparently develop or follow any particular traditions of martial arts in the sense that these were practiced by Buddhist monks in China and Japan. I am indebted to Vivienne Lo for raising this point.
12 Such edicts were religious injunctions rather than laws in the Western sense. But in this case the injunction was effective.
13 In 1949, the Tibetan Government also banned the Chinese game of *mah jong*, along with all other gambling games. *Mah jong* sets were to be surrendered to the government which offered 12 rupees for each set (PRO FO 371-76315-7611 1949).
14 Football has also developed within what is now the Tibetan Autonomous Republic of China. The China Tibet Information centre (www.tibetinfor.cc) reports that 'Lamas of Sela [*sic*, Sera?] ad Dazhao monasteries have their own teams and that many schools also play football.'
15 While predominantly a Western construction, this image has its parallels in Asian understandings of the Himalayas as the home of metaphysical beings and esoteric knowledge.'
16 The website of the Central Tibetan Administration (12 August 2003) does claim, however, that in the 1960s and '70s 'the Tsarong brothers, … invented the banana kick, later perfected by Pele'! It is also records that a Tibetan named Yeshi Bashi represented India at the 1972 Asian games in Bangkok.
17 The use of the term 'traditional' should not, of course, be taken as implying a static or ahistorical culture.
18 The Bhutanese club structure, incidentally, with an occupational rather than regional emphasis, may be better suited to the maintenance of national unity than the exile Tibetan system, which derives from the scattering of the exile communities throughout India and the Himalayan states.

10. Community, Identity and Sport: Anglo-Indians in Colonial and Postcolonial India

1 This chapter is keen to avoid the problem of characterizing Anglo-Indian communities as 'not-Indian' or 'not-British'. The tendency to judge them alongside idealized representations of what it is to be either British or Indian and then judging them as failures has dogged previous work (Gist 1967; Grimshaw 1958; Wright 1970). This tendency

also ignores the realities, possibilities and advantages of hybridity (Stoler 1989; Young 1995). See Mills (1996) for a fuller discussion of the conceptual problems involved in approaching Anglo-Indian history.

2 Thanks are extended to Mr. Subhasis Ganguly of the Indian Railway Service for information from archives in Orissa and West Bengal.

3 Mr. Blythe-Perrett was born in Sri Lanka and served the S.E. Railway from the 1940s to the late 1960s at which point he took retirement in England. He died in 1991 in Canada where his daughters had settled. I am grateful to Mrs. Carol McFarlane, now of Colorado, for her recollections of a sportsman who amassed hundreds of trophies through the course of his life.

4 The team's Anglo-Indians were: Goal – Allen, Bengal; Backs – Michael Rocque of the Central Provinces and Hammond of the United Provinces; Halfbacks – Penniger of Punjab and Cullen of UP; Forwards – Michael Gateley of Punjab, G.E. Marthins and Seaman of UP; General Utility – Rex Norris of the Central Provinces; Reserve – Deefholts of Bengal. Both Ernie and Willie G. Cullen played on Indian national teams as did L.G. Emmett. The team was managed by Mr. A.B. Rosser.

5 Melbourne's Noble Park Hockey Club would also benefit from Rudy Pacheco, Marcus Syms and Julian Maughey.

6 The Pearces were known as Lucknow Anglo-Indians. They emigrated from Jabalpur in 1947. Eric Pearce played in the 1956, 1960 and 1964 Olympics for Australia. Gordon Pearce played in 1956 and 1960; Mel Pearce in 1956, and Julian Pearce in 1960 and 1964.

7 The annual Lahore Gymkhana was once a focal point of South Asian hockey.

8 Other nations to benefit from Anglo-Indian hockey have done so through hiring coaches from the community. For example, Rex Norris coached the Dutch hockey team in 1954–1956, the Italian team in 1960 and then the Mexican team before the 1968 Olympic games.

9 Like many a sportsman of western India, Lawrence attended St. Mary's in Mazgaon.

10 Dickie Carr, Carl Tapsell and Joe Gallibardy are also said to have been former footballers.

11 Those turning their hand to coaching in Australia and India or both have been Merv Adams, Ralph Blazey, Cyril Carton, Patrick Jansen, Ivan Meade, Gordon Taylor and Ray Whiteside. At Australia's National Hockey Centre in Lyneham the third pitch has been named The Powell Field in recognition of the contributions to the game of an Anglo-Indian family. Mr. Bill Powell is a well-known coach and administrator. His brother, Chris Powell has also coached at the top level while Lisa and Katrina Powell have played for the Canberra Strikers and on the Australian national team.

12 Previously, Binny coached Karnataka and Goa and also, the Kenyan cricket team.

13 Mr. Bosen is the author of several titles pertaining to sports and coaching and twice won India's National Award for Sports Literature for *Training without Straining* (1972) and *The Complete Guide to Pole Vaulting*, (1977).

14 The novel and the film were considered offensive and lurid by Anglo-Indian readers. See The Calcutta Statesman: 3–4 March 2000.

BIBLIOGRAPHY

Introduction

Alter, J, 1992, *The Wrestler's Body: Identity and Ideology in North India*, Berkeley CA, University of California Press.

Alter, J, 2000, *Kabaddi*, a national sport of India: the internationalism of nationalism and the foreignness of Indianness. In Dyck, N (ed.), *Games, Sports and Cultures*, Oxford, Berg.

Alter, J, 2004, Body, Text, Nation: Writing the physically fit body in postcolonial India. In Mills, J, and Sen, S (eds), *Confronting the Body: The politics of physicality in colonial and postcolonial India*, London, Anthem.

Appadurai, A, 1995, Playing With Modernity. The Decolonization of Indian Cricket. In Breckenridge, C A (ed.), *Consuming Modernity: Public Culture in Contemporary India*, Minneapolis, University of Minnesota Press.

Armstrong, G, and Bates, C, 2001, Selves and Others: Reflections on sport in South Asia. In *Contemporary South Asia*, 10, 2, 191–205.

Armstrong, G, and Giulianotti, R, 2001, *Fear and Loathing in World Football*, Oxford, Berg.

Azoy, G, 1982, *Buzkashi: Games and power in Afghanistan*, Philadelphia, University of Pennsylvania.

Bains, J, and Johal, S, 1998, *Corner Flags and Corner Shops: The Asian football experience*, London, Phoenix.

Bakhtin, M, 1968, *Rabelias and his World*, Cambridge, Mass, MIT Press.

Bale, J, 1994, *Landscapes of modern sport*, Leicester, Leicester University Press.

Bandyopadhyay, K, 2003, Race, Nation and Sport: Footballing nationalism in colonial Calcutta. In *Soccer and Society*, 4, 1.

Basu, J, 2003, *Stories from Indian Football*, New Delhi, UMSPD.

Bose, M, 1990, *A History of Indian Cricket*, London, Deutsch.

Burton, R, 1997, *Afro-Creole: Power, Opposition and play in the Caribbean*, Ithaca, Cornell University Press.

Cashman, R, 1980, *Patrons, Players and the Crowd: The Phenomenon of Indian Cricket*, Delhi.

Chaturvedi, V, 2000, *Mapping Subaltern Studies and the postcolonial*, London, Verso.

Collins, T, and Vamplew, W, 2002, *Mud, Sweat and Beers: A cultural history of sport and alcohol*, Oxford, Berg.

Cronin, M, and Mayall, D, 1998, *Sporting Nationalisms: Identity, Ethnicity, Immigration and Assimilation*, London, Cass.

Dimeo, P, 2001, Football and Politics in Bengal: Colonialism, Nationalism, Communalism. In Mills, J, and Dimeo, P (eds), *Soccer in South Asia: Empire, Nation, Diaspora*, London, Cass.

Dimeo, P, 2002a, Colonial Bodies, Colonial Sport: 'Martial' Punjabis, 'Effeminate' Bengalis and the development of Indian football. In *The International Journal of the History of Sport*, 19, 1.

Dimeo, P, 2002b, The Local, National and Global in India Football: Issues of power and identity. In *Football Studies*, 5, 2, 74–87.

Dimeo, P, 2004, 'A parcel of Dummies'?: Sport and the Body in Indian History. In Mills, J, and Sen, S (eds), *Confronting the Body: The politics of physicality in colonial and postcolonial India*, London, Anthem.

Docker, E, 1977, *History of Indian Cricket*, Delhi, Macmillan.

Eagleton, T, 1981, *Walter Benjamin: Towards a revolutionary criticism*, London, Verso.

Eichberg, H, 1998, New Spatial Configurations of Sport? In Bale, J, and Philo, C (eds), *Body Cultures: Essays on sport, space and identity*, London, Routledge.

Fleming, S, 1995, *Home and Away: Sport and South Asian Male Youth*, Aldershot, Avebury.

Giulianotti, R, 1999, *Football: A sociology of the global game*, Cambridge, Polity.

Guha, Ranajit, 1982, On some aspects of the historiography of colonial India. In Guha, R (ed.), *Subaltern Studies I*, Delhi, Oxford University Press.

Guha, Ramachandra, 1998, Cricket and Politics in Colonial India. In *Past and Present*, 161, 155–190.

Guha, Ramachandra, 2002, *A Corner of a Foreign Field: The Indian history of a British sport*, London, Picador.

Guttman, A, 1994, *Games and Empires: modern sports and cultural imperialism*, New York, Columbia University Press.

Harvey, D, 1989, *The Condition of Postmodernity*, Oxford, Blackwell.

Heitzman, J, 1999, Sports and conflict in urban planning: The Indian national games in Bangalore. In *Journal of Sport and Social Issues*, 23, 1 (February), 5–23.

Hobsbawm, E, 2003, *Bandits*, London, Abacus.

Holt, R, 1989, *Sport and the British: a modern history*, Oxford, Clarendon.

Hong, F, 1997, *Footbinding, Feminism and Freedom: Liberation of Women's Bodies in Modern China*, London, Cass.

Klein, A, 1991, *Sugarball: The American Game, the Dominican Dream*, Newhaven, Yale University Press.

Klein, A, 1997, *Baseball on the Border*, Princeton, Princeton University Press.

Levine, E, 2000, *A Game of Polo with a Headless Goat*, London, Deutsch.

Ludden, D, 2002, *Reading Subaltern Studies: Critical history, contested meaning and the globalization of South Asia*, London, Anthem.

Maguire, J, 1999, *Global Sport: Identities, Societies, Civilizations*, Cambridge, Polity.

Mangan, J, 1985, *The Games Ethic and Imperialism: aspects of the diffusion of an ideal*, Harmondsworth, Viking.

Mangan, J A, 2000, *Superman Supreme: Fascist body as political icon*, London, Cass.

Mangan, J, 2000, Soccer as Moral Training: Missionary intentions and imperial legacies. In Dimeo, P, and Mills, J (eds), *Soccer in South Asia*, London, Cass.

Marqusee, M, 1995, Sport and Stereotype: from role model to Muhammed Ali. In *Race and Class*, 6, 4, 1–29.

Majumdar, B, 2002, The Politics of Soccer in Colonial India, 1930–1937, The Years of Turmoil, In *Soccer and Society*, 3, 1.

Majumdar, B, 2003, Forwards and Backwards: Women's soccer in twentieth-century India. In *Soccer and Society*, 4, 2/3.

Mason, T, 1990, Football on the Maidan: Cultural Imperialism in Calcutta. In *International Journal of the History of Sport*, 12, 1.

McDonald, I, 1979, Physiological Patriots? The politics of physical nationalism and Hindu nationalism in India. In *International Review of Sport Sociology*, 34, 343–358.

McKay, A, 1994, The Other 'Great Game': Politics and Sport in Tibet, 1904–47. In *The International Journal of the History of Sport*, 11, 3, 372–86.

McKay, A, 2001, 'Kicking the Buddhas Head': Tibet, Football, and Modernity. In Dimeo, P, and Mills, J (eds), *Soccer in South Asia: Empire, Nation, Diaspora*, London, Cass.

Mills, J, 2001a, A historiography of South Asian sport. In *Contemporary South Asia*, 10, 2, 207–222.

Mills, J, 2001b, Football in Goa: Sport, politics and the Portuguese in India. In Dimeo, P, and Mills, J (eds), *Soccer in South Asia: Empire, Nation, Diaspora*, London, Cass.

Mills, J, and Dimeo, P, 2003, 'When Gold is Fired it Shines': Sport, the Imagination and the Body in colonial and postcolonial India. In Bale, J, and Cronin, M (eds), *Sport and postcolonialism*, Oxford, Berg.

Nandy, A, 1989, *The Tao of Cricket: On Games of Destiny and the Destiny of Games*, New York.

Nielsen, K, 1995, The stadium and the city: A modern story. In Bale, J, and Moen, O (eds), *The stadium and the city*, Keele, Keele University Press.

Parkes, P, 1996, Indigenous polo and the politics of regional identity in northern Pakistan. In MacClancy, J (ed.), *Sport, Identity and Ethnicity*, Oxford, Berg.

Rodrigues, M, 2001, 'The Corporates and the Game: Football in India and the conflicts of the 1990s'. In Dimeo, P, and Mills, J (eds), *Soccer in South Asia*.

Rodrigues, M, 2003, *Batting for the Empire*, New Delhi, Penguin.

Rudé, G, 1964, *The Crowd in History*, London, John Wiley.

Sales, R, 1983, *English Literature in History*, London, Hutchinson London.

Sen, S, 2001, Enduring colonialism in cricket: from Ranjitsinhji to the Cronje affair. In *Contemporary South Asia*, 10, 2.

Sen, S, 2002, How Gavaskar killed Indian football. In *Football Studies*, 5, 2.

Sen, S, 2004, *Migrant Races: Empire, Identity and K.S. Ranjitsinhji*, Manchester, Manchester University Press.

Singham, A, 1968, *The Hero and the Crowd in a Colonial Polity*, London, Yale University Press.

Sreedhar, M, 2000, *Afghan Buzkashi: Power, games and gamesmen*, Delhi, Wordsmith.

Srinivas, S, 1999, Hot bodies and cooling substances: Rituals of sport in a science city. In *Journal of Sport and Social Issues*, 23, 1 (February), 24–40.

Tomlinson, A, 2002, Theorising Spectacle: Beyond Debord. In Sugden, J, and Tomlinson, A (eds), *Power Games: A critical sociology of sport*, London, Routledge.

Verma, G, 1996, *Winners and Losers: Ethnic minorities in sport and recreation*, London, Falmer.

Vertinsky, P, and Bale, J, 2004, *Sites of Sport: Space, Place and Experience*, London, Cass.

Werbner, P, 1996, 'Our Blood is Green': Cricket, identity and social empowerment among British Pakistanis. In MacClancy, J (ed.), *Sport, Identity and Ethnicity*, Oxford, Berg.

Zarrilli, P, 1995, Repositioning the Body, Practice, Power, and Self in an Indian Martial Art. In Breckenridge, C (ed.), *Consuming Modernity: Public Culture in a South Asian World*, Minneapolis, University of Minnesota Press.

Zarrilli, P, 1998, Kalarippayattu, *When the Body Becomes All Eyes: Paradigms, Practices and Discourses of Power*, New Delhi, Oxford University.

1. '*Kalarippayattu* is Eighty Percent Mental and Only the Remainder is Physical': Power, Agency and Self in a South Asian Martial Art

Alper, H P, 1989, *Mantra*, Albany, State University of New York Press.

Bhishagratna, K K, 1963, *The Susruta Samhita* (Vol. II). Varanasi, Chowkhamba Sanskrit Series.

Carter, A T, 1982, Hierarchy and the concept of the person in western India. In Ostor, A, Fruzzetti, L, and Barnett S (eds), *Concepts of person: Kinship, caste, and marriage in India*, Cambridge, Harvard University Press.

Chakravarti, P C, 1972, *The art of warfare in ancient India*, Delhi, [Originally published in Dacca, University of Dacca, Bulletin 21.]

Connerton, P, 1989, *How societies remember*, Cambridge, Cambridge University Press.

Daniel, E V, 1984, *Fluid signs: Being a person the Tamil way*, Berkeley, University of California Press.

Davis, M, 1976, A philosophy of Hindu rank from rural West Bengal, *Journal of Asian Studies*, 36(1), 5–24.

Dasgupta, G, 1993, *Dhanur Veda chapters, Agni Purana*, Unpublished translation.

Dutt Shastri, M N, 1967, *Agni Puranam*, Varanasi, Chowkhamba Sanskrit Series.

Eliade, M, 1975, *Patanjali and yoga*, New York, Schocken Books.

Freeman, J R, 1991, *Purity and violence: Sacred power in the Teyyam worship of Malabar*, Unpublished doctoral dissertation, University of Pennsylvania.

Gangadharan, N, 1985, *Agni Purana (Part II Chapters 101–251, Part III Chapters 252–311)*, Delhi, Motilal Banarsidass.

Gundert, Rev H, 1982, [1872], *A Malayalam and English dictionary*, New Delhi, Asia Educational Services.

Hart, G L, 1975, *The poems of ancient Tamil: Their milieu and their Sanskrit counterparts*, Berkeley, University of California Press.

Hart, G L, 1979, *Poets of the Tamil anthologies: Ancient poems of love and war*, Princeton, Princeton University Press.

Inden, R, 1986, Orientalist constructions of India, *Modern Asian Studies*, 20(3), 401–446.

Johnson, D H, 1992, *Body: Recovering our sensual wisdom*, Berkeley, North Atlantic Books.

Johnson, D H, 1994, *Body, spirit and democracy*, Berkeley, North Atlantic Books.

Kailaspathy, K, 1968, *Tamil heroic poetry*, Oxford, Clarendon Press.

Kakar, S, 1982, *Shamans, mystics, and doctors*, Chicago, University of Chicago Press.

Kondo, D K, 1990, *Crafting Selves*, Chicago, University of Chicago Press.

Kurup, K K N, 1977, *Aryan and Dravidian elements in Maslabar folklore*, Trivandrum, Kerala Historical Society.

Kurup, K K N, 1973, *The cult of Teyyam and hero worship in Kerala (Indian Folklore Series, No. 21)*, Calcutta, Indian Publications.

Marriott, M, 1976, Hindu transactions: Diversity without dualism. In Kapferer, B (ed.), *Transaction and meaning: Directions in the anthropology of exchange and symbolic behavior* Philadelphia, Institute for the Study of Human Issues.

Marriott, M, 1977, Symposium: Changing identities in South Asia. In David, K (ed), *The new wind: Changing identities in South Asia*, Chicago, Aldine.

Marriott, M, 1980, March, The open Hindu person and interpersonal fluidity. In *The Indian Self* (Session 19), Association for Asian Studies.

Marriott, M, 1990, *India through Hindu categories*, New Delhi, SAGE Publications.

Menon, A S M, 1979, *Social and cultural history of Kerala*, New Delhi, Sterling Publishers Pvt. Ltd.

Moore, L, 1983, *Taravad: House, land, and relationship in a matrilineal Hindu society*, Doctoral dissertation, University of Chicago.

Narayanan, M G S, 1977, *Reinterpretations in south Indian history*, Trivandrum, College Book House.

Narayanan, M G S, 1976, The ancient and medieval history of Kerala, *Journal of Kerala Studies*, 3(3–4), 441–456.

Narayanan, M G S, 1973, *Aspects of Aryanisation in Kerala*, Trivandrum, Kerala Historical Society.

Pant, G N, 1978, *Indian archery*, Delhi, Agam Kala Prakashan.

Pillai, A K B, 1987, *The culture of social stratification/sexism: The Nayars*, Acton, Mass., Copley Publishing Group.

Pillai, E K, 1970, *Studies in Kerala history*, Kottayam, National Book Stall.

Said, E, 1978, *Orientalism*, New York, Pantheon Books.

Shah, U P, 1968, Cattanam Madham-A gleaning from the Kuvala yamala-Kaha. In *Annals of Bhandarkar Oriental Research Institute (Golden Jubilee Volume)*, Poona, 250–252.

Shaner, D E, 1985, *The bodymind experience in Japanese Buddhism*, Albany, State University of New York Press.

Subramanian, N, 1966, *Sangam polity*, Bombay, Asian Publishing House.

Veluthat, K, 1976, Aryan brahman settlements of ancient Kerala. In *27th Indian History Congress, University of Calicut*, 24–27.

Veluthat, K, 1978, *Brahmin settlements in Kerala: Historical studies*, Calicut, Calicut University, Sandhya Publications.

Vogel, C, 1965, *Vagbhata's Astangahrdayasamhita*, Wiesbaden.

Zarrilli, P, 1989, Three Bodies of Practice in a Traditional South Indian Martial Art. In *Social Science and Medicine*, 28, 12, 1289–1310.

1992, To Heal and/or To Harm: The Vital Spots (Marmmam/Varmam) in Two South Indian Martial Traditions. Part II, Focus on the Tamil Art, Varma Ati. In *Journal of Asian Martial Arts*, 1, 2, 1–15.

1998, *Kalarippayattu: When the Body Becomes All Eyes: Paradigms, Practices and Discourses of Power*, New Delhi, Oxford University Press.

Zimmermann, F, 1983, 'Remarks on the conception of the body in Ayurvedic medicine'. In Pfleiderer, B, and Sontheimer, G D (eds), *South Asian Digest of Regional Writing, Vol. 8: Sources of Illness and Healing in South Asian Regional Literatures*, Heidelberg.

1986, *Susruta Samhita, Cikitsasthana xxiv, 38–49*, unpublished translation.

1988, The Jungle and the Aroma of Meats: An Ecological Theme in Hindu Medicine. In *Social Science and Medicine*, 27, 3, 197–215.

2. Empowering Yourself: Sport, Sexuality and Autoeroticism in North Indian *Jori* Swinging

Alter, J S, 1992, *The Wrestler's Body: Identity and Ideology in North India*, Berkeley and Los Angeles, University of California Press.

1995, 'The Celibate Wrestler: Sexual Chaos, Embodied Balance and Competitive Politics in North India', *Contributions to Indian Sociology*, n.s. 29(1,2), 109–131.

2004, *Yoga in Modern India: The Body Between Science and Philosophy*, Princeton, Princeton University Press.

Collingham, E M, 2001, *Imperial Bodies: The Physical Experience of the Raj, 1800–1947* Cambridge, Polity Press.

Dening, S, 1996, *The Mythology of Sex*, Sydney, Randomhouse.

Friedman, D M, 2001, *A Mind of It's Own: A Cultural History of the Penis*, New York, Free Press.

O'Flaherty, W D, 1976, *The Origins of Evil in Hindu Mythology*, Berkeley and Los Angeles, University of California Press.

Ram, Daya, 1985, *Jori. Samrika: Pratham Jila Jori Gada Pratiyogita-Jila Khelkudh Protsahan Samiti Awen Jila Mugdal Jori Gada Sangh Dwara Ayojit* (Govind Ram Bhargava ed.), Varanasi, Dr. Sampuranananda Stadium.

3. Indigenous Polo in Northern Pakistan: Game and Power on the Periphery

Alder, G J, 1963, *British India's Northern Frontier 1865–95: a Study in Imperial Policy*, London, Longmans (for the Royal Commonwealth Society).

Armstrong, G, and Bates, C, 2001, Selves and others: reflections on sport in South Asia, *Contemporary South Asia*, 10, 2.

Azoy, G, Whitney 1982, *Buzkashi: Game and Power in Afghanistan*, Pennsylvania, University of Pennsylvania Press.

Balneaves, E, 1972, *Mountains of the Murgha Zerin: between the Hindu Kush and the Karakorum*, London, John Gifford.

Barth, F, 1956, *Indus and Swat Kohistan: an Ethnographic Survey*, Oslo, Forenede Trykkerier.

Biddulph, J, 1880, *Tribes of the Hindoo Koosh*, Calcutta, Office of the Superintendent of Government Printing.

Bourdieu, P, 1990, Programme for a sociology of sport. In *Other Words*, Cambridge, Polity.

Bulley, T, 2001, *Halfway to Heaven. Cinema premiere internet advertisement.* At http://www.pologstaad.ch/htm/halfway_backinfo.shtml

Dani, A H, 1989, *History of Northern Areas of Pakistan*, Islamabad, National Institute of Historical and Cultural Research.

Diem, C, 1942, *Asiatische Reiterspiele, Ein Beitrag zur Kulturgeschichte der Völker*, Berlin.

Drew, F, 1875, *The Jummo and Kashmir Territories, a Geographical Account*, London.

Eggert, P, 1990, *Die frühere Sozialordnung Moolkhos und Turkhos (Chitral)*, Stuttgart, Franz Steiner Verlag (Beiträge zur Südasienforschung 134).

Elias, N, 1978, *The Civilizing Process*, Oxford, Basil Blackwell.

Frembgen, J, 1988, Polo in Nager, zur Ethnographie eines orientalischen Reiterspiel, *Zentralasiatische Studien*, 21, 197–217.

Ghufran, M M, 1962, *Nai Tarikh, e Chitral* [New History of Chitral, in Urdu, ed. Mirza Ghulam Murtaza], Peshawar.

Haserodt, K, 1989, *Chitral (pakistanischer Hindukusch): Strukturen, Wandel und Probleme eines Lebensraumes im Hochgebirge zwischen Gletschern und Wüste. In Hochgebirgsräume Nordpakistans im Hindukusch, Karakorum und Westhimalaya: Beiträge und Materialen zur Regionalen Geographie*, Berlin, Institut für Geographie der Technischen Universität Berlin.

Jettmar, K, 1975, *Die Religionen des Hindukusch*, Berlin, W. Kohlhammer.

Keay, J, 1979, *The Gilgit Game, the Explorers of the Western Himalyas*, London, John Murray.

Kreutzmann, 1991, The Karakorum Highway, the Impact of Road Construction on Mountain Societies, *Modern Asian Studies*, 25, 4.

Leitner, G W, 1889, *Dardistan in 1866, 1886 and 1893*, Woking, Oriental University Institute.

Lentz, W, 1939, *Zeitrechnung in Nuristan und am Pamir*, Berlin, aus den Abhandlungen der Preußischen Akademie der Wissenschaften, Phil., Hist. Klasse Jg. 1938 (reprinted 1978, Graz, Akademische Druck, u. Verlagsanstalt).

Lorimer, D, 1979 [1923–24]. *Texts on Hunza*, Library of the School of Oriental and African Studies, London (MS 181247), Ed. with commentary as Müller-Stellrecht, I (ed.),

Materialen zur Ethnographie von Dardistan (Pakistan) aus den nachgelassenem Aufzeichnungen von D.L.R. Lorimer, vol. I. Graz, Akademische Druck, u. Verlagsanstalt.

Mabey, M J, 2002, *The highest polo ground in the world, a summer journey to Pakistan's Shandur Pass*, Santa Fe Reporter at http://www.sfreporter.com/archive/06/12/02polo.html

Mahdisan, S, 1981, Chaughan or polo in Pakistan, its etymology and history, *Journal of Central Asia*, 4, 2, 29–31.

Mills, J, 2001, A historiography of South Asian sport, *Contemporary South Asia*, 10, 2.

Müller-Stellrecht, I, 1973, *Feste in Dardistan, Darstellung und Kulturgeschichtliche Analyse. Arbeiten aus dem Seminar für Völkerkunde der Johann Wolfgang Goeth*, Wiebaden, Franz Steiner.

1981, 'Menschenhandel und Machtpolitik im westlichen Himalaja, ein Kapitel aus der Geschichte Dardistans (Nordpakistan)', *Zentralasiatische Studien*, 15.

Parkes, P, 2000, Enclaved knowledge, indigent and indignant representations of environmental management and development among the Kalasha of northern Pakistan. In Ellen R, Parkes, P, and Bicker A (eds), *Indigenous Environmental Knowledge and its Transformations: critical anthropological perspectives*, Amsterdam, Harwood Academic.

2001a, Unwrapping rudeness, inverted etiquette in an egalitarian enclave. In Hendry, J, and Watson, C W (eds), *An Anthropology of Indirection*, London and New York, Routledge.

2001b, Alternative social structures and foster relations in the Hindu Kush, milk kinship allegiance in former mountain kingdoms of northern Pakistan, *Comparative Studies in Society and History*, 43, 1.

Robertson, G S, 1898, *Chitrál: the Story of a Minor Siege*, London, Methuen.

Schmid, A, 1997, *Die Dom zwischen sozialer Ohnmacht und kultureller Macht. Ein Minderheit im Spannungsfeld eines interethnischen Relationengeflechts*, Stuttgart, Franz Steiner Verlag.

Schomberg, R C F, 1935, *Between the Oxus and the Indus*, London, Hopkinson.

Schomberg, R C F, 1938, *Kafirs and Glaciers: Travels in Chitral*, London, Hopkinson.

Shahzad, M Y, 1995, A brief note on the Shandur Polo Tournament. In *Chitral: the Heart of the Hindu Kush, Souvenir of the 3rd International Hindukush Cultural Conference*, Chitral, Anjuman-e-Taraqqi.

Staley, J, 1982, *Words for my Brother: Travels between the Hindu Kush and the Himalayas*, Karachi, Oxford University Press.

Tahir Ali, 1981, Ceremonial and social structure among the Burusho of Hunza. In von Fürer, C, Haimendorf (ed.), *Asian Highland Societies in Anthropological Perspective*, Delhi, Sterling Publishers.

Trench, C C, 1985, *The Frontier Scouts*, London, Oxford University Press.

Turner, J, 1980, *Reckoning with the Beast: Animals, Pain and Humanity in the Victorian Mind*, Baltimore, Johns Hopkins.

Vigne, G T, 1842, *Travels in Kashmir, Ladak, Iskardo, the Countries Adjoining the Mountain, Course of the Indus, and the Himalaya, North of the Panjab*, London, H, Colburn.

Watson, J N P, 1986, *The World of Polo: Past and Present*, London, Sportsman's Press.

Watson, J N P, 1989, *A Concise Guide to Polo*, London, Sportsman's Press.

4. 'The Moral that can be Safely Drawn from the Hindus' Magnificent Victory': Cricket, Caste and the Palwankar Brothers

Anon, 1906, Hindu Cricket. In *Indian Social Reformer*, 16, 25, 18 February.

Antia, J D, 1913, *Elphinstone College Tours*, Bombay.

Briggs, G, 1920, *The Chamars*, Calcutta, Association Press.

Deodhar, D B, 1966, *I Look Back: An Autobiography*, Madras, Sport and Pastime.

Gandhi, M, *Collected Works of Mahatma Gandhi*.

Guha, R, 2002, *A Corner of a Foreign Field*, London, Picador.

Green, B, *The Wisden Book of Cricketers' Lives*, London, Queen Anne Press.

James, C L R, 1963, *Beyond a Boundary*, London, Hutchinson.

Keer, D, 1971, *Dr Ambedkar: Life and Mission*, Bombay, Popular Prakashan.

Langrana, N N, 1956, I Gaze into the Fire. In *Cricket Association of Bengal Silver Jubilee Souvenir*, Calcutta, CAB.

Mehta, C V, 1954, Beginnings of Hindu Cricket. In *Diamond Jubilee Souvenir of Parmanandas Jivandas Hindu Gymkhana, 1894–1954*, Bombay, Gymkhana.

Muckerjee, H C, 1911, *The Indian Cricketers' Tour of 1911*, Calcutta.

Nayudu, C K, 1953, Lessons from a Long Innings. In *MysIndia*, 25/10/1953.

Pandit, B J, 1959, *Khara Kheladu*, Poona, Vora and Company.

Pavri, M E, 1901, *Parsi Cricket*, Bombay, J. B. Marzban and Co.

Polishwalla, P N, 1919, *Representative Matches in India from 1892 to 1919*, Bombay.

Pyarelal, C, 1932, *The Epic Fast*, Ahmedabad, Navjivan.

Raiji, V, 1986, *India's Hambledon Men*, Bombay, Tyeby Press.

Roy, S K, 1945, *Bombay Pentangular*, Calcutta, Illustrated News.

1946, *India–England Cricket Visits, 1911–1946*, Calcutta, Illustrated News.

Sarkar, S, 1973, *The Swadeshi Movement in Bengal, 1903–1908*, Delhi, Peoples Publishing House.

Varerkar, B V, 1923, *Turungacha Darat*, Bombay, Lalitkaladarsha Natak Mandali.

Vithal, P, 1948, *Maze Crida-Jivan*, Bombay, Bharati Publishers.

Zelliot, E M, 1969, *Dr Ambedkar and the Mahar Movement*, unpublished Ph D dissertation, University of Philadelphia.

Bombay Chronicle.

Bombay Gazette.

The Sportsman.

The Tribune.

Mahratta

Navakal (Bombay).

Kesari and Bhala in Report on Native Newspapers for the Bombay Presidency in Oriental and India Office Collections, Britsh Library, London.

Palwankar, K V, 1996, Interview with author Bombay, November 1996.

Palwankar, Y B, 1999, Interview with author Pune, July 1999.

Pandit, B J, 1999, Interview with author Pune, July 1999.

Obituary clipping from Times of India in K. V. Gopalaratnam Collection, Sports Authority of India, New Delhi.

5. The Peasants are Revolting: Race, Culture and Ownership in Cricket

Appadurai, A, 1996, 'Playing With Modernity: The Decolonization of Indian Cricket'. In Carol A Breckenridge (ed.) *Consuming Modernity: Public Culture in Contemporary India*, Delhi.

Bose, M, 1991, *A History of Indian Cricket*, London.

Gavaskar, S, 1991, *Sunny Days*, Calcutta.

Lord Hawke, 1924, *Recollections and Reminiscences*, London.

James, C L R, 1963, *Beyond A Boundary*, London.

Magazine, P, 1999, *Not Quite Cricket*, Delhi.

Majumdar, B, 2001, 'The Politics of Leisure in Colonial India,' *Economic and Political Weekly*, September 1.

Mannathukkaren, N, 2001, 'Subalterns, Cricket and the 'Nation',' *Economic and Political Weekly*, December 8.

Nandy, A, 1989, *The Tao of Cricket: On Games of Destiny and the Destiny of Games*, New York.

Rushdie, S, 1991, *Imaginary Homelands*, New York.

Sandiford, K, 1994, *Cricket and the Victorians*, Scolar Press, London.

Sen, S, 2001, 'Chameleon Games, Ranjitsinhji's Politics of Race and Gender,' *Journal of Colonialism & Colonial History*, 2,3.

Wild, R, 1934, *The Biography of His Highness Shri Sir Ranjitsinhji*, London.

Cricket, September 17, 1896, no. 423, vol. xv.

Dawn

The Guardian.

The Independent.

Rediff.com.

The Sydney Morning Herald.

The Times of India.

6. The Social History of the Royal Calcutta Golf Club, 1829–2003

Alter, J, 1992, The *Wrestler's Body: Identity and Ideology in North India*, Berkeley, CA, University of California Press.

Anderson, B, 1991, *Imagined Communities: Reflections on the Origin and Spread of Nationalism*, London, Verso.

Bhabha, H, 1994, *The Location of Culture*, London, Routledge.

Brehend, J, and Lewis, P N, 1998, *Challenges and Champions: the Royal & Ancient Golf Club, 1754–1883*, St Andrews, The Royal & Ancient Golf Club.

Brown, J, 1994, *Modern India: Origins of an Asian Democracy*, 2nd edn. Oxford, Oxford University Press.

Carey, W H, 1906, *The Good Old Days of the Honourable John Company*, Calcutta.

Collingham, E M, 2001, *Imperial Bodies: The Physical Experience of the Raj, c. 1800–1947*, Cambridge: Polity.

Cook, S B, 1996, *Colonial Encounters in the Age of High Imperialism*, New York, Harper Collins.

Dimeo, P, (ed.), 2002, Football, Culture and Society in India, Special Issue of *Football Studies*, 5, 2.

Dimeo, P, and Mills, J (eds), 2001, *Soccer in South Asia: Empire, Nation, Diaspora*, London, Cass.

Gandhi, L, 1999, *Postcolonial Theory: A Critical Introduction*, New Delhi, Oxford University Press.

Gandhi, M, 1938, *Hind Swaraj*, reprint. Ahmedabad, Navjivan Publishing.

Hamilton, D, 1998, *Golf: Scotland's Game*, Glasgow, Partick Press.

Horne, W O, 1928, *Work and Sport in the Old I.C.S.* Edinburgh, William Blackwood.

Moorhouse, G, 1998, *Calcutta*, London, Phoenix.

Pearson, S, 1979, *The Royal Calcutta Golf Club*, Calcutta, Royal Calcutta Golf Club.

Phillips, M, 1990, Golf and Victorian Sporting Values. In *Sporting Traditions*, 6, 2, 120–134.

Playfair, H, 1984, *The Playfair Family*, Yeovil, Blackford House.

Stirk, D, 1998, *Golf: History and Tradition, 1500–1945*, Ludlow, Excellent Press.

Ward-Thomas, P, 1980, *The Royal and Ancient*, Edinburgh, Scottish Academic Press.

Zarrilli, P B, 1998, *When the Body Becomes All Eyes: Paradigms, Discourses and Practices of Power in Kalarippayattu, a South Indian Martial Art*, New Delhi, Oxford University Press.

7. Warrior Goddess Versus Bipedal Cow: Sport, Space, Performance and Planning in an Indian City

Alter, J, 1992, *The wrestler's body, Identity and ideology in north India*, Berkeley and Los Angeles, University of California Press.

1995, 'The celibate wrestler, Sexual chaos, embodied balance and competitive politics in north India.' *Contributions to Indian Sociology*, (n.s.) 29, 1 & 2, 109–131.

Augé, M, 1999, *An anthropology for contemporaneous worlds*, Stanford, Stanford University Press.

Bale, J, 1994, *Landscapes of modern sport*, Leicester, London, and New York, Leicester University Press.

BDA, 1995, *Comprehensive development plan (revised) Bangalore report*, Bangalore, Bangalore Development Authority.

1997, *Bangalore Development Authority annual report 1996–1997*, Bangalore, Bangalore Development Authority.

Brownell, S, 1995a, The stadium, the city and the state, Beijing. In Bale, J, and Moen, O (eds), *The stadium and the city*, Keele, Keele University Press.

1995b, *Training the body for China, Sports in the moral order of the people's republic*. Chicago and London, University of Chicago Press.

2001, Making dream bodies in Beijing, Athletes, fashion models and urban mystique in China. In Chen, N, Clark, C, Gottschang, S Z, and Jeffrey, L (eds), *China urban: Ethnographies of contemporary culture*, Durham and London, Duke University Press.

Census of India, 1981, Series-9 Karnataka. District census handbook, Bangalore district, Parts XIII-A and B.

Chamaraj, K, 1995, Choking a lung space. *Deccan Herald*, 25 February.

Cherian, T, 1997, Stage set for the beginning of a new era. *Times of India* 31 May.

CIVIC 1999, *City profile of Bangalore*, Bangalore, CIVIC Bangalore.

Eichberg, H, 1998, *Body cultures: Essays on sport, space and identity*, Edited by John Bale and Chris Philo, London and New York, Routledge.

Ferraz, J, 1997, 'Athletics competition tumbles into jeopardy over 'sub-standard' track.' *Times of India* 2 June.

Harvey, D, 1985a, *Consciousness and the urban experience*, Baltimore, MD, Johns Hopkins University Press.

1985b, *The Urbanization of capital*, Baltimore, MD, Johns Hopkins University Press.

Hasan, M. F, 1970, *Bangalore through the centuries*, Bangalore, Historical Publications.

Heitzman, J, 1999a, Corporate strategy and planning in the science city, Bangalore as 'silicon valley'. In *Economic and Political Weekly* 34: 5 (January 30–February 5), PE2–PE11.

1999b, Sports and conflict in urban planning, The Indian national games in Bangalore. In *Journal of Sport and Social Issues*, 23: 1 (February), 5–23.

2004, *Network City, Planning the information society in Bangalore*. New Delhi, Oxford University Press.

INRIMT. 1995, *Integrated resources analysis for structure plan of the Bangalore metropolitan region, Technical report*, Hyderabad, Indian Resources Information and Management Technologies Private Limited.

Kamath, S U, 1990, *Karnataka state gazetteer. Bangalore district*. Bangalore, Government of Karnataka.

Kapadia, N, 2001, Triumphs and Disasters: The story of Indian football. In Dimeo, P and Mills, J (eds), *Soccer in South Asia: Empire, Nation, Diaspora*, London Cass.

Keydar, C, 1999, *Istanbul: Between the global and the local*, Rowman and Littlefield Publishing.

Khan, I, 1997, Players perform amid chaos. In *Times of India*, 2 June.

Khan, I, and J. Ferraz 1997, On a night of shame, frayed tempers mar the spirit of the Games. In *Times of India* 10 June.

Loy, J, McPherson B, and Kenyon, G, 1978, *Sport and social systems: A guide to the analysis, problems, and literature*. Reading, MA, Addison-Wesley Publishing Company.

Madon, S, 1997, Information-based global economy and socioeconomic development: The case of Bangalore, *The Information Society*, 13, 227–43.

Mahalingam, T V, 1975, *Administration and social life under Vijayanagar, Part 2, Second edition*, Madras, University of Madras.

Narendra, K V, 1993, *Lakes of Bangalore: The current scenario*, Bangalore, Centre for Science and Technology.

1995, *Perspectives on ecology and development of Sankey Tank*, Bangalore, Centre for Science and Technology.

Nielsen, K, 1995, The stadium and the city: A modern story. In Bale, J, and Moen, O (eds), *The stadium and the city*, Keele, Keele University Press.

Orsi, R, 1999, *Gods of the city: Religion and the American urban landscape*, Bloomington/Indianapolis, Indiana University Press.

Rutheiser, C, 1996, *Imagineering Atlanta: The politics of place in the city of dreams*, London/New York, Verso.

Schenk-Sandbergen, L, 2001, Women, water and sanitation in the slums of Bangalore: A case study of action research, In Hans Schenk (ed), *Living in India's slums, case study of Bangalore*, Indo-Dutch Programme on Alternatives in Development (IDPAD) and Manohar.

Shiri, G, 1999, *Our slums mirror a systemic malady: An empirical case study of Bangalore slums*, Bangalore, Christian Institute for the Study of Religion and Society and Asian Trading Corporation.

Singhal, A, and Rogers, E M, 1989, *India's information revolution*. New Delhi, Sage Publications.

2001, *India's communication revolution: From bullock carts to cyber marts*, New Delhi/Thousand Oaks/London, Sage Publications.

Sorkin, M, 1992, *Variations on a theme park: The new American city and the end of public space*. New York, Hill and Wang.

Srinivas, S, 1999a, Remembering the city: The incarnation of the goddess and the boundaries of the metropolis. In Assayag, J, and Tarabout, G (eds), *Possession in south Asia: Speech, body and territory, Purusartha no. 21*, Paris, École des Hautes Études en Sciences Sociales.

1999b, Hot bodies and cooling substances: Rituals of sport in a science city. In *Journal of Sport and Social Issues*, 23: 1 (February), 24–40.

2001, *Landscapes of urban memory: The sacred and the civic in India's high-tech city*, Minneapolis, University of Minnesota Press.

Sundara Rao, B N, 1985, *Bengalurina itihasa [The history of Bangalore]*, Bangalore, Vasant Literary Library.

Taylor, I, and Ruth Jamieson 1997, 'Proper little mesters', Nostalgia and protest masculinity in de-industrialised Sheffield'. In Westwood, S, and Williams, J (eds), *Imagining cities: Scripts, signs, memories*, London/New York, Routledge.

Viswanathan, P R, 1997, 'A blessing for infrastructure development'. In *The Hindu*, 31/05.

8. 'Nupilal': Women's War, Football and the History of Modern Manipur

Ansari, S, 1991, *Manipur: Tribal Demography and Socio-Economic Development*, Delhi, Daya.

Appadurai, A, 1995, Playing with modernity: the decolonisation of Indian cricket. In Breckenridge, C (ed.), *Consuming Modernity: Public Culture in Contemporary India*, Minneapolis, University of Minnesota Press.

Arambam, L, 2002, Some aspects of lai haraoba, In Sarma, P (ed.), *Traditional Customs and Rituals of North-East India*, Chennai, Vivekananda Kendra Institute of Culture.

Basanta, N, 1998, *Socio-Economic Change in Manipur*, Imphal.

Chaki-Sircar, M, 1984, *Feminism in a Traditional Society, women of the Manipur Valley*, New Delhi, Shakti Books.

Chatterji, J, 1996, *Customary Laws and Women in Manipur*, New Delhi, Uppal.

Clark, A, 1993, *Gender and Political Economy: Explorations of South Asian systems*, Delhi, Oxford University Press.

Dena, L, 1984, *British Policy Towards Manipur, 1891–1919*, Imphal.

Dev, B, and Lahiri, D, 1987, *Manipur: Culture and Politics*, Delhi, Mittal.

Dimeo, P, 2001a, 'Team Loyalty Splits the City into Two': Football, ethnicity and rivalry in Calcutta. In Armstrong, G, and Giulianotti, R (eds), *Fear and Loathing in World Football*, Oxford, Berg Oxford.

2001b Football and Politics in Bengal, Colonialism, Nationalism, Communalism. In Dimeo, P, and Mills, J (eds), *Soccer in South Asia*, London, Cass.

Dimeo, P, and Mills, J (eds), 2001, *Soccer in South Asia: Empire, Nation, Diaspora*, London, Cass.

Dunn, E W, 1886, Gazetteer of Manipur 1886. In Sanajaoba, N (ed), *Manipur: A British anthology*, New Delhi, Akansha Publishing House.

Ghosh, G K, and Ghosh, S, 1997, *Women of Manipur*, New Delhi, APH Publishing.

Giulanotti, R, 1999, *Football: A sociology of the Global Game*, Cambridge, Polity Press.

Guha, R, 1998, Cricket and Politics in Colonial India, *In Past and Present*, 161, 155–190.

Guha, R, 2002, *A Corner of a Foreign Field: The Indian history of a British sport*, Oxford, Picador,

Grimwood, E, 1975, *My Three Years in Manipur*, Delhi.

Hargreaves, J, 1994, *Sporting Females: Critical issues in the history and sociology of women's sports*, London, Routledge 1994.

Hong, F, 2001, Freeing Bodies, Heroines in History. In *International Journal of the History of Sport*, 18, 1.

Joykumar Singh, N, 1992, *Social Movements in Manipur, 1917–1951*, New Delhi, Mittal.

2002, *Colonialism to Democracy: A history of Manipur 1819–1972*, Delhi, Spectrum.

Kumar, N, 1994, *Woman as Subjects: South Asian histories*, Charlottesville, University Press of Virginia.

Lokendra Singh, N, 1998, *Unquiet Valley: Society, Economy and Politics in Manipur 1891–1950*, New Delhi.

Majumdar, B, 2002, Kolkata Colonized, Soccer in a sub-continental Brazilian Colony. In *Soccer and Society*, 3, 2.

Majumdar, B, 2003, Forwards and Backwards, Women's Soccer in Twentieth-Century India. In *Soccer and Society*, 4, 2/3, 2003.

Mangan, J A, 1987, *From 'fair sex' to feminism: Sport and the socialization of women in the industrial and post industrial eras*, London, Cass.

Mangan, J A, 2001, Soccer as Moral Training, Missionary intentions and imperial legacies. In Dimeo, P, and Mills, J (eds), *Soccer in South Asia: Empire, Nation, Diaspora*, London, Cass.

McDonald, I, 1999, Between Saleem and Shiva, The politics of cricket nationalism in 'globalising India'. In Sugden, J, and Bairner, A (eds), *Sport in Divided Societies*, Aachen, Meyer and Meyer.

Mills, J, and Sen, S, 2004, *Confronting the Body: The politics of physicality in colonial and post-colonial India*, London, Anthem.

Murthi, R, 1984, Daring Dames of Manipur. In Ahluwalia, B, and Ahluwalia, S (eds), *Social Change in Manipur*, Delhi, Cultural Publishing House.

Nandy, A, 1989, *The Tao of Cricket: On games of destiny and the destiny of games*, New York, Oxford University Press.

Nelson, M B, 1998, 'Introduction'. In Smith, L (ed.), *Nike is a Goddess: The History of Women in Sports*, New York, Atlantic Monthly Press.

Nilakanta Singh, E, 1986, Historical and Cultural Relations between Manipur and Bengal. In Ranbir Singh, H (ed.), *Historical and Cultural Relations between Manipur, Assam and Bengal*, Imphal, Manpuri Sahitya Parishad.

Parrattt, J, and Parrratt, S, 1992, *Queen Empress vs. Tikendrajit, Prince of Manipur: The Anglo-Manipuri Conflict of 1891*, New Delhi, Vikas.

Parratt, S, and Parratt, J, 1997, *The Pleasing of the Gods: Meitei Haraoba*, New Delhi, Vikas.

Parratt, S, and Parratt, J, 2001, The Second 'Women's War' and the Emergence of Democratic Government in Manipur. In *Modern Asian Studies*, 35, 4, 905–919.

Phukon, G, 2003, *Ethnicisation of Politics in Northeast India*, New Delhi, South Asian.

Rizvi, S, and Mukherjee, S, 1998, Meitei. In Horam, M, and Rizvi, S, *People of India: Manipur*, Calcutta, Seagull.

Sharma, M, and Vanjani, U, 1993, Engendering Reproduction, The political economy of reproductive activities in a Rajasthan village. In Clark, A (ed.), *Gender and Political Economy: Explorations of South Asian systems*, Delhi, Oxford University Press.

Singh, K, 1998, Foreword. In Horam, M, and Rizvi, S, *People of India: Manipur*, Calcutta, Seagull.

Suryanarayan, S R, 2003, Manipur rules, unambiguously. In *The Hindu*, 25/06/2003.

Tarapot, P, 2003, *Bleeding Manipur*, New Delhi, Har-Anand.

Venkata Rao, V, Gangte T, and Bimola Devi, K, 1991, *A Century of Government and Politics in NE India*, vol. 4 (Manipur), New Delhi, Chand.

Vijaylakshmi Brara, N, 2001, Meira-Paibis, an Introspection. In *The Imphal Free Press*, 23/12/01 (reproduced on manipuronline.com).

Zehol, L, 1998, *Ethnicity in Manipur: Experiences, issues and perspectives*, New Delhi, Regency.

Media Reports.

One dies as torch-rallyists defy curfew. In *The Imphal Free Press* 05/07/01: (reproduced on www.e-pao.net).

Naga union tells Meiteis not to interfere in Indo-Naga issue. In *Matamgi Yakairol* 11/06/01: (reproduced on www.e-pao.net).

Women Power. On *www.manipuronline.com* 13/09/2003

9. 'Playing for the Tibetan People': Football and History in the High Himalayas

Bishop, P, 1989, *The Myth of Shangri-La: Tibet, Travel Writing and the Western Creation of Sacred Landscape*, London, Athlone.

Dhondup, K, 1986, *The Water-Bird and Other Years*, Delhi.

Diehl, K, 2002, *Echoes from Dharamsala: Music in the Life of a Tibetan Refugee Community*, Berkeley, Uni. of California Press.

Dodin, T, and Räther, H (eds), 2001, *Imagining Tibet: Perceptions, Projections and Fantasies* Boston, Wisdom Press.

De Filippi, F, 1932, *An Account of Tibet: The Travels of Ippolito Desideri of Pistolia S.J., 1712–1727*, London, Routledge.

Finkel, I L, 1995, Notes on two Tibetan Dice Games. In de Voogt A J (ed.), *New Approaches to Board Games Research: Asian Origins and Future Perspectives*, Leiden, IIAS.

Goldstein, M, 1989, *A History of Modern Tibet, 1913–1951: The Demise of the Lamaist State*, London.

McKay, A, 1994, The Other 'Great Game', Politics and Sport in Tibet, 1904–47. In *The International Journal of the History of Sport*, 11, 3, 372–86.

2001, 'Kicking the Buddhas Head', Tibet, Football, and Modernity. In Dimeo P, and J, Mills (eds), *Soccer in South Asia: Empire, Nation, Diaspora*, London, Frank Cass.

Mills, J, 2002, Sport, History and Asian Societies. In *IIAS Newsletter* 28.

PRO FO 371-76315-7611. *Lhasa mission report* May 1949.

www.cphpost.dk

www.eloratings.net

www.friends-of-tibet.org.nz

www.hummel.dk

www.logic.at

www.mypage.bluewin.ch

www.news.bbc.co.uk

www.Tibet.net

www.tibetanyouthcongress.org

www.TimesofTibet.com

www.zen.co.uk

10. Community, Identity and Sport: Anglo-Indians in Colonial and Postcolonial India

Anglos in the Wind (2000) Chennai.

Anthony, F, 1968, *Britain's Betrayal: The Story of the Anglo-Indian Community*, New Delhi, Allied.

Arnold, D, 1979, European Orphans and Vagrants in India in the Nineteenth Century. In *The Journal of Imperial and Commonwealth History*, 7, 2, 104–127.

Bala, R, 2000, Aaj Ka MLA. In *Cricket Talk* (Calcutta) 13/04/2000.

Bannister, J, 1998, Chakradharpur Through the Eyes of an Anglo-Indian. In *Indian Railways* July–August, 69–71.

Blunt, A, 2003, Geographies of diaspora and mixed descent: Anglo-Indians in India and Britain. In *International Journal of Population Geography* 9, 4, 281–294.

Caplan, L, 2003, *Children of Colonialism: Anglo-Indians in a Postcolonial World*, Oxford, Berg.

Carton, A, 2000, Beyond 'Cotton Mary': Anglo-Indian categories and reclaiming the diverse past. In *The International Journal Of Anglo-Indian Studies* 5, 1, (http://www.alphalink.com.au/~agilbert/cover9.html).

D'Souza, C, 2000, Indian hockey needs money. In *The Chandigarh Tribune* 06/05/2000.

Gist, N O, 1967, Cultural versus Social Marginality: The Anglo-Indian Case. In *Phylon* 28, 361–375.

Gist, N O, and Wright, R D, 1973, *Marginality and Identity: Anglo-Indians as a Racially Mixed Minority in India* (Monographs & Theoretical Studies in Sociology & Anthropology in Honour of Nels Anderson) Leiden, Brill.

Grimshaw, A D, 1958, The Anglo-Indian Community: The Integration of a Marginal Group. In *The Journal of Asian Studies*, 18, 1, 227–240.

Hawes, C, 1996, *Poor Relations: The Making of a Eurasian Community in British India; 1773–1833*, London, Curzon.

Ismail Merchant's film "Cotton Mary" testifies. In *The Calcutta Statesman*: 3–4 March 2000.

Masters, J, 1954, *Bhowani Junction*, London, John Murray.

Mills, M S, 1996, Some Comments on Stereotypes of the Anglo-Indians. In *The International Journal of Anglo-Indian Studies*, 1, 1.

Moore, G J, 1986, *The Anglo-Indian Vision*, Melbourne, A.E.Press.

Reuters, E B, 1918, *The Mulatto in the United States including a Study of the Role of Mixed-Blood Races Throughout the World*, Boston, Gorham.

Rizvi, M M, 1999, Eliza Nelson Looks Back. In *Mid-Day* (Bombay) 10/10/1999.

Stoler, A, 1989, Rethinking Colonial Categories: European Communities and the Boundaries of Rule. In *Comparative Studies in Society and History*, 31, 1, 134–161.

Stracey, E, 2000, *Growing Up in Anglo-India*, Chennai, East West Books.

Smith, A D, 1992, Chosen Peoples: Why Ethnic Groups Survive. In *Ethnic and Racial Studies*, 15, 436–456.

Wright, R D, 1970, *Marginal Man in Transition: A Study of the Anglo-Indian Community of India*, Unpublished PhD thesis, University of Missouri-Columbia.

Young, R, 1995, *Colonial Desire: Hybridity in Theory, Culture and Race*, London, Routledge.